HOW TO LEARN LANGUAGES
AND WHAT LANGUAGES TO LEARN

Enlarged Edition

How to Learn
LANGUAGES
and What
LANGUAGES
to Learn

Enlarged Edition

BY

MARIO PEI

Professor of Romance Philology, Columbia University

HARPER & ROW, PUBLISHERS

NEW YORK, EVANSTON, SAN FRANCISCO, LONDON

Acknowledgment is hereby gratefully made to the Modern Language Association, which furnished most of the statistics on languages in the schools and colleges that appear in Chapter 16; to the private language schools, notably Berlitz and the Language Guild, that supplied percentage figures for the private study of languages; to the language recording publishing houses, notably Dover and Living Language, which furnished similar percentage figures for sales of recordings in the various tongues; and to my good friends and colleagues, Professor John Fisher of Fairleigh Dickinson University and Professor Paul Gaeng of Montclair State College, who painstakingly went over this work in manuscript and offered numerous valuable emendations and suggestions.

HOW TO LEARN LANGUAGES AND WHAT LANGUAGES TO LEARN (ENLARGED EDITION). Copyright © 1966, 1973 by Mario Pei. All rights reserved. Printed in the United States of America. No part of this book may be used or reproduced in any manner whatsoever without written permission except in the case of brief quotations embodied in critical articles and reviews. For information address Harper & Row, Publishers, Inc., 10 East 53rd Street, New York, N.Y. 10022. Published simultaneously in Canada by Fitzhenry & Whiteside Limited, Toronto.

STANDARD BOOK NUMBER: 06–013323–6

LIBRARY OF CONGRESS CATALOG CARD NUMBER: 72–79685

CONTENTS

Part II—WHAT LANGUAGES TO LEARN

Introduction

This book is designed specifically for the learner or would-be learner of languages, and only incidentally for the language teacher. It is meant to be an answer to the many requests for advice and aid that have come to me over a period of more years than I care to count, from people all over the nation and the world, who said: "I would like to learn Spanish (or French, or Russian, or Swahili). How can I best do it? These are my circumstances." There would usually follow a lengthy account of background, previous training, geographical location, financial availabilities. Some had an excellent education and had learned, or at least studied, one or more languages besides the one they now wanted to acquire; others had a very poor educational background, even to the extent of never having studied a foreign language. Some were located in large cities, where the language-learning opportunities were many, even at no financial cost, and it was only a matter of choosing the most suitable; others were in isolated, remote spots, where they had access to no schools, no colleges, no teachers, no native speakers, often not even a local radio or TV program offering language lessons. Some could buy the best that Columbia University, or Berlitz, or Linguaphone had to offer; others were desperately poor, and had only a few hard-earned dollars to spend on books, recordings, or other materials. Could I help them? Would I advise them?

There were many other questions in the letters I received. Could a person with a low IQ really learn a foreign language? Or was this type of learning a prerogative of the brilliant? Would previous study of another language help? Or would it hinder? Could two, or even three, languages be learned at once? Or was it better to concentrate on just one at a time? What about all the touted short cuts to language learning, French in three weeks or Russian in six days? Where regular courses and native teachers were not available, could records really replace them? Should one concentrate at first on speaking or on reading the foreign language? Would travel abroad do the trick?

Occasionally (but only occasionally), there would be a statement of purpose: "I want to learn German in order to read scientific periodicals in that language"; or: "I want to train myself for a job as a simultaneous interpreter at the UN"; or: "My firm is sending me to its office in Sweden, and I want to learn enough Swedish to get by." More often, I would be left in the dark as to why a certain language was wanted, and my answer would have to be couched along general lines, outlining the various possibilities adapted to the various possible purposes.

The statement of purpose was often accompanied by a dilemma: "For what I want to do, is it better for me to study Spanish or French?" But far more often the dilemma came all by itself, in a vacuum, so to speak: "In high school I took two years of Latin and three of French; now, in college, I can either continue my Latin and French or switch to German and Russian. Which is it better for me to do?"

Once in a while there were questions so highly pinpointed as to tax my ingenuity in getting some sort of sensible answer on a single sheet, even if single-spaced: "How much of the French I am now learning in high school will I remember ten years from now?"; "What can I do with just one year of a language?"; "How can I get around the Russian alphabet?"; "I studied Italian for two years, and seemed to progress quite rapidly; but now I have reached an impasse; no matter how much more I study, I don't seem to make any further headway"; "I used to speak German all the time at home when I was a boy; then I moved away from my family and forgot it; what can I do to bring it back?"

Nearly ten years ago, when my *Language for Everybody* appeared, the review written by Theodore Huebener in *Modern Language Journal* said in part: "Part VI, 'Some Practical Language Hints,' gives such valuable suggestions that one wishes there were many more than the 28 pages in this section. It is such an excellent beginning that we hope an entire book will be devoted to this subject. Pei, who has learned a dozen tongues in entirely different ways—from traditional classroom instruction to casual chats at a lunch with a Japanese waiter—can offer some valuable practical advice to the learner."

This suggestion, voiced by a man who was at the time Director of

Languages in the New York City public schools, stuck in my mind, and finally led me to action.

Language and languages are, after all, the indispensable vehicle of human communication and understanding. Anything that can be done to encourage and spread their study must of necessity have some social value. But, in addition, languages are perhaps the one field of human knowledge that pays immediate and abundant dividends, from the very outset of the learning process. It is simply not true that you must learn a language thoroughly, to the point of speaking, understanding, reading, and writing it like a native, in order to enjoy its fruits. There is no area where the rewards of even a little learning are greater. A word, a phrase that we can speak or understand may have untold value in hundreds of ways; above all, in what the modern world euphemistically calls "public relations" or "image building." Few indeed are those native speakers of foreign languages who will not unbend and feel more friendly toward the man or woman who proves that he or she has an interest in their culture and language by speaking even a few words of the latter. On the purely practical side, the ability to read properly a sign in a station, an office, a shop, a street, may save us untold embarrassment, sometimes even safeguard us from danger. It is safe to assert that no time spent in learning any fraction of a language, however infinitesimal, is ever wasted. Once out of high school and college, I may never have occasion for the rest of my life to use my binomial theorem, my knowledge of equations and cosines, my memory of secondary historical dates, my table of chemical elements; but even if I do nothing but view TV, I shall have occasion to hear words and phrases of the many tongues that appear on so many of the programs and commercials, recognize the written signs in foreign films, even if I don't understand the dialogue, be able properly to identify at least some of those foreign words and expressions that loom so large in the literary output of my own language.

A few words in a foreign language have enabled me to give help and constructive directions to Puerto Ricans and Frenchmen and Germans and Israelis lost in the mazes of the New York subway. (The Israeli case was particularly good, because he spoke nothing but Hebrew and Arabic, and those are far from being among my best languages.) A few words in a foreign language have in turn made me the recipient of full aid, even to the shifting of a tire, from a Hungarian-born police sergeant on a lonely Jersey road.

Not everybody can learn a foreign language (or, for that matter, his own language) to perfection. Nobody, of course, can learn all languages, even imperfectly. But there is no one able to speak who cannot learn some portion, however small, of another language, and once it is learned, put it to use.

This book is dedicated to the world's language learners, the people who want to know, in the hope that it may assist them to understand and overcome their problems, by placing their needs and wants in juxtaposition with their available supply of language ability (which fluctuates widely from person to person, but of which all persons have some, as proved by the fact that they speak their own language, however well or poorly); of time (something extremely important in this modern age, when most of us bite off far more than we can chew); of geographical location; even of money.

If professional language teachers find anything here that is worth their consideration, they are more than welcome to it. But language teachers ordinarily are steeped in language-teaching methodology (there is a very large number of excellent books on the subject of how to teach languages effectively); they have normally been fully indoctrinated in the methods of their particular pedagogical school; they work under conditions which, while often burdensome, are nevertheless advantageous by reason of the fact that they have a captive audience which must subscribe to their method or forgo any advantage from the course they are taking. They really do not need my help, though they may find, in glancing through this book, a point or two that they may be able to use.

The man for whom this book is really written is the Utah rancher who writes: "I live fifty miles from the nearest town, a hundred and fifty miles from the nearest college. I work ten hours a day. I want to learn some Spanish. There are no Spanish speakers in my area. Shall I buy a grammar book? If so, which one? Shall I get a set of records? If so, how do I use them?"; or the boy just entering college who writes: "I studied French for two years in high school. I mean to become an oil engineer. Is it better for me to continue my French, or to switch to another language? If so, which one?"

PART I

How to Learn Languages

I

Can Anybody Learn a Foreign Language?

Native Endowment—The Musical Ear and the Sense of Grammatical Coordination—The Field of Interest—Pretesting for Language Ability—The Time Element—Learning and Unlearning a Piece of a Language

IN his *Outline Guide for the Practical Study of Foreign Languages,* Leonard Bloomfield, one of America's most revered linguists, makes the following statement:

"The process of acquiring a language, whether in infancy or in later life, is essentially the same. . . . There is no special 'gift for languages,' possessed by some but not by others."

He goes on to claim that anyone not deaf or idiotic has fully mastered his native language by the end of his fifth year, no matter how difficult or complex it may seem to strangers; and he further states that whoever has accomplished this feat can go on, at any later age, to master one or more foreign languages. All that is needed is a reliable source of information (preferably in the form of one or more native speakers), plenty of time for the task, and going about it the right way.

Bloomfield is stating the proposition in the broadest possible terms, in a fashion so oversimplified as to be misleading.

The process of acquiring a language in infancy and in later life is not quite the same. The child's mind is a blank sheet, on which one may write at will. The adult's mind is like a palimpsest, already inscribed, on which erasures must be made in order to overlay the new information. The child enjoys certain other specific advantages which do not extend to the adult: infinite time, with infinite possibility of trial and error, imitation and repetition; a fresher and uncluttered memory; utter lack of self-consciousness. The adult, on the other hand, has certain advantages that do not accrue to the child: the typically adult faculties of abstraction and generalization, and the ability to reason deductively as well as inductively.

Many will take issue with Bloomfield's strange-sounding state-

3

ment that "everyone who is not deaf or idiotic has fully mastered his native language by the end of his fifth year," and wonder, if this is truly so, why our schools need to bother with English instruction. What Bloomfield really means is that by the end of his fifth year the individual has mastered the sound scheme of his own language, along with the basic (but only the basic) grammatical structure. He has not, of course, mastered the vocabulary that he will need in later life, even if we restrict "vocabulary" to the thirty to sixty thousand words that are the normal equipment of the average educated adult, rather than the one million words, more or less, which constitute the full word stock of English or any other highly developed language. Nor has he mastered the full structure of the language, the ability to use words in any but elementary groups of subject, verb, and object with a few modifiers. Of course he has not mastered spelling, reading, composition, punctuation, and all the other things that the school teaches; but remember that to Bloomfield and members of his school "language" means only spoken language, not writing or anything connected with writing.

Where Bloomfield really comes to a head-on collision with reality is in his statement that "there is no special 'gift for languages,' possessed by some but not by others." Here it is the equalitarian philosopher who speaks rather than the practical, hardheaded linguist.

The phrase "all men are created equal" holds true in only two fields, religion and the law. Elsewhere, we have but to look around us to see that all men are not born with the same endowment. Physically, some men are superbly endowed, to the point where they can develop into heavyweight champions, long-distance runners, Olympic athletes; others are born puny and weak, and remain that way throughout their lives. Some come into the world with built-in health, and live to be a hundred if they are not killed off by accident or war; others have a predisposition to all sorts of diseases, that carry them off long before their allotted span as determined by life insurance statistics. Some are equipped with fantastic IQs, and turn into geniuses of science, art, and literature; others have IQs so low that they can hardly become literate, no matter how much time and effort are spent on them. Some are born with tremendous advantages of financial and social status and background, the proverbial "silver spoon in their mouths"; others, to use terms favored by the sociologists, are born "underprivileged" or "disadvantaged."

Inequality, rather than equality, seems to be the law of nature. Even the stock phrase "equality of opportunity" does not mean too much, in view of the basic inequality of personal equipment. All that society can do beyond equalizing opportunity is to see to it that the overprivileged by heredity, inheritance, or environment do not take advantage of their less fortunate fellow men.

It is equally true, however, that within the limits set by nature each individual is free to cultivate his own patch of good qualities, be it large or small. The man whom Mother Nature has "disadvantaged" in the matter of health and physical constitution can, by living more carefully than others and deliberately running fewer risks, prolong his life and enjoy such health as is given him. Financial fortunes have as often been built on hard, unswerving labor as on inherited wealth or sheer luck. Intellectual qualities can be cultivated by unremitting effort to the point where a man who is not endowed with the IQ of a genius can turn out very creditable work, and even achieve high distinction in his chosen field.

In the matter of language, it is a commonplace to find people of approximately identical social and educational background who are far more articulate and precise in their speech than others, whose diction is far superior, whose use of constructions and vocabulary is far more effective. Of two men, born in the same social class, having gone to the same schools and colleges, one turns into a polished orator, a charming conversationalist, a sought-after speaker, while the other seems tongue-tied, stumbles all over himself every time he speaks in public, flounders about seeking the right word even in ordinary conversation, poses as a strong, silent man not because he really feels inclined that way but because he doesn't trust himself to speak in anything beyond monosyllables and grunts. What makes the difference? It is precisely that "gift for languages" which Bloomfield claims does not exist. One man is naturally endowed in the field of language, just as Cassius Clay is naturally endowed for prizefighting; the other man is not. But this doesn't mean that the second man cannot assimilate the basic elements of the art or self-defense, if not in fisticuffs and shadowy footwork, then at least in a few judo or karate holds.

The same elements of natural endowment that go into the handling of one's own language, which some people handle well, others poorly, enter the learning of another language, at the child or at the adult

stage. It is idle to blind ourselves to the differences of native equipment. But this does not mean that those who are less generously
endowed must give up all hope, any more than those who are born
frail must resign themselves to a life of ill-health and an early death,
or those who are born poor must resign themselves to an entire existence of poverty and privation. Within the limitations of one's natural equipment, everyone can do something about his particular situation. While there's life there's hope. If you are not bountifully
endowed, it means greater effort on your part, and perhaps you will
never achieve the heights so easily attained by another whose native
gifts outstrip yours. But within your own limitations, you can attain
and achieve, sometimes to amazing degrees.

While some people seem to speak only in grunts and monosyllables,
they nevertheless speak. Without fully mastering his own language at
the age of five, everyone who is not deaf or idiotic does manage to
communicate, in one fashion or another, perfectly or imperfectly.
What he can do in his own language he can also do in another.

The fact of the matter is that in language learning three faculties
are involved, two of which pertain to the individual's natural, inherited equipment, while the third is a matter of personal choice,
though it, too, may in the final analysis turn out to be an inherited
trait.

The first item, on which even equalitarian mechanists of the Bloomfield type would agree, is the faculty of accurate hearing and accurate
reproduction of the sounds heard. Not all people hear equally well.
You don't have to be deaf to be tone-deaf, unable to reproduce or
carry a tune, seize the delicate overtones that are as much a part of
language as they are of music. It is not altogether certain whether the
language ear coincides precisely with the musical ear, though it is
extremely seldom, in my experience, that the two fail to go together.
A musical or a language ear can to some extent be cultivated, but
basically, what you don't hear you don't hear, and cannot reproduce.
Some people have a language ear so finely attuned that they can
catch not merely the nuances of a national accent, but even those of
the speech of an individual, and reproduce them to perfection. Others
are like the young Army lieutenant I observed in a Portuguese class
at the U.S. Army Language School in Monterey. The Brazilian lady
instructor pronounced a very simple word for him at least ten times

(three repetitions had sufficed for each of the other class members). When he gave it back to her wrong for the tenth time, she gave up and went on to the next man. The lieutenant was neither deaf nor idiotic. He simply lacked a language ear. He eventually graduated, but not with flying colors.

A child learns to speak by imitation of the people around him, coupled with endless repetitions. It is only careful observers without axes to grind who notice how many false starts are made, how many corrections are needed, what infinite patience must be exercised, when the child first begins to speak, and how much more this has to be done with some children than with others. Fortunately for the human race, and for our own thesis, all children eventually "learn to speak," in the Bloomfieldian concept of speaking. But it must be obvious to any impartial observer that all children do not progress at the same rate, that some have a quick and fluid gift of gab, while others of the same age group stumble and hesitate over the simplest utterances. This may to some extent be due to a difference in IQ. It is more likely to be due primarily to a difference in hearing equipment and the faculty to reproduce what one hears.

But very quickly a second inherited faculty comes into play, one that is more often associated with adult than with child speech. Yet the child, too, must possess and exercise it, otherwise his speech comes forth in the form of meaningless gabble. This is the associative faculty, one of the many functions of the brain, whereby certain sounds and sequences of sounds are linked to certain meanings. Here is where native IQ, the intellective function, begins to play a part. Later ramifications of this intellective function are the processes of selection and discrimination, quickness of perception and response, ultimately the power of abstraction and generalization that is exemplified in the mastery and application, even on a purely inductive plane, of the so-called rules of grammar, the ability to determine that if several nouns that one is already familiar with form their plural in a certain way, a new and unfamiliar noun that has the same characteristics and uses will probably also form its plural in that fashion.

The rational faculty is the common property of all human beings, but not to the same degree. After all, such terms as "bright," "dull," "quick-witted," "slow-witted" were not coined out of thin air or out of prejudice (though they may sometimes be applied with prejudice in the back of one's mind). They represent reality, a reality which may seem harsh to some of our equalitarian theoreticians but is reality nevertheless. At the same time it must be recognized that there are many different applications of this rational faculty, not all of them by any means equal. The man who fails at learning a language may do brilliant work in mathematics, physics, or chemistry.

There is not too much one can do about improving his language ear (short of surgical operations which to the best of my knowledge have not yet been tried), his basic IQ, or his specific logical faculty as applied to language. All are part of our heredity, and for them, as individuals, we can neither claim merit nor accept blame. We can, however, cultivate to the utmost the language ear and basic IQ we possess. No one need really despair. The man who falls within what is accepted as a normal range, and who cannot learn as much of a language as he really wants to learn, is yet to be born.

The third quality involved in language learning is far more subjective and individual, and at the same time altogether universal. This is the quality of interest in what you are doing or want to do, what you are learning or want to learn.

There are people who have no interest whatsoever in language or languages. There are others who view a language only as a tool to something else they want to achieve, like my colleague at Columbia who had gone deeply into Latin, Greek, French, German, and Italian in pursuit of his philosophical studies, but had never bothered with Spanish or Russian because he claimed they had produced little in his chosen field. There are still others to whom all language holds out a fascination and a spell. Psychologically, we tend to remember what we want to remember, and forget what we are not interested in and basically don't want. Interest supplies the answer to the remarkable ability of some people to recall baseball scores, batting averages, league standings, what actor or actress played what role in a play or picture that appeared twenty years ago, or what grandma said on a certain distant occasion. Everyone remembers what he likes and is interested in. If you have a basic interest in languages you will remember them; if you don't, you will forget them. It's as simple as that.

Interest, too, can be cultivated. If the incentive is attractive enough, some measure of interest normally develops. Pedagogical experts are well aware of this, and call it "motivation."

Interest often goes hand in hand with an occupation or calling, and memory goes with it. I was once talking to my automobile mechanic while he was repairing my car. We had known each other for a long time. He knew I was a good linguist; I knew he was a good mechanic. He was wondering how I could possibly remember all the various facts about all the various languages that I am supposed to be familiar with. Wasn't this some sort of superhuman gift? I countered by asking him how many individual parts there are in the average car. "About two thousand," he replied. "And they differ, do they not, from model to model and from year to year?" "Oh, yes." "Therefore you, in your repair work, have to know what to do with two thousand parts, multiplied by at least twenty makes, multiplied by at least twenty years. That makes you an expert in nearly one million separate items, about as many as I have to keep track of." It just so happened that his interest was cars; mine was languages. He made his living with his field of interest; I made my living with mine.

There are limits to interest and memory both. The human memory is a storehouse of facts, important and unimportant. Some storehouses are larger, others smaller (again, the size of your storehouse is part of your native endowment, and you should neither boast of it nor apologize for it). Psychologists are not agreed whether for every new fact that comes into our memory storehouse an old fact goes out, but there is certainly a relative position of accessibility to which the new or old fact is assigned. Some items, usually the ones that most interest us, are at our fingertips. Others lie buried so far back that it takes time and labor to dig them out. These are not necessarily the least important. They are the ones our mind considers least important, because they are least interesting to us. Again, if the motivation is there, we may consciously and deliberately assign a high priority to the ones we select.

It is the combination of these three factors—our language ear, our IQ, as applied to the field of grammatical coordination, and our interest, spontaneous or motivated—that constitutes our language-learning ability, and determines our success in acquiring a language. Within limits, the third may compensate for deficiencies in the first two.

Linguistic interest is rather easily pretested. The pretesting, in fact, can be left to the individual. Does language in the abstract, or do languages in the concrete, stir you to enthusiasm? Do they arouse a thirst for greater information? Do you shrink with distaste from a foreign-language program or commercial on radio or TV, and wonder why they had to put it on? Or do you joyfully accept it, and try to figure it out? When a foreign personality speaks in his own tongue, and the interpreter's voice quickly drowns out his utterance, do you experience relief or resentment? If you chance across a newspaper in a foreign language, do you quickly avert your eyes from it and go on to something else, or do your eyes linger lovingly on the strange words and characters? If someone speaks to you in a strange tongue, is your instinctive reaction "Aw, why don't you speak English?" or "Keep talking! Let's see if we can't get together on some common ground?" To take the proposition from another angle, do you feel that one or more languages are sufficiently important to you to warrant your attention, time, and labor?

Interest, as described above, can be spontaneous and instinctive. But it can also be motivated by the prospect of certain advantages, rewards, or punishments. We may not be basically interested in language or a language, but we may want to use it for some specific purpose. If so, we are like the manual laborer who does not really like his job but figures that's the only way he can earn the money he wants. Not as good as loving the game for its own sake, but effective nevertheless.

On the other hand, pretesting the other two basic language faculties, the "language ear" and grammatical coordination, can be placed on an altogether scientific basis.

When I was working as linguistic consultant at the U.S. Army Language School in Monterey, I insisted upon submitting myself to the type of entrance examination that was administered to all student entrants, officers and enlisted men alike. I had not previously seen the test, but it had been developed, under the direction of John B. Carroll, Harvard's linguistic psychologist, by Stanley Sapon, one of my own former graduate students, who had become a professor of linguistics in his own right. The test was in written form, and dealt exclusively with the faculty of grammatical coordination. You were given a certain length of time to familiarize yourself with some words in a constructed language called Temtem, and with some of the basic grammatical rules of this imaginary tongue. Then you were called upon to answer, in writing, one hundred questions testing your ability to apply the rules and vocabulary you had just learned. In the amount of time given you, fifty answers were about as many as anyone could give. The answers could, of course, be wrong as well as right. The scoring was automatic. My score was 48, which placed me, not too surprisingly, among the very top entrants. What might have been surprising to some, but not to me, was that there were two young officers in the entering class whose scores were higher than mine. I had, of course, far more experience than they. However, their native sense of grammatical coordination, which meant their theoretical ability to acquire languages, was greater than mine. Following their later careers at the school (one specialized in Italian, the other in Russian), I observed that they both did brilliantly. Both had an extensive language background from high school and college.

By way of contrast, some of the entering officers had scores as low as 3 and 7. They undoubtedly were experts in gunnery, or military engineering, or something else. Their sense of grammatical coordination was nevertheless weak. I doubt that this was a reflection on their general IQ—merely on that segment of it which involves the language faculty.

This formed, at the time, the entire prognostic test for the entrants. Considering that the method of instruction used in the Army Language School is almost entirely of the aural-oral variety (infinite imitation of native speakers and repetition, sound tapes, grammar assimilated inductively, through masses of examples, rather than intellectively, by precept and rule), it struck me as strange that the test should not include something designed for the language ear. Such tests had been tried, I was told, but they were very difficult and expensive to administer. Later tests, devised by Carroll and Sapon, are designed to remedy this deficiency. What I suggested at the time was a series of tapes, permanently inscribed with sounds, syllables, words, phrases, and entire sentences from an imaginary language, with blank, erasable spaces for repetition by the student. Fully inscribed and played back by the examiner, the tape would give a fairly exact prognosis of the student's ability to hear and reproduce what he heard.

I still think that a combination of the repetition tape to test the language ear and the written questions to test a student's faculty of grammatical coordination represent as nearly perfect a pretest of his native language ability as can be devised at the present time. A combination of the two, plus appropriate devices for self-administration, could give any individual the answer to the question: "How well and how fast can I learn another language?", so far as mechanical, inherited factors are concerned. To the question: "How interested or how well motivated am I?", he should be able to supply his own answer. To my mind, the last is the true determining factor in answering that other question so often asked: "*Can* I learn another language?"

Time, as Bloomfield states, is important. All other things being equal, results will be in direct ratio to the amount of time expended upon the language. But let us not overestimate the time element. Enough of a language can be learned in the time you ride the bus to work each morning to produce good, often striking results.

2

What Is Your Purpose? Your Available Time? Your Convenience?

The Individual: His Equipment; His Needs; His Motivation—Language for Tourism or for Literary Pursuits?—The Specific Need vs. the Generic Desire to Learn—Knowing What You Want, and Why —Where Do You Live?—How Much Time Have You?—How Much Do You Really Want to Learn?

THE individual's native equipment for language learning, his language ear, his sense of grammatical coordination, are what they are; and they differ from one person to another.

The matter of spontaneous interest in language and languages is likewise an individual proposition. If it is there, you are bound sooner or later to act on it, in one way or another. If it is not, you may nevertheless be interested, not by instinct but by motivation.

This brings us to the question of purpose. Why do you want to learn a particular language? Consider the proposition first in its grossest, most material aspect.

We are often amazed at the way ignorant, sometimes illiterate immigrants to our country manage to learn, in a relatively short time, enough American English to get by and enable them to participate in the nation's economic and even social life. We envy them. How do they do it? Are they more highly endowed than we are?

Not at all. They are more highly motivated. They *must* learn English if they want to make a living. Therefore, consciously or unconsciously, they make a massive effort, the kind of effort that we, too, would and could make if we found ourselves in their position; not the puny sort of effort that is exerted by the majority of our tourists abroad, who know they can always fall back on the linguistic facilities that are provided for them in exchange for their money, such as hotel clerks, guides, interpreters, waiters, porters, who speak their language.

Americans have proved time and again that they can learn foreign languages as fast and as well, within their individual limitations, as do foreigners, when they are placed in the sort of situation where a language *must* be learned. American war prisoners in Germany have been known to learn German well enough to pass for natives when they wanted to escape.

Compare the motivation of the European and the American student of foreign languages. The European knows from the time he begins to reason that a few hours on a train will take him to a land where his own language has no currency. He can hear foreign broadcasts on his radio, see foreign programs on TV, by merely flicking his switch. He is acutely aware of the reality and immediacy of foreign languages. The American student knows that he can travel for days and never encounter anything but his own American English, with slight local variations. There may be foreign speakers in his immediate environment, but he doesn't have to defer to them; they have to defer to him. There may be foreign travel in his future, but he normally does not know that until shortly before it happens.

Consequently, as he takes, in high school or college, a brief course in a foreign tongue, his motivation is altogether different from that of the European. There is a language requirement for graduation (just as often there is none), and he therefore faces language study as a boresome but indispensable chore associated with getting the diploma or degree that is his real goal.

This makes all the difference in the world. The European student, even though he is not highly endowed by nature for the acquisition of languages, yet considers them worth while for their own sake; the American student all too often thinks of them as something to be forgotten as soon as the final exams are over.

In recent times there has been some shift in the American attitude. There has been more travel abroad, there have been more foreign contacts. Above all, there have been more practical outlets for languages, more ways of putting them to work for material purposes rather than for the esoteric, ethereal literary or philosophical pursuits which have always been, and continue to be, the prerogative of a chosen few.

This supplies us with a new motivation and a new interest, still of a material order, to be sure. A good many people are now interested in a language not because of any spontaneous enthusiasm for it but because it leads to some sort of material benefit. But purposes still differ.

Columnist Robert Ruark, satirizing the sort of language instruction he claimed to have encountered in his French phrase book ("Nothing diverts me like a cat in the farmyard"), once said that what he really wanted to know how to say was: "Which way to the black market, *monsieur le gendarme?*" His was a legitimate complaint, if that and "What's in the hash, Giuseppe?" was what he really wanted to say. On the other hand, language has been described as the most IBM-like process of the human mind, something that enables us to express the most delicate shades of meaning as well as the most basic emotions. In approaching language in general or a language in particular, we should have some sort of clear notion of what we want it for. To read fine literature in the original? To understand a scientific paper? To read a letter from a pen pal? To make a speech before an audience? To read the signs and the menus? To chat pleasantly with a member of the opposite sex? To order a beer in Singapore? To do all of these things?

If it is the last, we may as well resign ourselves to the fact that the road will be long and difficult, that it will take many years of intensive work, of different varieties, to bring about the desired result. If our basic goal is only one or two of the above items, then the ideal way to go about it will be different in each case. The best way to learn to speak a few essential tourist phrases is not necessarily the best way to learn to translate a diplomatic document.

Schools and colleges must of necessity strike some sort of balance among the various goals and needs of their masses of students. The individual is under no such compulsion.

It used to be fashionable for the schools and colleges to present language study as the sort of thing that would lead to the enjoyment of literature, the appreciation of higher cultural values, the rounding out of the individual. This was at a time when the schools and colleges catered to an elite. Today, with democratic tendencies in the saddle and education for everybody, the trend in the schools and colleges is to favor the colloquial approach, on the theory that more people talk than read or write. But the needs of the individual are still varied, particularly at the grown-up stage, where people have some idea of their future plans and activities. This fact is recognized particularly by the colleges, which often distinguish between colloquial and literary courses. There is a perfectly good reason why their catalogues list courses in "Conversational French," "Scientific German," "Business Spanish," even "Tourist Italian," along with specific courses for the training of interpreters and translators, and courses in higher literary criticism.

You, as an individual, should have a fairly clear purpose in mind as you embark upon the study of a language. By and large, it is best to learn to speak and understand, to read and write, in the foreign language. But your purpose may call for something more specific.

If you are studying a language in regular classes at an institution (be it high school, college, Berlitz-type school, or school of adult education), there is little you can do about the basic program and method, save to supplement it intelligently with special regard for your own private requirements. Subject matter, methodology, textbooks, are all prescribed for you. You may discover to your sorrow after a time that they do not coincide with your native equipment and your needs. It is worth while making that discovery before you are too deeply committed. This you normally can do by means of a few pointed, well-directed inquiries.

If you are thrown upon your own resources, as many are, you may lack guidance, but you at least have the advantage of being able to make your own choice of books, recordings, native speakers. Since this book is directed primarily at those who are in this position, these matters will be discussed in detail later on. What may be stressed at the present time is the desirability of an avowed purpose in language study.

Consider the things that language may serve for under specific circumstances. If you are a lover of language in general, you may wish to turn into a professional linguist, a scientist of language, of whom there are said to be over two thousand in the United States, all gainfully employed by educational institutions, government agencies, nonprofit organizations, and private industry. Here you need a thorough grounding in the principles of linguistics (descriptive or historical, or both), plus a fairly deep knowledge of a few languages, plus structural information concerning many more. At the other end of the line, as a tourist or traveler for mere pleasure, all you really need is the ability to speak and understand a certain number of well-chosen phrases, with an accent which does not at all have to be that of a native, plus the ability to read signs and menus; but for best results, you should be able to do this in the language of each of the countries you propose to visit. Remember also that the more extensive your knowledge the more intense will be your enjoyment; there are few sadder sights than that of a tourist who is completely tongue-tied and utterly dependent on his hotel clerk and guide, or on the ability of the natives to speak and understand his language.

A UN or other diplomatic interpreter, particularly of the simultaneous variety, needs to know his two languages thoroughly and faultlessly, and to have the acuteness of hearing and the readiness and facility of speech to render into one what someone else is saying in the other. Here the ability to speak and understand has to be at its maximum. By way of contrast, the translator, be he diplomatic, commercial, or literary, needs no spoken-language ability whatsoever. He has time for reflection at his disposal. But his reading ability must be of the highest. In the case of the technical translator, he must possess not merely the two languages but the jargon of the particular field he is dealing with; if he is not specialized in this, all the conversational fluency in the world will avail him nothing (as I regretfully discovered when I had to return, untranslated, an Italian banking document that had been sent to me for translation into English; English and Italian are the tongues in which I am most fluent, and in which I can lecture extemporaneously and write without the slightest hesitation; but I did not know, and still do not know, the technical terminology of banking, in either language). To such an extent is the art of translating divorced from the spoken language that the UN actually has people who translate currently and accurately from written Chinese into English, and who are completely unable to read the Chinese text out loud, or speak a word of conversational Chinese.

A singer needs faultless diction and a native-speaker accent, but only in a restricted area. He need not even know what he is saying, provided he pronounces it correctly. Many opera singers can sing well in languages that they can neither speak, understand, read, nor write, but of which they have mastered the sound scheme.

A director of work crews in a foreign land (say an American oil engineer in the Arabian oil fields) needs a given number of spoken phrases in a specialized area. It does not matter too much if he is unable to read the Koran in the original.

Librarians, publishers and editors, museum curators, need a limited reading knowledge of a number of languages, which they may never be called upon to speak, plus the ability to identify several additional ones. A good reading knowledge of a language or languages, unaccompanied by the ability to speak or understand what is spoken, will normally suffice for research work in such far-flung fields as medicine, science, philosophy. A good conversational knowledge, even of the colloquial and slang variety, is needed by airline hostesses, tour leaders, foreign correspondents, for use abroad, and by salesmen, bank clerks, storekeepers, policemen, firemen, welfare and hospital workers, teachers, for use within our own borders, in areas where foreign-born populations are heavy. The Foreign Service and officers of the armed forces stationed abroad should be able to speak, understand, and read the language of the country to which they are assigned. Advertising men should have some knowledge of customs and points of view, as well as of the written languages, of the countries where they expect to sell their products. Broadcasting staffs should at least know how to pronounce with some degree of correctness personal and place names. For military intelligence and secret police work, the foreign language should be handled to perfection, with native-speaker accent. Export and import houses and international banking establishments need primarily the written language, even though a good deal of their correspondence comes in stereotyped formulas.

What we have listed above are only a few of the many purposes you may have in mind in connection with your study of a language or languages. Your specific needs are different in each case. You should know them, and weigh them.

But now comes another important item. Where are you located? In a large city, where you have the possibility of taking regular language courses at a school or university? In a smaller town, where you could perhaps arrange for private instruction from the local high school teacher of French or Spanish? Out in the open wastes, where your main contact with culture is through radio and TV? Out at sea a good part of the time?

Your environment more often than not determines your behavior. You are freest where you have the broadest choice: a school of general studies, or of adult education; a private school; individual person-to-person instruction; radio or TV lessons; recordings and tapes; books of all sorts. Some forms of instruction are fairly expensive, others less so, others practically or altogether free. Some place definite restrictions upon you, others do not. If you join a regularly constituted class at a school, public or private, you have a fixed commitment, which must be met under penalty of missing essential parts of the instruction and falling hopelessly behind; at the same time, this acts as an incentive to continue to attend the course till the bitter end, since you have already invested your money in it. You can ask a private tutor to skip the lesson for one day or one week, but not the French 3 instructor at Columbia University or N.Y.U. You can make a date with a recording, but you can also break it, with no immediate dire results, since you can always pick up where you left off; on the other hand, you may be tempted to break the dates too often. Books are something you can even carry around with you, to occupy time that would otherwise be wasted, such as bus and subway rides, or waiting periods between trains.

The question of time as well as of money comes up. It is all very well to say: "I'm going to learn Russian in my spare time." How much spare time do you really have? If you have it now, are you sure it will remain that way next month? Are you distraction-prone?

Some schools of psychology claim that we always do what we really want to do. If this is true, it means that your resolution to learn Russian in your spare time will not be broken by anything that may happen, short of a real personal or national disaster. But if you go to the movies instead of listening to your Russian recordings, it is because basically you like the movies better than you do Russian.

It is interesting to see to what lengths people will go to study languages when they really want to. In Oxnard, California, a group of businessmen wanting to learn Spanish couldn't agree on a suitable evening class time. A morning hour was suggested, and the group finally settled on 5 to 7 A.M., Tuesdays and Thursdays. The newspaper account does not inform us how many stuck to their resolve, or for how long. New York school children, desiring additional conversational practice in the languages of their choice, turned up voluntarily forty minutes before official school opening time to enjoy a class in conversational drill.

So far as language learning is concerned, time does not differ materially from native equipment and money. Where there's a will there's a way. One finds time to do what one really wants to do. And there is such a thing as utilizing every scrap of time.

3

How Many Different Ways
of Learning a Language Are There?

Being Born to It—Residing in a Foreign Country—The Dangers of Biculturism—The Spoken-Language Course and the "Army Method"—Reading and Writing—The Value and Use of Recordings—The Private School and the Correspondence School—Studying a Language All by Yourself

BY far the best way of learning a language (or more than one) is to be born into a family that speaks it (or them). This may sound paradoxical, but it isn't meant to be.

Bloomfield, whom we quoted above, is right at least to the extent that everyone not deaf or idiotic will have picked up, by the age of five, the basic sound scheme, structure, and essential speaking vocabulary of the language or languages he hears spoken around him. He couldn't help himself even if he tried. In one fashion or another (and fashions may differ radically) all people, with the exceptions noted, manage to speak their own language. Often they speak more than one, if more than one was spoken around them before they reached school age.

In a home where another language than the one native to the country is spoken, and the children are encouraged or compelled to speak it, they will normally grow up bilingual, because they will invariably pick up the national tongue on the outside, in the course of their play, their schooling when they get to school age, or their other activities.

The reason I am thoroughly bilingual in English and Italian is that my parents resolutely set their foot down against my speaking English at home, and refused to allow me to speak it to them. Similar cases are too numerous to count. Unfortunately, far too many parents are too busy, or tired, or indifferent to bother, and take the course of least resistance, adapting their own speaking habits to the language the child brings in from the street or the school, and which they themselves have learned or are learning. Sometimes they do this deliberately, under the mistaken notion, fostered by certain unwise psychologists and educationists, that the child's development is hindered and confused by two languages, and that neither language will come out perfectly. Nothing could be further from the truth. Psychological development is quickened by the sense of comparison between two modes of expressing the same concept, and the child is prevented from establishing the ironbound link between concept and speech symbol that all general semanticists deplore. Not merely two, but three or four, perhaps more languages will all come out equally well, if they continue to be practiced and used. I am one living example. Others are the two daughters of the *Reader's Digest's* roving editor, J. P. McEvoy, now deceased; their command of idiomatic English, French, and Spanish was and is absolute, and their psychological development was anything but impeded. Still another is Charles Berlitz, who spoke four languages before he reached kindergarten, still speaks them today (plus a few more learned at the adult stage), and does not seem to be at all inhibited, frustrated, or confused. The facts of the matter are: 1. that the possession of more than one language builds up self-confidence, since it gives you a decided advantage; 2. that the person who would speak poorly two or more languages would speak a single language just as poorly.

In the kindergartens and schools of both New York and Texas, children of different language backgrounds have been set at the task of talking their respective languages to one another, with the result that little Mexicans and Puerto Ricans come out speaking good English as well as Spanish, and children of other groups acceptable Spanish as well as English. At the UN nursery school, children of as many as ten different language backgrounds are encouraged to use their respective languages to one another. Though English and French predominate, the results are excellent. American language teachers are becoming more and more sold on the proposition that the best time to begin foreign language study is as early as possible, preferably in kindergarten.

Under the circumstances, we would submit that it is not merely illadvised but little short of criminal for parents who have the possibility of imparting an extra language to their children by the most effective and most natural method yet devised to fail to do so, either because of silly and outdated psychological theories, or because they are indolent and indifferent, or because they foolishly give in to the child's protests, born of the tendency to conformity that occasionally sweeps the younger generation, that "he doesn't want to be different from the other children."

Next to growing up with a second language, the most effective way of learning is probably foreign travel and residence. But this has its own peculiar drawbacks, as will be seen in a later chapter. If it is not done the right way, it may do more harm than good. It is often done under the official auspices of educational institutions, but at the adult stage. Some colleges (and they are no longer mainly women's colleges) have junior years abroad, which means that the students, with professorial guidance from their own institution, spend a year in France, Germany, Italy, Spain, or Mexico, as the case may be, attending classes at the local universities, mingling with the local populations and their native fellow students, often living with local families. An attempt is made to duplicate foreign residence conditions at summer institutes like that of Middlebury, where the students are placed on their honor to use nothing but the language they are studying, even to one another, but it's not quite the same thing, because two students talking imperfect French to each other will tend to copy each other's imperfections. At any rate, the Junior Year Abroad and the Foreign Residence form part of the official language offering of regular institutions, and involve special requirements of money, time, and even age level. Conversational practice with native speakers, often on a basis of exchange ("We'll talk my language to each other one day, yours the next") can be an effective replacement for residence abroad if consistently followed.

Regular courses in high school, college, and university will be discussed in a separate chapter, as will be their assorted methodologies, old and new. This is as good a place as any, however, to voice a warning against the dangers of what might be styled biculturism, or psychological over-specialization, which is often fostered by high school and college teachers of individual languages. This occurs when the learner becomes so immersed in the language and culture of the group whose language he is learning that he forgets or tends to look down upon all others, save, of course, his own. This is not quite, but almost as bad as monolingualism and monoculturism, where we view all foreign groups and languages without exception as inferior. Native teachers of a language often impart to their students the notion that nothing is of importance outside their own culture and tongue. In these cases, it is up to the learner to keep his eyes and ears open and retain his sense of balance. Non-English contributions to civilization are many, and they come from many sources, not perhaps to an equal degree, but sufficiently to prevent us from becoming Anglo-French, or Anglo-Spanish, or Anglo-German, or Anglo-Italian cultural snobs.

This warning goes hand in hand with another in connection with what might be termed over-specialization of interests, as represented by the man who thought Spanish and Russian beneath his attention because, in his concept, they had contributed little to his favorite philosophical pursuits. One should have his field of specialization and seek his sources where they exist. But a man of true culture should also be interested in and recognize contributions from other fields. The range of beauty and learning is infinite. An open mind never hurt anybody.

In addition to regular high school and college courses, which are necessarily subject to the broader requirements of the curriculum of which they form a part, there are the private language schools which make it their business to impart only the language or languages the learner may be interested in, with no side issue of requirements or degrees. These are often favored by people who really want to learn a language and have no further ax to grind. Language courses for so-called non-matriculated students were, and still are, offered by a good many universities in their University Extensions or Schools of General Studies; but the tendency is perceptible in many of these institutions to look with disfavor upon the non-matriculated student as one having insufficient preparation and cluttering the academic landscape, and to restrict their offerings to degree-seeking adult students, with all the side requirements that such a degree-seeking status implies. The fact that the man who is willing to invest his money and time in a language, and wants nothing else, must necessarily be strongly motivated in connection with that language apparently makes no difference to the administrators. In all events, courses offered by Schools of General Studies do not normally differ in methodology or procedure from those of the regular undergraduate college.

When one speaks of the private language school, his thoughts run naturally to the mighty Berlitz chain, with ramifications and branches throughout not only the United States but the rest of the world as well. Yet there are numerous other excellent private schools of languages, some even more highly specialized and tailored to fit individual requirements. The Language Guild in New York, for instance, features crash courses in unusual languages, on an individual or group basis, for business, industrial, and government personnel destined for overseas service. There are special schools for interpreters, in various fields, and for translators, both of the literary and the technical variety. There are schools that specialize in imparting certain segments of the language, such as the medical or legal jargon. In the case of the Berlitz schools, there is a specific methodology based on the motto that "The Eye is the Enemy of the Ear," and on the principle that the learner's native language must never appear. Initially, everything is presented, explained, defined in the language that is being learned, with objects, pictures, gestures, play-acting coming into play as often as necessary. Not everyone reacts favorably to this method, but it has become popular enough to have been appropriated by a certain school of linguistics and widely imitated, with variations, particularly in institutions under government control, such as the Army Specialized Training Program (ASTP) during the Second World War, and most of the armed forces language schools today, not to mention a good many high schools, colleges, and universities that accept government grants for language teaching; but the latter normally run their Berlitz-type courses side by side with the more traditional variety. Other private language schools have their own points of view and methodologies, which cover a surprisingly wide range.

Needless to say, the Berlitz and other private schools, like academic institutions, call for a specific outlay of money and time. Even if you pay higher rates for individual instruction, you must make your appointments with your instructor in advance, and endeavor to keep them. Also, these schools, public, academic, and private, are by no means available everywhere, though they are likely to be found in all fair-sized cities. Private tutoring is merely a private school on an individual basis.

For those who are forced to study by themselves, without the aid of a teacher, several ways are open. They split into two great divisions, the one that makes its appeal through the ear and stresses the spoken language, and the one that makes its appeal through the eye and stresses the written language. Recordings are typical of the first, books of the second. Of course, they are often blended. All recordings, to the best of my information, are accompanied by some sort of booklet that presents the written form of what one is learning through the ear, while the fashion is growing of producing grammar books for class or individual instruction with an accompanying recording or series of recordings that present the spoken form of what one is learning primarily through the eye.

Language recordings have been in existence for quite a long time, though their real vogue began after the Second World War. Cortina-phone and Linguaphone were among the earliest. Today, the number of recorded courses is legion, to the point where their producers are encountering the law of diminishing returns because of too much competition. The merits and drawbacks of various types of recordings will be discussed in a separate chapter. One of their greatest claims is that they present the voices of native speakers, not of American-born, American-trained teachers whose pronunciation of the foreign language may leave something to be desired, and who were all too numerous in the high schools and colleges of earlier decades. It must be stressed that the application of recordings is left to the purchaser-learner, and this means that they are often in one way or another misused. More on this later.

A compromise between the regular or private language course under full supervision and the individual form of study based on recordings or books is a new type of correspondence course which has recently gained considerable vogue in Europe, has spread to countries of Asia and Africa, and now seems about to enter the American market. Correspondence courses in all sorts of fields, including languages, used to be featured by a good many of our most prominent institutions of higher learning, as a part of their Extension offering. The course would be planned and imparted by regular staff members and subscribed for by students who lived too far away from the university to be able to attend its regular classes. The student would receive by mail textbooks and other materials, precise instructions as to what to do each week, quizzes to be answered and sent in to the university, where they would be corrected and sent back to him so that he could see where he was deficient, and a final exam at the end of the course, with questions which he could answer and send in for an evaluation, with a diploma or attestation, or even regular academic credits, conferred upon him upon successful completion of the term's work. Among the reasons that led to the gradual decay of the correspondence course were probably the difficulty of administering it properly, the labor and expense involved in the grading and mailing of papers, and, for what concerns the field of languages, the fungus growth of the newfangled recordings.

But now the correspondence course bids fair to come back to life. Such organizations as Denmark's Nature Method and Sweden's Nu-Methoden combine the correspondence features with such devices as progressive reading in the foreign language, with notes and grammatical explanations, or the presentation of a foreign literary text done in excellent translation, with, at first, only a few words and phrases in the original foreign language injected into the translated text, going on progressively to less translation and more original, until at the end one reaches lessons presented entirely from the original text. While these devices bear necessarily upon the written (in fact, the literary) rather than the spoken language, the addition of recordings where the foreign words and phrases are spoken by a native for repetition by the learner supplies the spoken-language feature.

Variations on this basic theme are the language lessons presented by many stations on radio and TV (these offer the attractive feature of being altogether free); foreign-language movies (for purchase or hire, or on TV); the taped or recorded lecture, given in a foreign language; and even the lecture telephoned by long-distance wires by a speaker located in one section of the country and amplified in a lecture hall for a student audience a thousand or more miles away, with the added bonus to the audience of seeing their lecturer's picture, or the written text of his address, flashed on a large screen before their eyes. The radio and TV lessons are predicated upon your being in the area where they are given, and upon your being free at the time of their occurrence, while the telephone lectures are institutional. Foreign-language movies with English captions are of aid once the elements of the language have been assimilated, and there are even special instructional films which can be rented or bought, and used at home or in the classroom.

Books for language instruction are the earliest known form of such instruction on record. The speakers of Sanskrit, Greek, and Latin had grammarians who codified the language and prescribed usage, in written works that have come down to us. But these were for the language's own speakers. Bilingual grammars came later, one of the earliest on record being Aelfric's Latin grammar for the instruction of Anglo-Saxon speakers, which appeared about A.D. 1000.

Grammars are normally directed at the written rather than the spoken language. This is not as great a drawback as might appear on the surface, especially in these days of extensive literacy and widespread use of the written tongue. But there are also attempts to teach the spoken language through written devices, ranging all the way from the spelling by ear employed in medieval pilgrim phrase books to the so-called "English transcription" of the GI and tourist manuals, and the International Phonetic Alphabet (IPA) transcriptions, or the more sophisticated phonemic transcriptions appearing in many up-to-date grammars and dictionaries.

Learning a language in written form does not, as a rule, confer upon you the ability to speak and particularly to understand the spoken language, though if you have thoroughly assimilated the grammatical rules and vocabulary in written form it will be far easier for you to speak and understand after you have been exposed for a time to native speakers and have attuned your ear to the sounds of the language, a process which may take anywhere from a few weeks to a year or two, depending upon your language ear and the nature of the language.

On the other hand, learning a language for reading purposes only presents certain advantages. Reading gives you time for reflection, comprehension, and full assimilation; speaking does not. If you miss a key word in speech, it may throw your entire understanding out of kilter; if you come across an unfamiliar word in your reading, you can look it up in a dictionary, and go on from there. In using our own language, it is easier to pick up the phone and speak than to write a letter; the opposite is often true when dealing with a foreign tongue.

More will be said later about the effectiveness of grammars, dictionaries, and phrase books, and the qualities that are desirable or undesirable in connection with them. Certain special written-language devices are worth mentioning here. The system of language through pictures, recently brought back into vogue by I. A. Richards of Basic English fame, has a fairly remote ancestry. There is, for example, a Swedish A-B-C book for children, published in 1822, with pictures of objects and equivalent words in Swedish, French, German, and English, so that the picture of the roots of a tree is accompanied by *Rot, Racine, Wurzel,* and *Root.* The present-day series of *Languages Through Pictures,* extending to such unusual tongues as Arabic and Hindi, is far more elaborate.

Another written-language device is the dual reader, with a literary text on one page and its English translation on the page facing. This facilitates the reading process to the extent that instead of wasting time looking up unfamiliar words in the dictionary, or in the vocabulary at the end of the book, you can glance across and pick up the meaning, at the same time that you can compare the syntactical construction in the two languages. This type of reader can be used effectively only if you have some previous knowledge of the language; it definitely is not recommended for beginners. Its classroom use is marred by the possibility of its being used as a trot in the preparation of assignments.

Grammars, readers, dictionaries, even phrase books or idiom lists are all, of course, used in regularly constituted language courses, particularly those of the traditional variety, where they form the basis of instruction. They can also be used for self-instruction. The techniques for using them are the same, but checking yourself for progress and accuracy is not always easy. Keys to exercises are often included in grammars, particularly those specifically designed for self-instruction, where the learner is not likely to misuse them as a short cut to a passing grade. Programmed learning, recently developed and at present used in some schools, is still in the experimental stage. Here the learner checks his own progress at every step by means of mechanical devices, and progresses naturally, and at his own speed, from one

stage to the next. It presents entrancing possibilities for self-instruction, but also certain difficulties of application which are in the
process of being ironed out.

As you see, the means of learning a new language are many and
varied, and such as to suit practically any purpose, time schedule,
and pocketbook. It is up to you to select the one that will best fit
into your scheme.

4

The Old or the New Method?

The "Quickie" Claims—Learning a Piece of a Language—Stress on Speaking and Understanding—Time-Wasting Procedures—The Written Language and Its Practical Importance—What Is "Correct" in Language Learning?—Comparisons Not Always Odious

IT was typical of the old-line language teacher that he guaranteed you nothing. He did not stress the ease of learning of the language he tried to impart; if anything, quite the contrary. He would emphasize the difficulties and complexities of the task you faced, the time and sweat and labor it would cost you to assimilate his language properly. By properly he meant with full command of all the intricacies of grammatical forms, all the minor exceptions, all the complex vocabulary. But if you dutifully put in your three or four years of classroom instruction, at the rate of three hours a week, supplemented by long poring over homework assignments, he allowed that you might eventually come up with enough knowledge of French or German or Latin to be able to read and enjoy the classics of the language.

During the Second World War and the years that followed, the new school of language teaching made altogether different claims. By using the aural-oral or audio-lingual method, learning as a child does, by constant imitation and repetition, with high concentration of time, plus certain special, mysterious techniques about which there was a magical aura and which were never quite clearly defined, you could become a fluent speaker of a foreign language in a very, very short time.

Some of the claims were debatable, but at least halfway reasonable: "A student learns a language more quickly and more soundly by an intensive oral approach than he would in the same number of hours devoted to the traditional slow study of reading and writing"; "Students taught entirely in French have a better grasp on all phases of the language than those taught by the conventional bilingual method"; "When the pupils reach the third grade, they take a course in oral

31

French; it is amazing how easily many of them read and speak the language before they get into the fourth grade"; "Students can learn in two years' study to speak and understand ordinary conversational French."

On the other side of the ledger were some rather wild pronouncements made at the time of the Army Specialized Training Program, that in six weeks or less the soldier-students had become fluent speakers of the languages they were studying intensively. As recently as May, 1965, a very popular Sunday newspaper magazine supplement featured an article with the astounding title: "How to Learn a New Language in Five Days." This described an experiment in something called Total Immersion, where the student spends the sixteen hours of his waking day with three native instructors, working in three shifts, and using nothing but the target language, which the learner is also forced to use by gentle persuasion coupled with a little bullying. Result: the creation of a Russian or Italian speaker in five days of such concentrated instruction.

The wilder of these claims are based on a partial truth: that anyone can learn a *piece* of a language in a very short time. How large the piece is depends partly on your native equipment of ear and grammatical coordination, partly on your previous language background, partly on the effectiveness of your instructors. How much of that piece you will retain after the lapse of a year, a month, or even a week, unless there is a steady follow-up, is a matter of conjecture.

In contrast to these rather extravagant claims, we have the sober statements of the real experts in the audio-lingual field. The Yale Linguistics Program, for instance, says: "A large proportion of the student's time must be devoted to this one task, at least for the first semester. Three-hour courses are utterly inefficient; maximum efficiency certainly cannot be attained in less than eight hours a week in the classroom, and probably a still larger proportion of the student's effort during the first months would save time in the end." The U.S. Army Language School at Monterey has a schedule of six hours a day, five days a week, with the native instructor changing every hour, so that the students will not get used to only one instructor's pronunciation and be able to understand no one else; plus three hours of "homework" per night (this consists mainly of listening to tapes or recordings, repeating the utterances and answering the questions asked on the tapes); and this goes on for six months in the case of the "easier" languages (such as French, Spanish, Italian, German); nine months for the medium-hard ones (Russian, Arabic, Turkish, Persian); and twelve months for the truly difficult ones, particularly the tone languages (Chinese, Thai, Burmese, Vietnamese). It is submitted that anyone endowed with anything even faintly resembling a normal ear and coordination equipment, relieved of all other duties and preoccupations, can indeed become a fluent speaker of a language with such an outlay of time and effort. If one studies an "easy" language, such as French, under this system, he will have 780 hours of classroom work in his six-month course, which is the full equivalent of six and a half years of the ordinary high school or college course at the rate of three hours a week, with a school year consisting of the normal forty weeks. A good deal can be and has been accomplished also in six and a half years of high school and college French, as will be testified by many former students who have had such a sequence and are just as fluent speakers of French as many of the Army Language School graduates. Ten years of college Russian, and thirteen years of college Chinese (the equivalents in time of the Army School courses) have also been known to produce excellent results, even by the traditional method.

It is time to stop kidding ourselves about short cuts to *full* language ability. Plenty of results can be obtained in short periods of time, but they will be only partial results; how partial depending, as usual, on the individual's native equipment and his motivation and effort. This does not at all mean that the partial results are not worth while striving for. It is highly desirable to have a hundred, or even a dozen high-frequency phrases at the tip of one's tongue, to be able to understand as many when spoken by a native speaker, to be able to read a few signs and headlines. But this is not *full* possession of the language. It is a highly desirable smattering, but a smattering nevertheless. Full possession of a language means being able to do with it pretty much what we do with our own: speak it unhesitatingly, and on a variety of topics; understand practically all that is said to us at normal conversational speed; read all the material that it interests us to read; write at least an acceptable friendly or business letter. Note that not all people, even in their own tongue, are fluent after-dinner orators, or even charming conversationalists; that things can be said to us in one of the professional jargons, or one of the language's dialectal forms, that we will not understand; that we cannot read all books on all subjects; that not all of us are qualified to write technical reports, or even publishable short stories; and that there is no reason why we should be required to do in a foreign language what we cannot do in our own.

So much for the "quickie" claims. When it comes to the full audio-lingual methodology as contrasted with the traditional one of learning the grammar out of a book, and then applying that grammar in reading, writing, and speech, there are other considerations.

The aural-oral methodology advocated and applied by the innovators has in itself certain built-in weaknesses as well as certain contradictions. The child learns by imitation and repetition, followed at a distance by an inductive mental process based largely on analogy. The adult is not a child. He tires of imitation and repetition, which are purely mechanical processes. He has acquired inhibitions and self-consciousness, and does not delight in "monkey-sees-monkey-does" activities. He has also acquired faculties of abstraction and generalization which are largely deductive in nature, and which clamor to be put to work. Hence it is quite usual in places like the Army Language School to hear the students complain that they would learn much faster if the instructors would lay down for them certain grammatical rules of the language, so that they would know the reasons for some of the shifts in the phrases they are asked to repeat like parrots, and if they were then left free to apply these rules. This is precisely what the traditional method does. Many adult students resent being turned into parrots, and having their adult intellective faculties relegated to oblivion.

The child normally gives no thought to the written language until he comes to it. The adult knows that the language he is studying has a written form. He resents having it kept a dark secret from him until several weeks after he has started his instruction; partly because he thinks it is important; partly because he does not like to be an adult illiterate, even temporarily; partly because he thinks it would clarify visually what he does not always hear perfectly. He accepts without protest transcriptions of languages like Chinese, where the written character bears no relation to the spoken sound; but he does not see why this is necessary in the case of languages that have some sort of phonetic alphabet and sound-for-symbol relationship, which he feels capable of grasping, even if it is imperfect. He knows it might confuse him, but he feels it will confuse him anyway when it is finally presented to him, no matter how much he may have assimilated the spoken forms of the language, just as he was confused by his English spelling when he first began learning it, after having learned to speak.

It used to be fashionable in audio-lingual circles to advocate that the learner should divorce himself from his own language as he learned another, and the methodology is still followed, as in the Berlitz schools, of never saying "book," but holding up a book and saying *"livre,"* in the hope that a mental link will be created between the object and the foreign word that will bypass the English word. But the adult has already formed a mental habit of associating the object book with his English name for it. Translation can be done mentally as well as orally, and a great deal of this mental process goes on even in a class ostensibly conducted by the new methodology: "What I want to say at this point is 'Give me the book'; but I want to say it in French; 'give me' is *donnez-moi;* 'the book' is *le livre;* therefore what I must say is *'donnez-moi le livre.'* "

This process of mental translation, however, if sufficiently repeated, ultimately becomes automatic, with the result that the English is eventually skipped, and *Donnez-moi le livre* comes out spontaneously in given situations. This is what the old methodology relied on, and its translation exercises were aimed at eventually producing an automatic response. A man learning to drive is at first acutely conscious of his clutch, his brake, his gas pedal, his steering wheel. His driving process is at first largely a matter of conscious directions transmitted from the brain to the muscles. Eventually, they become automatic reflexes that bypass the conscious brain. It takes time. It also takes time for the imitation and repetition to sink in to the point where they become automatic.

Of late, interestingly, a certain number of audio-lingual advocates have gone back on the original Bloomfieldian maxim, "Forget all the languages you know, particularly your own, when learning a new one," in favor of a new principle of detailed comparison of the sound scheme, grammatical structure, and vocabulary of your own language and the target language. This ultra-modern approach, advocated particularly by Robert Lado, begins to resemble the old traditional method, which was in essence precisely that: a comparison of the new language with your own.

Learning to speak and understand a language by imitation and repetition presupposes, of course, the appearance at the point of contact of one or more native speakers whom it is safe to listen to and imitate. Best for the purpose are speakers of the standard language (rather than one of its dialects) who are fairly cultured and educated, but without being over-refined or inclined to use literary terms and expressions that are often outmoded or not current in ordinary speech. To the extent that the instruction is of the traditional, predominantly written-language type, this requirement wanes; under these circumstances, a non-native instructor who is acutely conscious of the differences between the two languages and of the psychology of the learners is often indicated, even if his pronunciation leaves something to be desired. We shall see further on how these features work out in practice, both in academic courses and in private instruction.

One more feature of the new methodology to which attention may be drawn is the doctrine of the basic pattern. Many followers of the aural-oral school believe that it is not at all essential to acquire a large vocabulary at the outset, but that the instruction should rather be centered on those phrase and sentence types which are of most frequent occurrence in the language. This means taking a basic, frequently used expression, such as "Where is the ——?" or "I am going to the ——," and repeating it until it is thoroughly assimilated, with suitable, but not too numerous substitutions for the blank space ("Where is the church?"; "Where is the school?"; "Where is the police station?", etc.). The theory is that once all basic pattern structures are thoroughly assimilated, vocabulary can be expanded at will and according to individual needs. There is undoubted merit to this method, which is in many ways the opposite of the traditional learning-for-reading methodology which concentrated on abundant and rapid expansion of the vocabulary.

On the other hand, it must be pointed out that in the long run, for purposes of complete language learning, the outstanding difficulty lies in the vocabulary. Sound schemes, basic grammatical structures, systems of writing (at least in any alphabetic form) may present formidable problems, but they can be overcome, and normally are, at the end of one or two years of conscientious instruction. But the normal speaking vocabulary of the average cultivated speaker consists of at least 30,000 words. These have to be learned, usually the hard way, by a process of memorization, and there is no known device by which this labor may be minimized. (Grouping words by roots and prefixes, or referring to etymological origins or English cognates, is only of limited help; languages are too idiomatic and illogical to be seriously circumvented by these devices.) It is not of too much help, from the conversational standpoint, to be able to say "How do I go to ——" and then be stuck on the word designating the place to which you want to go. "I want some ——" is fine, but is it water, wine, beer, milk, or bread that you want? Occasionally, the bare noun, or verb, or adjective, properly spoken, is of greater use than the basic phrase.

All that has been said so far seems to point to two basic conclusions. The first is that thorough language learning, as distinguished from a bigger or smaller smattering of a language, is a long, difficult, and tedious process, with no royal road. To be able to handle a foreign language with anything like the facility with which we handle our own, many weary hours must be spent in study, of one type or another, according to our specific needs. This does not at all mean that the smattering is to be despised. Much can be done with a fraction of a language, and no time spent in acquiring that fraction is wasted.

The second conclusion is at least equally far-reaching. In the absolute, there is no such thing as a "good" or a "bad" method, a "correct" or an "incorrect" method for learning a language. There is only an effective and an ineffective method, for you as an individual, and for the purpose to which you want to put what you are learning. Generally speaking, the most effective method is a "catch-as-catch-can," or altogether eclectic method, based on your particular needs and circumstances. Granting that the quality of instruction in various methods is equally good, and that you have full choice of methods, you should still consult your specific needs, inclinations, and native equipment. The conversational, direct, audio-lingual method is indicated if your primary purpose is to communicate orally, to speak, understand, and be understood. (Realize, however, that under any circumstances you will probably never speak quite like a native, or be mistaken for one; but that is no great tragedy, unless you are engaged in espionage work; and espionage work calls for special techniques and training.)

Realize also that for purposes of basic communication there is no such thing as a "better" or a "worse" type of language, by which we mean language that is more or less "correct" from the standpoint of grammatical structure or native-speaker accent. There is only effective and ineffective language. Does what you say get your meaning across, and do you, in return, seize the gist of what is being said to you? If so, your spoken language is effective; if not, it fails in its purpose. But remember also that the purpose for which you are using the language may be a different one. You may be speaking for rhetorical effect, in which case you need a type of language that no one can criticize or laugh at.

On the other hand, you may want the language only, or primarily, for the purpose of reading scientific treatises, or restaurant menus, in which case if you can get the burden of the written or printed message your control of the language is effective. Or you may want it to extract from works of literature in the original their full flavor and aesthetic nuances, in which case your control of syntactical and stylistic devices and of high-flown vocabulary must be well-nigh perfect.

Both in the audio-lingual and in the traditional grammatical method there is bound to be at first a process of laborious translation, mental even if not spoken, which eventually turns into automatic control. If you are learning Portuguese by ear and run up against the peculiar Portuguese fashion of naming the days of the week, you will see or hear *quarta-feira,* and your initial reaction will be to start counting on your fingertips: "Monday is the second day, Tuesday the third day, Wednesday the fourth day; that's it!" But it won't be long before you are automatically using *quarta-feira* with the same degree of unconsciousness with which you use "Wednesday." Do not let this worry you, no matter what your Berlitz instructor tells you.

Professor John B. Carroll of Harvard, probably America's foremost linguistic psychologist, described in the May, 1965, issue of *Modern Language Journal* the most comprehensive experiment tried out to date to determine the efficacy of the two basic methodologies, the audio-lingual (or aural-oral) and the cognitive code-learning (the old traditional method based primarily on the written language). This experiment was conducted over a period of two years, with three hundred students divided into two groups, under the auspices of the U.S. Office of Education and the University of Colorado. At the end of the first year, the aural-oral group was significantly better in listening and speaking, but somewhat behind the traditional group in reading and writing. By the end of the second year, the traditional group was still slightly ahead in writing ability, but the two groups no longer differed at all in listening and reading. The suggested conclusion was that it does not make material difference which method is used, provided the quality of instruction is uniformly good. Additional conclusions formulated by Dr. Carroll are to the effect that meaningfulness works out better than automaticity; that materials presented visually are more easily learned than comparable ones presented aurally; and that conscious, associative features facilitate learning. His final suggestion is that the audio-lingual methodology is ripe for major revision, particularly in the direction of combining it with some of the better elements of the cognitive code-learning, or traditional, system.

All this is of scant comfort to theorists who hold that there is "only" one correct method to impart or learn languages. But it ties in pretty well with what we have chosen to label the "catch-as-catch-can" system, with particular attention to the needs and native equipment of the individual.

5

How Did YOU Learn Languages?

A Bit of Personal Linguistic History—The Easy and the Hard Way—Teaching as an Aid to Learning—The Drawbacks of a Native-Speaker Accent—Speaking Knowledge vs. Structural Knowledge—"Which Language Do You Dream in?"

LET me preface my statements with an avowal: in the matter of languages, I am tremendously, almost disgracefully, overprivileged. I have a good ear for music and for language, with the capacity for accurate imitation and reproduction of sounds. This is coupled with an analytical, logical, quasi-mathematical mind, and ability in grammatical coordination. This is not at all a boast, for in all this there is nothing to boast about. These traits are God-given or inherited, as you choose to view them. I was born with them. I had nothing whatsoever to do with them, save to put them to good use.

Along with this wealth of native equipment, I was almost fantastically lucky for what concerns languages. I happen to have been born in Rome, of a cultured middle-class family. This means that my first language was a fairly literary brand of Italian, unmarred by any heavy dialectal features (though my Roman accent is noticeable in my Italian, along with a whiff of Tusco-Umbrian from my Orvieto-born mother), or by excessive upper- or lower-class traits. At the age of seven, after I had had two years of schooling in Rome and had learned to read and write Italian with facility, my family came to the United States, where I had to learn American English (New York variety, but again shorn of excessive class features) and start my schooling all over again in my new language.

Spoken English came to me largely by a process of osmosis, in school and at play, and I do not have any too vivid recollections as to how I acquired it. I remember being intrigued by the enormous spread between English spelling and English pronunciation, and particularly by the flash cards that were used in school to speed our reading process. In Italian, all they have to do is teach you the alphabet, then give you syllabic combinations: *a, e, i, o, u; ba, be, bi, bo, bu,* etc. There are a few snags, such as the insertion of *h* after *c* before *e* or *i* to represent the *k*-sound, or of *i* before *a, o,* or *u* to get the *ch*-sound; but these are few, fairly simple, and easily remembered. After that, you know how to read and write Italian, and it is rather hard to make a mistake in spelling or reading, save for an occasional misplaced accent. But in English every word, it seemed, was a law unto itself. I hit upon the expedient of memorizing the spoken word with its English sound, and also with the sound the word would have if read with Italian rules of pronunciation: this meant that *enough* was eh-NOWG and *catch* was KAHTK. With this little trick, I quickly became the best speller in the class.

By the time I left St. John Evangelist Parochial School at the age of thirteen, my New York English was all there, with the inclusion of one or two localisms that had to be eliminated later (*sing-er* pronounced *sin-ger;* but to the best of my recollection, I never said *dem* for *them,* or *tree* for *three,* or *goil* for *girl*), plus one or two misconceptions concerning English phonemic structure that came from my native Italian (one of my chums, at one time, called my attention to the fact that I was saying *znow* for *snow;* a professor of public speaking at City College later made me realize that the degree of openness of the *o* vowel in words like *rose* and *soul* (or *sole*) is a matter of speaker's choice, and not, as in Italian, phonemically significant; but this leads to no practical error, and to this day it is my tendency to pronounce the name of the flower and *soul* with a more open *o*-sound than the past tense of *rise* and the synonym for *only*). My English today is so native-speaker that it occurs to no one who does not know me intimately to think I'm foreign-born; and a Californian once said to me: "My, you have a strong New York accent!" Since I don't use the more evident New York localisms in my speech, he must have been referring to my threefold distinction in *marry, Mary, merry,* my lack of distinction between *horse* and *hoarse,* my evanescent *r*'s in *farther,* and the *o* in my *orange,* all general Eastern U.S. traits.

Going back to my Italian, it was saved from extinction by two things: one was the fact that my parents put their foot down hard in the matter of what I spoke at home, and insisted that Italian should be the national language of the household (to their evident disadvantage and my profit). The other was that at first my reading matter (and I was a voracious reader) consisted, outside of school books, of a dozen or so books I had brought with me from Italy (*Le Mille e Una Notte, I Reali di Francia, Il Libro del Giannetto,* de Amicis' *Cuore,* a Bible History with beautiful colored illustrations are among those I remember), plus the Italian-language daily *Il Progresso Italo-Americano,* which my father brought home every day. It was at least three years before one of my school chums revealed to me the treasure trove of the New York Public Library (East 58th Street Branch). From then on, most of my reading was done in English. But it so happened that this particular branch had fairly abundant collections of books in several foreign languages, Spanish among them. Spanish looked easy to me with my Italian background, so I borrowed and made a stab at reading a few of those. One that I recall was a history of ancient Egypt.

So far, I had grown up thoroughly bilingual, with only an occasional library excursion into Spanish and one or two conversational stabs at French, which my family, like all good, educated Italians of the period, had a smattering of. At thirteen I won a scholarship to St. Francis Xavier High School. This meant not merely a continuance of my Catholic education, with the respect for authority and attention to fundamentals that the term implies, but a Jesuit form of training than which, at the time at least, there was no whicher. The good Jesuits believed that a thorough high school education should include four years of Latin, three and a half of Greek, and three of a modern foreign language; this in addition to plenty of English in all its forms, lots of mathematics (algebra and geometry in all their ramifications), considerable history (ancient, medieval, modern, American, English, even civics), considerable science (physical geography, biology, physics, chemistry), and even a little Christian Doctrine, with the bare rudiments of philosophy, theology, logic, and ethics. There were sports and athletics, too, but not on a very highly organized basis. Conspicuous by their absence were courses on garbage disposal, courtship and marriage, automobile driving (but remember that there were few automobiles in those days), and problems of democracy, or how to view the criminal as a victim of society.

Now, in the space of two successive years, three new languages came my way. Latin and Greek were, of course, taught as Classical languages, with little emphasis on their spoken use (though in our very first year our Jesuit teacher gave us a startling demonstration of Latin as a spoken tongue, when a Chinese Jesuit who spoke no English came to visit our class, and the two of them conversed fluently in Latin, with English translations to us). Stress was on grammar, reading, two-way translation, free composition, vocabulary drills. My initial reaction at being introduced to Latin was that here was a language of which I could recognize almost every word; what I couldn't do was to put the words together so that they would make sense—at least, not until after I had mastered some grammar. Our four years of Latin, five times a week, carried us through the basic grammar, Caesar's *Gallic War,* Cicero's *Orations,* Virgil's *Aeneid.* In the second half of the first year we were introduced to the Greek alphabet and taught to read it; then there was a year of grammar, a year of Xenophon's *Anabasis,* a year of Homer's *Iliad.* Plenty of attention was devoted to parsing and the analysis of word, phrase, and sentence structure, with side excursions into etymology and the connection of the Latin and Greek roots we were studying with the English we spoke.

At the beginning of our second year we were given the choice of three years of French, German, or Spanish. The year was 1915. German was already beginning to become unpopular. Spanish had just been introduced, by reason of a hypothetical expanding Latin-American trade. In previous years the choice had been between French and German only, with German in the lead by reason of the heavy percentage of Germans in the New York population of those days. Now, one of the problems facing the Jesuits was to find one of their number who could teach Spanish. There happened to be none. A man who ordinarily taught physics was told to prepare himself to take on a beginning Spanish class at the end of the summer. This he did conscientiously and well, and when he first faced his eager audience he told them: "Boys, we're all starting from scratch, I as well as you. But this I will promise you: I will always keep at least three lessons ahead of you." He kept his promise.

From the standpoint of methodology, it did not make too much difference that he had not specialized in Spanish. The three modern languages (I happened to select French, in accordance with the European tradition that no person could consider himself truly educated unless he knew some French) were imparted in exactly the same fashion as Greek and Latin. Grammar, two-way translation, composition, occasional dictation, irregular verbs, vocabulary, parsing and analysis of structure. Little or no conversation, not even for such purposes as passing the time of day or telling a student to go to the board. Under the circumstances, a native speaker was not really necessary. Our first two teachers of French were both Irish-born, and such French as they spoke in the classroom was slightly tinged with brogue. But they knew their French vocabulary and structure. In our senior year we drew an Alsatian Jesuit, who was a native speaker of both French and German. "Now," we gloated, "we'll really get to do some talking!" Not at all! The Alsatian gave us classroom directions in his heavily accented English, and the classroom procedure went on exactly as before.

This account is calculated, though not deliberately, to make the hair of audio-lingual advocates stand on end. No one would dream of using such a methodology these days. Yet it had its merits. The grammatical structure of the language (Latin, Greek, or French) was assimilated with absolute thoroughness. The two-way translation exercises eventually led to at least semiautomatic responses. Reading proficiency was good, since it was based on reading and still more reading. Those verbs and their vagaries were really memorized, to the point where you could pick out the right form fast, and put it either to written or spoken use. We got next to no training in what is admittedly the toughest thing about languages, the ability to understand a native speaker when he speaks at normal speed. But this, I discovered later, was something you could pick up when you came in contact with native speakers. Utter confusion at first, then a gradual picking up of the distinctive sounds, to the point where you could identify part of the utterance, then most of it, then all of it. For a man with my ear, a month at the most sufficed.

As I emerged from high school and began my teaching career at the age of seventeen (Xavier put me in to teach the sixth grade in their elementary school as soon as I had my diploma), my preference for languages was not at all established. I wanted to be a civil engineer. I had an uncle who had come to New York from Rome with a civil engineering degree in 1904, and had played a major role in planning the very first New York subway. I admired him, and wanted

to follow in his footsteps. Why not? True, I had won the general excellence prize in high school for four years running, and that was
based primarily on Latin, Greek, and English; also, I had won the
French prize for three years. But I had also won the mathematics
and science prizes for the four years. It was only after a grueling
year spent in attending City College's night courses in engineering
for six nights a week while I taught by day that I came to the realiza-
tion that my languages stood up better than my math and sciences.
I switched to an A.B. course, but at that stage it included no languages except for a continuation of Latin, of which I took four more
semesters, with Horace, Livy, and more Cicero, still imparted by the
traditional method. Later in my evening A.B. course I had a full
year of French (Racine and Corneille) and one of Spanish (Cervantes and Lope de Vega).

My teaching in Xavier Grammar School went on for two years.
Next came a year in Cuba, as private tutor to the nephews of Presi-
dent Menocal. They taught me colloquial Cuban Spanish, and I
taught them everything else, including English and French. But I
had already studied Spanish on my own, out of an old grammar book,
in my spare time, along with German and Russian, a little Hebrew,
and a little ancient Egyptian. At this point, my interests were mainly
cultural and literary. I wanted especially to be able to read the
classics of each language in their original version—Goethe and
Schiller in German, Tolstoi and Dostoevsky in Russian, the Old
Testament in Hebrew, the Book of the Dead in hieroglyphics. It was
only after a time that I discovered that as my literary interests waned,
my purely linguistic interests grew. I struck up an acquaintance with
a Russian political exile and a German former U-boat commander,
and traded lessons with them, at the same time that I went through
grammar books in the fashion in which I had been trained at Xavier.
This was the catch-as-catch-can method at its purest and fullest.
Memorize grammatical rules and vocabulary out of a textbook, the
hard way; write out translation exercises and get them corrected;
attempt to converse with the speakers, listening to and imitating their
utterances, including their mistakes and misconceptions in English
(my Russian informant, for instance, was teaching me the sound of
Russian *yeri,* which is a high, back *i,* with lips shaped for *reel,* and
tongue in position for *food*; nearest English equivalent is the *y* of

rhythm; he used to tell me: "Eet eess exactly de same sound dat you get in *wing*"; and his *wing* had a beautiful Russian *yeri*-sound). My German informant, coming from Bremen, would say: "Vy do you say *shpielen, shtehen?* It should be *spielen, stehen*"; and he would use the Low German *sp, st* sounds in place of the High German *shp, sht;* but I knew enough not to imitate his dialectal feature.

In 1921 I was one of thirty-two students of Italian birth or descent selected by the Italian government for a three-month scholarship tour of Italy. This lovely experience undoubtedly strengthened my Italian and brought it up to date. It also led to the beginning of my career as a language teacher, for on my return, too late to get a regular teaching job, I had to accept a part-time post teaching French and Spanish at Fordham Preparatory School. This led to a similar but full-time position at the private Franklin School in New York for -one year, and finally to my appointment to the Romance Department of City College and its preparatory school, Townsend Harris, two years before I finally achieved my A.B. from the evening session of the same college. Again, this would make many scalps tingle in horror, but in those days there was not so much preoccupation with degrees as there is now. For two years I taught by day and studied by night. My A.B., *magna cum laude,* came through in 1925, and now my schedule changed to the extent that I taught French, Spanish, and Italian in Townsend Harris by day, Latin in the City College evening session three nights a week.

Here, again, let me point out how fortunate I was, at least from the standpoint of languages. What you teach you learn. As you go over the same material, the same texts, term after term, year after year, expounding them to your students, pronouncing for them, conversing with them, drilling them, correcting their mistakes, a tremendous amount of what you are doing rubs off on you. I knew Italian quite well, French, Spanish, and Latin moderately well, when I began teaching them. After fifteen years of delving into their most obscure points of grammatical structure, their vagaries of spelling and pronunciation, their vocabularies as reflected in the works of literature presented to my classes, I knew them much better than when I had started. Also, in the course of my teaching, I had long and affectionate association with colleagues who were natives to the languages they taught, people like José Martel in Spanish, Pierre Courtines in

French. Constant association and conversation with them could not fail to improve my grip on their languages. When I began my graduate studies at Columbia I came in contact with more native-born professors and scholars, such as Henri François Muller in French and Angel del Río in Spanish, both of whom invariably lectured in their own tongues, conversed with you in them, and even insisted that you should translate from the Vulgar (or Late) Latin of Gregory of Tours or the medieval French and Spanish of the *Chanson de Roland* and the *Cid* into modern French and Spanish. This meant that my hold on these languages in spoken, written, historical or descriptive form simply had to become firmer and firmer.

Today, when people marvel at the native-speaker accent, ease and fluency with which I handle both French and Spanish, they forget that I have been studying them, reading them, handling them, conversing in them, writing in them, teaching them, in one way or another, for over four decades. It would be surprising indeed if I did *not* handle them well. I have put in on them not hundreds but thousands (many thousands) of hours of training.

Not too much is to be said about my coverage of numerous ancient and medieval languages, because none of them, with the exception of Latin and, in modified modern form, Greek, is for spoken use. My graduate work in Columbia included courses in Sanskrit, ancient Greek dialects, Oscan and Umbrian, Old High German, Gothic, Old Church Slavic, on the one hand, Vulgar Latin, Old French, Old Provençal, medieval Romance dialects, on the other. Here a reading knowledge, often reinforced by the use of a dictionary and a reference grammar, is all I can lay claim to.

More to the point are such languages as German and Russian, in which I have never had a formal course. These are languages I have been learning since the age of eighteen (and the process is far from completed) by the catch-as-catch-can method—perusal of a grammar here, reading for pleasure or research there, a little conversational practice where opportunity offers, a certain amount of travel in German-speaking countries. I haven't really mastered them yet, though I've had the pleasure of being mistaken for a German speaker by German speakers. For one thing, German and Russian do not offer the similarities of grammatical structure and vocabulary to one of my two "native" languages that are offered by French, Spanish, or

Portuguese. For another, I haven't had the constant practice in them
that I have had with the others. Lastly, I have never fully taught
them. In both, I can be thrown for a loss by a word or turn of phrase
I don't grasp or understand. In both, I have to use the conscious
translation process occasionally instead of throwing myself into the
language's gear and using fully automatic reflexes. In both I have a
native-speaker accent which is anything but an unmixed blessing,
because my native interlocutor, hearing me speak so well and correctly what I can speak, comes at me with a flood of rapid-fire talk
in which there are bound to be things I can't grasp offhand; then he
looks surprised, aggrieved, and slightly suspicious when I ask him
to repeat or speak more slowly. "What! You speak so well, and you
want me to repeat? You must be kidding!" his eyes seem to say.
Some of the experiences can be embarrassing, others ludicrous. On
a shore excursion in Messina from the *Vulcania,* on which I was re-
turning to the United States, I noticed four or five German passengers who obviously were not profiting from the explanations the
guide was giving in English and Italian. Being warmhearted by nature, I took it upon myself to summarize for them in German what
was being said. After a while my German ran out, and I found myself
floundering for a word, at which point I started to apologize for my
imperfect German. *"Sie sind nicht Deutscher?"* one of them said in
surprise. *"Nein, ich bin Amerikaner." "Ach, so!"* came the amazed
exclamation, and anyone who knows German knows how much
amazement a German can put into that little utterance. It goes far,
far beyond our English "Oh, really?"

I thought I knew Portuguese, having studied it philologically and
done some reading in it, until I crossed the border from Spain and
began to eavesdrop on the Portuguese bus driver and guide. Then I
realized that, while I might know written Portuguese, I did not know
spoken Portuguese. There was only one way to remedy that. I was
scheduled to take a ten-day motor tour of Portugal with my good
friend and colleague Alexander Prista, who at that time taught
Portuguese at Columbia. He was waiting for me at the Lisbon bus
stop. "You must speak nothing to me but Portuguese, and allow me
to speak nothing to you but Portuguese, for the duration," I told him.
He smiled, and began at once correcting the Hispanicisms that crept
willy-nilly into my spoken Portuguese. *"Em português se diz cedo,*

não temprano; diz-se perto de, não cerca de." It worked very well. On my next visit to Portugal, for ten weeks instead of ten days, I enforced the same rule with all my hotel help and all my English-speaking Portuguese friends. After two weeks I was able to give an acceptable lecture in Portuguese at the University of Coimbra.

Such Japanese as I know was started at a Japanese sukiyaki restaurant in New York, where a highly intelligent and cooperative waiter undertook to tell me how to say various things connected with a meal, along with the amenities. Later, this aural-oral information was supplemented by grammatical structure out of a textbook and other items. But to this day, while I can astound a dinner guest whom I take into a Japanese restaurant with my seeming command of the language, I do not venture much beyond that.

My smattering of spoken Chinese comes from the three initial weeks of a regular course in the Army Language School in Monterey. Having been assigned to the post of linguistic consultant, where one of my duties consisted of familiarizing myself with the methods used and later reporting on their effectiveness, I decided at once that the only way to do an effective job was to turn myself into a guinea pig, take three weeks of a language I knew only slightly and structurally, and see how it would take on me. Did they have a beginning course in either Chinese or Arabic that I could join? Chinese was available, with six enlisted men and a non-commissioned officer for classmates. Six hours a day, five days a week, for three weeks, I not merely sat in on the course, but participated actively as a student. At the end of the three weeks, I reluctantly had to leave, to attend to my other duties. But those three weeks were the full equivalent of a semester of the language in a civilian college, and on the basis of my own progress I was able to report that the methodology was highly effective for the purpose desired. What I got out of it was a certain amount of spoken Mandarin, some of which I still remember and use on occasion.

My linguistic interests, my official duties as Professor of Romance Philology at Columbia, and in particular the course in the World's Chief Languages, which I convinced the authorities to institute at the time of the war for the benefit of selected segments of the armed forces and government bureaus, have led to my acquiring both a structural knowledge and a spoken- and written-language smattering of a number of other languages—Dutch, the Scandinavian tongues, Romanian, Slavic languages beside Russian, modern Greek, Hungarian, Turkish, Finnish, Arabic, Hindi. Some I can read and translate, with the help of a dictionary and plenty of time at my disposal. In others I can say a few essential phrases, which always impress people because of my native-speaker accent, due to my faithful reproducing ear. But this is neither knowing nor speaking the languages. It is precisely what I describe it to be—a structural knowledge, which means knowing various things about the language, including its basic grammatical principles, something about its history, development, and affiliations, its distribution and speaking population, the ability to sing folksongs in it, the ability to speak and understand a few words and phrases—from as few as half a dozen to as many as a hundred. Regardless of what anyone says, I insist that this is neither knowing nor speaking the language, though it can be extremely useful on occasion, and can be expanded at will if the need arises.

I am not the first to claim that there is an intimate relationship between languages, on the one hand, geography and history, on the other. The anthropologists put language in the very first rank of that complex of characteristics which they style a group's "culture." Next to knowing and speaking a language, it is highly desirable to know various things about it.

On the other hand, there is no true substitute for the full possession of a language in both spoken and written form. Oral smatterings, literary appreciation, linguistic structural knowledge, etymology and linguistic history, the study of a people's "culture" in the anthropological sense, cannot replace full knowledge of a language in the sense of spoken and written mastery.

Spoken and written mastery, as you have seen, is hard to come by. It takes either birth and upbringing or many long, weary years of study and effort. Do not let anyone tell you that he can turn you into a fluent speaker of a language in a few days, or even a few weeks or months. A few years barely suffice, if you have the equipment.

At the same time, do not look with scorn upon smatterings, or anything short of native-speaker knowledge. Language is something that can be put to work at any stage and in any amount. Also, you may be surprised how much more you know than you think you do. At least according to the psychologists.

I was once asked at a press conference a question that stumped me at the time: "What language do you dream in?" I had never given the matter any thought. From then on, I began to watch my dreams. I was amazed to find that they came in a variety of languages. My native Italian and English were most frequent, but I would wake up remembering French and Latin conversations, and even addressing large audiences in languages in which I would have no trouble doing so, such as Spanish, but also in languages where I would not trust myself to make a public address, save from a prepared text, such as Russian. I asked a psychologist what the significance of this might be.

"In your dreams you discard your inhibitions," came his surprising reply. "You no doubt could make that speech in Russian if you weren't afraid to try."

Maybe so. I'd still be afraid to try.

6

Is There an Ideal Grammar Book?

THE primary function of a grammar is to act as a short cut to the language. The child learns by endless imitation and repetition, finally making choices and discriminations based on repeated experiences. The adult, having developed faculties of abstraction and generalization, is supposed to be in a position to be given a general rule, which he applies to specific cases. The child is told many times. The adult is told once and for all, and thereafter left free to work out his own salvation.

This is the basic principle of all grammars, from the skeleton abstracts that appear in tourist phrase books to the most complex reference and historical grammars. In between are the grammars used primarily for classroom or self-instruction, which give you rules with examples, then reading and translation exercises that test your assimilation of the rules. Or, in more modern versions, they may follow an inductive rather than a deductive procedure, giving you first a number of examples, or a reading passage that contains such examples, then asking you to build up your own rule on the basis of the examples you have read, and finally testing your assimilation of both examples and rule.

Grammars have been around for a long time. About 300 B.C., an Indian grammarian named Panini constructed a grammar of the Sanskrit language, in which references appear to much earlier grammars that have not come down to us. There were among the Greeks and Romans numerous grammarians who composed grammars, some of which have found their way down to us. These ancient grammars were composed, presumably, for speakers of their respective languages who wanted to speak in more acceptable fashion; that is, in accordance with the rules laid down by the grammarians. What the grammarians based their rules on is a matter of conjecture, but they must to some extent have been based on usage, contemporary or previous, perhaps the usage of a ruling class rather than of the lower ranks of the population. Under the circumstances, exercises were not really necessary, though examples of the "right" usage often appear accompanying the rules. In fact, there are occasionally examples of "wrong" usage, which the reader is cautioned against.

Bilingual grammars (that is, grammars for the learning of one language by speakers of another) do not appear till about A.D. 1000 (Aelfric's grammar of Latin for the use of Anglo-Saxon speakers). From that time on, bilingual grammars appear more and more frequently. Earlier ones, as a rule, offer little if any exercise or reading material, limiting themselves largely to rules and examples. Today, they would be called reference grammars, and would be used for instructional purposes only after the student has had a thorough grounding in the language he is learning.

True instructional bilingual grammars, of the type used in our high school and college courses, with all the trimmings of attractive presentation, motivational devices, reading material, exercises, and two-way vocabularies, are largely the product of the nineteenth and twentieth centuries, when mass education became general and widespread illiteracy began to wane.

Today, the type of monolingual grammar common among the ancients is still with us, under the form of manuals and dictionaries of usage. Its main function is to get people to speak and write better in their own language. The bilingual grammar of the reference or historical type is in use also, but mainly for specialists. The bilingual instructional grammar is the one that really concerns the language learner, and here the question of what to include and how to present it is paramount.

The older, traditional grammar was largely concerned with regularity and symmetry of presentation. If verbs in a given language fall into various conjugational classes, these classes would be presented in sequence, preferably throughout their entire scheme. Irregular verbs that do not fall into any of the main patterns would be presented later, regardless of the fact that in real life they are of very frequent occurrence, and you can hardly put a sentence together without them. Nouns and adjectives would be presented the same way, declension by declension, or type after type, with all exceptional forms presented immediately after each type, no matter how seldom they might occur in actual speech. The various tenses of the verb would come in sequence, though some might be far more useful than others. Eventually you would have all the rules of the language, but without any "value judgment" as to which are most important and should be learned first.

Something similar happened with examples of use, and even more specifically with vocabulary. Words would be presented not on the basis of how relatively useful they might be but on the basis of how they might serve to illustrate certain rules (this, by the way, explains *la plume de ma tante*). If any thought was given to their occurrence, it was their occurrence in the loftiest works of literature. This meant the inclusion of "twilight" and "celestial," but the exclusion of "beefsteak" and "toilet," as well as of phrases of extremely common occurrence in real life, but not in literature, such as "Hi!" and "What time shall I meet you?"

The first application of the doctrine of frequency of occurrence came in vocabulary. Many teachers of language pointed to the inconsistency of students being able to talk in terms of cantos and infernal apparitions while still not knowing how to ask their way to the railroad station or explain that their car had run out of gas. Vocabulary frequency lists began to appear, and to find their way into instructional grammars. But there was still a question of choice. Relative frequency in what? Molière's *Tartuffe?* Or the latest edition of *Le Figaro?* Or the exchange of compliments between two Paris taxi drivers?

How these difficulties were smoothed out is a story in its own right. Suffice it to say that at the present time fairly reliable and reasonable frequency lists appear for the major languages, and are generally utilized, more or less conscientiously, by the compilers of instructional grammars.

Next came the question of relative frequency of grammatical forms and constructions, and, above all, of colloquial phrases and sentences. Here the choice was more difficult, both to make and to apply, but the guiding principle was the same. Present at the outset not only those words, but also those phrases and sentences, those grammatical forms, such as verb tenses, which are of most frequent occurrence in the language. Then keep on repeating them in later lessons, as new material is presented, so that they will stand the best chance of being assimilated by sheer force of repetition. Relegate to the later lessons, with less chance of repetition and assimilation, those forms and constructions which are least frequently used in real life, particularly in everyday speech.

There is no question that certain words are used over and over again, to the point where it is impossible to speak without them. In English, they would be such article forms as *the, a, an,* such prepositions as *in, on, by, with, without, for, from, to,* such adverbs and conjunctions as *well, badly, fast, slowly, not, and, but, if, when, where, today, yesterday, tomorrow,* such pronouns as *I, me, you, he, him, they, them, who, which, what, that.* In the case of nouns, adjectives, and verbs, the choice is broader and more difficult, but there is no doubt that *man, woman, boy, girl, child* appear more frequently than *illustration, preponderance, forgetfulness, recollection, escrow; good* and *bad, hot* and *cold,* more frequently than *ethereal, philosophical, abstract* and *concrete; come* and *go, walk* and *sit,* more often than *cogitate, perambulate, reflect,* and *predict.* These words of extremely common occurrence, or their equivalents, must appear very early in a practical instructional work.

It is also ascertained that a great deal of conversational interchange, at least of the casual variety, comes in frequently used, ready-made clichés, which have their equivalents in practically all languages: "good day," "how are you?", "please," "thank you," "don't mention it," "excuse me." A hundred or so of these clichés, presented early in the course of instruction, serve a double purpose: they are of intensely practical use, even if one does not "know" the language, since they elicit favorable attitudes; and they build up the learner's confidence, since he is at once using the language he is learning, even though on a very limited scale. There is no point in reserving them until after so-called "basic patterns" are learned. They lend themselves to assimilation through imitation and repetition, and do not at all interfere with basic patterns.

Most difficult of all is discriminating, in the construction of a practical use grammar, among the various grammatical forms and constructions that must all eventually be learned. There is a very definite hierarchy of frequency in such forms and constructions. In French, for example, the demonstrative *adjective* (*ce livre, cet homme, cette femme*) is of extremely frequent occurrence; the demonstrative *pronoun* (*celui-ci, celle de ma soeur*) is not, and can furthermore be replaced by a repetition of the noun (*ma maison et la maison de ma soeur*). Symmetry and regularity of presentation would call for the demonstrative pronoun to come right after the demonstrative adjective in a grammar, and in many traditional grammars that is precisely what happens. Practical considerations, however, dictate that the demonstrative adjective should come very early in the course, while the demonstrative pronoun can be postponed until the latter part of the book. The past definite tense in French is definitely part of the verb scheme; it coincides in form with the English past, and *je fis* is the theoretical equivalent of *I did* or *I made*. Practically, it is very seldom used in conversation, though it appears in literature, and is replaced by *j'ai fait,* "I have made." Under the circumstances, *j'ai fait* should come very early in the grammar, while *je fis* can come close to the end of the book.

The principle of priority of appearance where there is frequency of occurrence is basic to a good grammar, even more basic than completeness. It should not be assumed that the student who begins using a grammar will use it all the way through. He may drop out of the course, or his interest may flag, or he may become too busy to continue. What he really learns must necessarily come at the beginning, and it should be the most useful part of the language.

There are in each and every language certain grammatical points that have very limited application in the language, spoken or written, but are tricky enough to lend themselves beautifully to trap questions on exams and quizzes. These are overstressed by certain grammars and by certain teachers, as well as by certain types of examinations (example: French *ce dont,* or *dont* as opposed to *duquel*). Grammars should not be constructed, or instruction given, for the convenience of the teacher, who already knows the language, but for the convenience of the student, who still has to learn it. Exams, quizzes, and textbook exercises should not be based primarily on the fine points of the structure, which are of little practical value, but on the big points, which come into play a hundred times a day.

A somewhat similar principle applies to reading material. It is easy and cheap to construct a reader out of material from one to three hundred years old, on which the copyright has expired. It is somewhat more difficult and expensive to construct it out of present-day materials and authors. But the present-day language is the one that is being spoken now. If you must be literary, then the present-day authors are the ones who will reflect not only the language in use today but also present-day psychology and attitudes on the part of the speaking group. A publisher's editor once told me how a rival house, tired of French readers everlastingly constructed out of Daudet, Maupassant, Mérimée, and other authors over a century old, had put on the market a book, constructed at some expense by reason of copyright payments to living authors and publishers, which represented the very latest word in contemporary French writing. The publishing house was not surprised when its book sold 50,000 or more copies in its first year, because they expected it to go over big. They were very surprised when it sold fewer than a thousand copies the following year. The reason? The teachers of French didn't like it, because it was composed in a brand of French they did not fully understand. They had been brought up on a diet of Daudet and Maupassant, and that, to them, was the "real" French language, regardless of the facts of language change in the course of time.

How much spoken-language material should a written grammar of a language contain? Should it limit itself to summarizing the rules of relationship between speech and writing, plus a few rough English-language approximations of the sounds of the language to be learned? Should it go into elaborate discussions of the sound structure of the language, running the risk of losing the interest of beginners by reason of complicated descriptions, phonemic charts, and transcriptions based on the International Phonetic Alphabet, with which few beginners are familiar?

Today, grammars composed for classroom use generally presuppose the presence of an enlightened teacher in the classroom, who is capable of supplementing the written explanation and supplying the appropriate drilling. Grammars for individual use are very often accompanied by recordings with native-speaker pronunciations of the sounds that are being described. Beyond this, there is no point in being overprescriptive in print. A grammar of scientific German,

constructed for people who are specializing in the written form of
the language for a specific purpose, need not go into elaborate
phonetic explanations. On the other hand, almost everyone who
learns a language would like to be able to use it in spoken form on
occasion, even if only to read out loud to himself. Without making
a cult of native-speaker accent and pronunciation, some information on that point should be offered.

What form of speech is it desirable to present? That of the most
highly cultured classes, perhaps overrefined and somewhat artificial?
That of the very lowest classes, with its peculiarities of sound and
slang forms? Something in between? Where a language is split into
dialects none of which has a clear-cut standing as representing the
national standard (this happens in our own English as well as in
Spanish), which form shall be presented?

It is desirable to avoid class excesses, and to base oneself primarily on what might be styled the middle-class standard in its colloquial form. To exemplify from English: such forms as *ain't, it's me,
who did you see?* are sufficiently widespread to warrant inclusion in a
grammar of English for foreigners, not in replacement of the more
"correct" forms, but for presentation as substitute forms, with the explanation that, while somewhat substandard, they are nevertheless in
widespread, nationwide use, and the learner may expect to run into
them frequently. This is neither violating the canons of the language
nor deifying vulgarisms; it is simply stating the facts, which the
learner is entitled to know. In composing a French grammar, I had
given as the possible equivalents of *"Avez-vous un livre?"* "Have you
a book?", "Do you have a book?", "Have you got a book?" The editor struck out the third form, on the ground that it was a rank col-
loquialism. Perhaps so; but in normal U.S. conversational exchange
it occurs far more frequently than its more prim and British counterpart "Have you a book?"

Where a certain local standard form of pronunciation is presented
to the exclusion of another, the fact should be stated. It is quite all
right to present the Castilian pronunciation of Spanish (though it
happens to be used by a minority of the speakers); but reference
should be made to what you may hear in other parts of the Spanish-
speaking world in the way of consistent sound structure (*sielo* for
Castilian *thielo; cabayo* for *caballo,* etc.).

Save for highly specific purposes, there is no point to seeking native-speaker perfection in pronunciation, and in any case a written grammar is not the thing to achieve it with. Water will tend to find its own level, in language learning as in everything else.

Morphology and syntax should be presented, at least at the outset, in their most basic forms, uncluttered by exceptions, save where the exception is a very high-frequency word. It is safe to state at the outset, for example, that in Spanish, generally, nouns ending in *-o* are masculine, those ending in *-a* are feminine, and about the only two significant exceptions, for the beginner, are *mano* and *día*. It is quite safe to overlook the French imperfect and pluperfect subjunctive, save perhaps for second-semester presentation.

Vocabulary and phrases should definitely be based on frequency of occurrence, which in these two segments of language is now fairly well established. Specialized vocabularies can be introduced for specific purposes a little later, when and as needed.

Comparison with other languages, including the learner's own, is good, both as a mnemonic device, to reinforce memorization, and for sheer pleasure. There is absolutely no reason why language learning should be turned altogether into a drab, mechanical chore. Language is alive and picturesque, and full advantage should be taken of those features. One of my Spanish colleagues stresses in one of his textbooks what a linguist has termed "contrastive phrasal doublets" (Spanish *blanco y negro* as opposed to English "black and white," with order reversed). Whatever the intrinsic value of this may be, there is no question that after this point is so interestingly presented the learner will never forget how to say *black* or *white* in Spanish.

Involved grammatical and linguistic technical terminology should be shunned in beginner's grammars. Few beginners know the meaning of *suprasegmental phonemes* and *complementary distribution*. On the other hand, there is no reason why terms consecrated by usage should be avoided, provided they are presented with an accurate explanation. Such moronic devices as "Nouns in form 1, 2, 3 and 4" instead of "nominative, genitive, dative, accusative," or *"der-, die-* and *das*-nouns" instead of "masculine, feminine, and neuter nouns," or "unreal" instead of "subjunctive," in a German grammar are insults to the learner's intelligence and interest.

The ideal grammar should, above all things, be subdivided into short and easily manageable units. There is a definite limit to the strain that can be placed upon the assimilative capacity and the retentive memory. A brief unit, thoroughly gone over and assimilated, gives the learner a sense of completion, achievement, and satisfaction. If he can master a unit in half an hour instead of having to plow through it for three hours, there will be an enormous psychological as well as practical advantage. Success breeds an appetite for more success. Also, it is wise to utilize brief stretches of time in language learning. If you have only half an hour at your disposal before train time, and you see your way clear to covering a two- or three-page unit in that time, you will do so. But if the lesson is twelve pages long, you realize you cannot do it in that time, and you put the whole thing off until a rainy day when you have the whole afternoon before you.

Perhaps all that has been said in this chapter looks as though it were addressed more to the teacher, and particularly to the textbook writer, than to the learner. But you, as a learner, have a very definite choice in the selection of a textbook if you are studying on your own, and have to shop for your own texts. Look before you leap, and browse before you buy. Does the grammar you are examining on the bookshop counter contain all, or most, of the features we have described as desirable? That you are in a position to determine for yourself, even without a knowledge of the language.

I am not primarily, nor do I consider myself to be, a writer of textbooks. Nevertheless, I have embodied the principles enumerated above in one regular grammar for classroom or individual use (*First-Year French,* by Edmond Méras and Mario Pei, originally published by Dryden Press, and at present by Holt, Rinehart, and Winston, a book in which I supplied the basic presentation, while my coauthor did the exercises and reading material). Here the reader will find the application of these principles: (a) the presentation of a reasonably correct, yet thoroughly colloquial language, with stress on real life situations in the Conversations that head each chapter; (b) expressions of the cliché type in extremely common use, presented in the early lessons, and repeated throughout, for maximum assimilation; (c) grammatical forms, regular and irregular verbs, syntactical constructions, vocabulary, arranged by frequency of occurrence, with diminishing emphasis on less frequent ones as you go along, and constant repetition of essential ones.

The principle of condensation of basic grammar and vocabulary, the latter to some extent for specific purposes, appears both in my manuals for the use of tourists (*Getting Along in French, Italian, Spanish, German, Portuguese, Russian,* published by Harper & Row, with Bantam paperbacks)* and my *World's Chief Languages,* originally designed for military use, published by Vanni Publications in America and by Allen & Unwin in Britain. The latter work also contains abundant information of what might be styled a geolinguistic nature, of particular interest to the layman—where and in what form the languages are spoken, as primary or secondary and colonial tongues, the extent and nature of their speaking populations, the uses to which they may be put, the possibility of using them as substitute languages in given areas, their political, military, scientific, and cultural potential—information which is to some extent repeated in the second part of this book and which, for an enlightened understanding of the world of language and languages in general, can hardly be overstressed.

* The hard-cover Portuguese and Russian are out of print, but copies are available directly from the author; the Bantam paperback series lacks the Portuguese volume.

7

Special Learning Aids:
Phrase Books and Dictionaries

Older and Newer Phrase Books—"English" Transcriptions, their Crutch Value and Drawbacks—The Imported Dictionary—The Antiquated Dictionary—Words and Idiomatic Word Groups—A True American Bilingual Dictionary

THE tourist phrase book is a venerable institution. As far back as the eighth century of our era, we can find phrase books for the use of pilgrims from the German-speaking to the Romance-speaking lands, with such interesting, practical, and up-to-date expressions as "Give me a haircut" and "Shave the back of my neck" presented in the spoken vernacular of the two languages.

The English, who were the great globe trotters of the nineteenth century, have perhaps the most extensive stock of tourist phrase books, like the old Marlborough series, which covers a surprisingly large range of unusual languages (the books are all styled "——Self-Taught"; in my own collection I have Hungarian, Japanese, Hindustani, Turkish, Arabic, Persian, modern Greek). Lyall's *Languages of Europe* (Sidgwick & Jackson, Ltd., London, 1935) contains, in parallel columns, words and phrases in five Romance languages, then in five Germanic languages, then in five Slavic languages, next in five Uralic and Baltic tongues, lastly in such unrelated languages as Greek, Albanian, Turkish, Arabic, and Esperanto.

In all these rather well-constructed aids there is some description of the language's sound scheme and written notation, brief sets of useful expressions, written signs, numerals, months and days of the week, then sentences of the type a tourist may be expected to use, then a limited vocabulary, which may be arranged alphabetically or by topics (the world and its elements, metals and minerals, time, mankind and relations, the human body, food, etc.). There may or may not be a summary of grammar.

During the war the Army brought out booklets in dozens of strategic languages, containing phrases that might be of use to military personnel. These, from all accounts, served their limited purpose rather well. With the postwar boom in the tourist trade, more ambitious phrase books were composed, containing tourist phrases classified by topic (landing, customs inspection, railroad station and plane terminal conversation, restaurant, hotel, sightseeing, motoring, etc.), with fairly substantial grammatical outlines and two-way vocabularies. The Berlitz, Dover, and Harper-Bantam phrase books in various languages (the last-named compiled by this writer) are illustrative of the present-day trend. This type of phrase book can not only see you through language difficulties and permit a limited amount of "Getting along in" whatever language you may be faced with; it can also, if judiciously used, serve as a general introduction to the language in its most basic spoken aspects, to the point of serving as an introductory textbook. The phrases are extremely practical, and the vocabulary is fully colloquial and up-to-date, with no archaisms or literary features whatsoever. The books have the added merit of being paperbacks or having paperback editions, so that they are light and very easy to carry on your person, particularly when traveling. From a purely practical standpoint, the phrase book can serve a useful purpose even if no words are spoken. One can pick the phrase he wants and point to it in its foreign version, thus making himself understood.

The Dover "Say It" phrase book series, retailing for 75 cents apiece, contain 1,000 useful phrases in quite a large variety of languages: Danish, Dutch, Esperanto, French, German, Greek, Hebrew, Italian, Japanese, Norwegian, Polish, Portuguese, Russian, Spanish, Swedish, Turkish, Yiddish, and English for German, Spanish, and Italian speakers. More pretentious and expensive colloquial manuals, with prices up to $4, add Arabic, Czech, Hindustani, Persian, Roumanian.

The Berlitz "Phrase Books for Travelers" ($1 paper bound) include French, Spanish, Italian, German, the Scandinavian languages treated en bloc, Russian, Hebrew, Japanese, Greek, while a single larger book, selling for less than $3, gives you 16 languages, including Arabic, Chinese, Dutch, Indonesian, Swahili, and Urdu-Hindi.

The Harper "Getting Along in——" series, with Bantam paperbacks for 60 cents, include French, Spanish, German, Italian, Russian, and Portuguese (but see p. 61 note). They also feature an outline of basic grammar in each language.

From the spoken-language aspect, a word of caution is necessary. For the convenience of the tourist who is not a linguist, all these phrase books carry what is known as an English transcription of the foreign phrases. This can only be an adaptation and approximation to the actual foreign-language sounds. It is normally impossible to render precisely, in the orthography of one language, the spoken sounds of another (in fact, not even the native orthographies manage to do this, as abundantly proved by English spelling). At best, the English transcription can be viewed only as a makeshift, a temporary aid, a crutch, which permits you to get around spoken-language difficulties, but only haltingly and imperfectly. It is under no circumstances to be viewed as exact or scientific. A scientific transcription (and it would still be short of perfect) would be a phonetic one, in IPA (International Phonetic Alphabet) characters; or a phonemic one, which would require far more technical knowledge than the average tourist can be expected to possess. Writers of tourist phrasebooks usually protest at being required to work out English transcriptions for their phrases, on the ground that the crutch can be, and often is, habit-forming, and tends to confirm the user of the book in his American accent when he attempts to speak the foreign language. The publishers just as often insist, on the ground that the buying public wants the crutch, and feels bewildered and cheated if it is not offered. A compromise remedy has been worked out, whereby the phrase book with its English transcription is flanked by a recording in which native speakers give the authentic pronunciation of the phrases. This means that the tourist or traveler may train on his phrase book and its recording in advance of his trip; but he cannot carry the recording with him as he travels, and must fall back on the authentic spelling of the language and/or the English transcription, which at least indicates for him the place where the accent falls. In short, the phrase book is a very useful tool, but the learner must be cautioned against accepting its English transcriptions at face value.

The bilingual dictionary is an even more venerable institution than the phrase book, for bilingual word lists, in Akkadian and Sumerian, inscribed in cuneiform characters and baked into clay tablets, appear in our museums.

The modern bilingual dictionary can be a useful tool, but most of the ones on the American market display glaring imperfections. Since the cost of producing a dictionary is high, and the return is interfered with by excessive competition, American publishers have generally gotten into the convenient practice of bringing out American editions of pre-existing British dictionaries, with or without adaptation to the American brand of English. This is normally of little importance for what concerns literary terms, which are fixed and standardized for the whole English-speaking world. It can and does play havoc with the colloquial, everyday language. Before investing in a dictionary, it will be well for the learner to inspect it with a careful eye for words and word groups dealing with certain areas of modern life. If he discovers that he has the French or Spanish equivalents for *cheque, programme, gaol,* and *tyre* instead of *check, program, jail,* and *tire,* he should begin to get suspicious. His suspicions should increase if he finds *bonnet, boot, demister, windscreen, sump, cubby locker, fascia, trafficator,* and *spanner* instead of *hood, trunk compartment, defroster, windshield, crankcase, glove compartment, dashboard, directional signal* and *wrench.* Many originally British dictionaries now include American terms, but they still leave something to be desired. What America needs is bilingual dictionaries that will translate into and from American English.

Secondly, dictionaries have a way of becoming antiquated and falling behind the times. Modern civilization is a fast-moving thing, and many terms that were unknown twenty and even ten years ago are commonplace today. Here again, while straight English dictionaries are regularly brought up to date by the publishers, bilingual ones seldom are. It is ever so much easier and cheaper for the publisher to bring out a new printing than a fully revised and modernized edition. Look for some of the terms that have appeared in very recent years before you buy. Does the dictionary you are examining give you the French equivalent of *feedback, fallout, laser, escalation, cookout, Dolce Vita?* Does it give you only older meanings for words that have acquired new ones? Look for *lane* in the automotive sense. Italy and Spain have "four-lane highways" too, and in that sense they do not use the same word they use for *footpath,* as we do.

Observe what actually happens. Spanish uses *faja,* which normally means "waistband," as correctly reported in both sections of one of three comprehensive dictionaries in my possession; another gives "auto lane" as one of the translations of *faja,* but in the English-Spanish section worries only about sea lanes and air lanes. The third ignores the problem altogether.

For Italian, one large and generally satisfactory dictionary fails utterly to recognize the car lane in either section. The most comprehensive Italian dictionary on the American market, with over 2,000 pages and retailing for over $17, recognizes it to the extent of giving you "four-lane motor road—*autostrada a quattro corsie*"; but when you look up *corsia* in the Italian section, you find "gangway," "passage," "aisle," "hospital ward," "dormitory," even "race track," but no automotive lane. You are left with the impression that *corsia* is what Italian uses, but you get no confirmation. In reverse, *scaricabarili* (*giocare a*) is correctly rendered as "to pass the buck," but neither "pass" nor "buck" in the English section elicits any information as to the idiom.

Lastly, watch for idiomatic word groups. Any bilingual dictionary will give you the foreign-language equivalent of *call, put, look, run, see.* But does it give you, under those headings, *call up, call down, call for, put through, put out, put up with, look out, look for, look in on, run out of, run out on, see through something, see something through?* There are still on the market a few old cheap dictionaries that give you only single words in English with a single foreign-language translation. This means that the user of such a dictionary will translate *ash tray* into French as *plateau de frêne,* "tray of ash-wood."

Unlike others in language learning, the dictionary field is one in which much work still remains to be done. It is perfectly true that vocabulary is the division of language that is forever changing at whirlwind speed, while the division of speech sounds, which forms the stamping ground of recordings, and the division of grammatical structure, which is covered by grammars, are relatively stable over much longer periods. Nevertheless, publishers of bilingual dictionaries can do a much better job than they are doing at present. At the very least, they can construct or adapt their product for American users, who constitute their market, instead of remaining forever dependent on our British cousins and their brand of English. Recommended procedure would be to take a good, practical American dictionary, like Webster's *Collegiate* or *New World,* and combine it with a purely foreign dictionary of the same type, like the *Petit Larousse* in French. By "combining" I mean finding and giving the precise French equivalent of each and every meaning of each and every word in the American dictionary, and the precise American English equivalent of each and every meaning of each and every word in the French *Larousse*. This way we would have both languages in their most authentic and up-to-date form.

8

What Should Our Schools Do About Language?

The Lessons of Sputnik—Importance of the Teacher's Personality —Methods Courses—Crackpotism in the Schools—Uses of Laboratory Equipment—The General Language Course and Coordination in Languages

I have before my eyes a group of clippings from the days, that now seem so remote, before Sputnik put the fear of the Lord into the linguistic isolationists and aroused the linguistic interest of both government and education. One such clipping voices the complaint, commonly heard in the early fifties, that more and more high schools are abolishing language courses and replacing them with home economics and other gadgetry. Another bemoans the fact that far too many colleges have done away with any and all language requirements, either for admission or for graduation. There is one that points out, with the greatest of justification, that you cannot expect out of a two-year language course at the rate of three hours a week what other nations accomplish in eight or ten years. There is a horrendously impressive 1958 chart which shows the United States at the very bottom of a long list of nations (36, to be exact) on two counts: starting age (14 for us, 6 to 12 for everyone else); and number of years of continuous study (2 for us, 10 for Ceylon and Iraq, 9 for Egypt and Germany, 8 for Austria, Thailand, and Yugoslavia, and so on down the line). One clipping says that perhaps it would be worth while to teach languages in our schools and colleges, if only to promote world friendship and understanding, and is borne out by another that points to the far-reaching results in that field accomplished by subjecting foreign students at one of our colleges to an intensive course in English. From Canada comes a plea for imparting languages at an earlier age; but this is countered by a blast from the New York State Department of Education, which does not want the curriculum cluttered up with too many subjects, and reminds supervisors that "since a mother tongue constitutes the instrument for thought which a child has to use all his life, this tool should be developed to a fairly high degree of efficiency before he is encouraged to start a second language."

There are not too many things for which we, as a nation, have to be grateful to the Soviets, but our change of views and pace in the matter of languages is definitely one of them. Today the study of foreign languages is taken for granted. The trend toward the abolition of language studies is definitely and altogether reversed. The federal government has gotten into the picture to the extent of declaring languages a "critical" study area, along with mathematics and science (whatever "critical" may mean in this context), and even of subsidizing the study of certain languages at certain institutions, mostly of higher learning.

Languages are here to stay. The next question is: "How may the schools and colleges impart them more efficiently?"

Here also there is ground for optimism. The old-fashioned aim of imparting a reading knowledge of a language so that it might be used for the aesthetic appreciation of literary masterpieces is generally on its way out. (Be it noted that there is absolutely nothing wrong with such an objective; only it should not be foisted on the majority of learners, who want languages for other and more practical purposes.) Replacement has been, generally, with a speaking-and-understanding objective which is fostered through aural-oral methods, mechanical aids, and relatively highly concentrated doses of classroom instruction based largely on imitation, repetition, and conversation. Clippings of a slightly later vintage speak glowingly of individualized instruction, small classes, and long hours, following the lead of wartime Army Specialized Training Programs and peacetime Army Language Schools.

By and large, there is little to worry about so far as language instruction in our regular institutions of learning is concerned. All signs point in the direction of expanding language programs, possibly to the point where all high school and college students without exception will be exposed to at least one language in the course of their studies; more time devoted to language learning, so that the favorite American two-year, three-hour-a-week program may eventually develop into a minimum of four years, which will almost bring it into line with the average for other civilized nations; an earlier beginning of language instruction, possibly in the grade schools or even the kindergartens, where the language has the best chance of being assimilated naturally; more stress on the language of conversation and less on the language of literature; and an ever-increasing use of laboratory equipment to supplement classroom instruction and supply needed drill in imitation and repetition.

Certain problems connected with language learning in the schools and colleges are perennial, and not at all limited to language courses. First among these is the problem of the instructor's personality and his training.

Some teachers are infectiously dynamic and enthusiastic in the way they affect their group students. Others are plodding, lackadaisical, indifferent, and put classes to sleep. Some make the language they teach live, vibrate, throb with interest; others treat it as something lifeless, dead, that the learner must work on as on a mummy to be embalmed. With the former, study is a pleasure; with the latter, it is a boresome chore, something that must be gone through with to accumulate the credits necessary for graduation.

This happens in all fields of study. It is perhaps more noticeable in languages, because languages are so much a part of the human content of education. All sorts of personality and psychological tests have been devised by the schools of education to make sure that only people qualified by temperament and approach get into the teaching system, but to no avail. Bad teachers continue to crop up, and a teacher can make or break a class, or a subject.

The question often comes up whether it is better to have a native or a foreign teacher of a language. Place of birth has absolutely nothing to do with the qualities of enthusiasm and personality just described. Among the very best language teachers I have known, the American-born and the foreign-born appear in about equal proportions. The most that can be said is that the teacher who is native to the language he is teaching has a better grasp of at least the sounds of the language, while the American-born and American-trained teacher has a better grasp of the learner's psychology, outlook, and learning problems. Both these qualities, or the lack of them, can be of great importance. A teacher who is attuned to the thought processes and mental habits of the students because he comes from the same background, but has a very imperfect knowledge of the language he is teaching can give no more than he has it in him to give, and the students are bound to acquire most of his imperfections. On the other hand, I have seen class discipline and the learning process go very quickly to pieces in the hands of a foreign-born teacher who had no idea how to handle American students, antagonized them with his attitude of lofty superiority, and made himself ridiculous from the very start. The ideal language teacher is, of course, one who combines perfect command of the language to be taught, in all its aspects, spoken, written, and literary, with thorough command of the language of the learners and knowledge of their psychology and thoughtways; plus personality, enthusiasm, and a general interest in language. Be it said to the credit of our professional language teachers that a surprisingly large number of them have been steadily approaching this ideal, particularly in recent times. Part of the credit for this is due to the increasingly rigorous training they receive, part to the barriers against incompetents set up by school administrations, part to the spirit of the times.

The question of methodology has relatively little to do with the efficacy of language instruction. There are specific methods of teaching specific languages, but these tie in rather with content than with actual form of presentation. In the general language teaching methods courses now in vogue in our teachers' colleges, the prospective teacher is instructed in the mechanics of the classroom, is given some hints on how to arouse motivation and interest, and how to prepare a lesson plan, so that the hour spent in the classroom will blend into an organic unit instead of being a series of disjointed exercises. It is not safe to go too far beyond this, and be too prescriptive about how the teacher shall conduct his class, under penalty of stifling initiative and turning him into a robot rather than a human being. (The quality of being human is of superlative importance in language classwork.) We no longer have the excesses of methodology whereby a prospective teacher would flunk his class test by reason of spending one fifth rather than one fourth of the class period doing blackboard exercises, as sometimes used to happen in the past.

Individual schools and colleges have their own individual ideas about the proper blend of spoken-language and written-language content and methodology to be employed, and the student who joins a language class must be prepared to submit in advance to the prevailing system, and not expect it to be changed for his benefit, though he may at times make what amounts to constructive and acceptable suggestions.

Methodological crackpotism in classroom instruction should be, and generally is, avoided. The mere fact that a thing may be done a certain way does not mean that it may not be done as effectively another way. The learner should be suspicious of any school or instructor who says or implies: "My way of learning a language is the *only* good and correct way; all others are a waste of time." The best methodologies and textbooks in the world can be mishandled if they fall into the hands of the wrong person. Conversely, lots can be done even with antiquated methods and materials by the real natural-born teacher. It is not at all unusual to find, in certain free-wheeling institutions, that the instructor sidesteps both official method and official textbook and sets up what amounts to his own personal course.

Some teachers, particularly of the native variety, exhibit a tendency to forget that their main function is to teach the language, and show a fondness for going off on repeated side excursions into the history, geography, economics, literature, and linguistics of the country whose language they are supposed to teach. While a certain amount of this is legitimate and desirable, and even forms part of the official methodology, it should not be overdone. One can learn an infinite number of true, useful, and interesting facts about a nation's culture without learning its language. The primary purpose of a language course is to learn the language.

The use of mechanical equipment and what are styled "language labs" has of late become a vogue. The language lab is equipped, among other things, with listening booths, earphones, recordings and tapes, and these are used either individually, to give the student the necessary drilling in imitation and repetition of a native speaker, or en masse, for group instruction, with a live instructor, who utters phrases and sentences for imitation; these are repeated by the students, and transcribed on a blank tape as they are repeated. The instructor then corrects each individual pronunciation, and the process is repeated until the instructor is satisfied, or worn out. A student may enter the lab in his spare time, listen to a half-inscribed tape with native-speaker phrases, repeating each phrase. His utterances are in-scribed in erasable fashion after each authentic, permanently inscribed phrase. He then listens to the entire tape, comparing his own repetition with the original and correcting himself as he goes along. He will then repeat the whole procedure until his own phrases come out to his satisfaction.

There is considerable value to the language lab, but there is also a tendency on the part of its advocates (I almost said "addicts") to overstress its value. It is true that the mechanical equipment never tires, flags, or gets hoarse. It does not, however, possess the dynamic qualities of a living person. Above all, it cannot answer questions or give explanations, or make precise, to-the-point corrections where needed. The language lab supplements but can never replace the teaching staff. It also goes without saying that the lab functions only for what concerns the spoken language, and only for that portion of the spoken language which is purely mechanical. It marks, however, a very definite advance in language teaching.

Schools and colleges should continue to refine and perfect their pro-cess of teacher selection, making sure that only persons with the right personality, motivation, and interests enter the field of language teach-ing. They should recall that content is, in the absolute, more im-portant than method, and that while we teach students, we also teach languages. They should avoid absolutism in methodology and ap-proach, realizing that there are many possible ways of attaining the same objective. They should obtain and use mechanical equipment to the best of their financial capacities, but not deify it, since it does not supply the single answer to their problems. They should be forward-looking in the matter of devoting more time to language courses, hav-ing smaller classes, and beginning language instruction at a progres-sively earlier age. Above all, they should view the language program not as something that interferes with other curriculum subjects, but as something that aids and furthers all subjects. The second (or third or fourth) language does not interfere with the native tongue; it helps to clarify it and make it more effective.

Again, all that we have said seems to be aimed rather at the teacher and administrator than at the language learner. But again, you, as a language learner, generally have an intelligent choice to make. If you are in a position to avail yourself of standard classroom instruction, the chances are that you are also in a position to choose among different institutions with different methods and time schedules. Before signing up for a course, try to find out something about it. Who is the teacher? How well qualified is he, by degrees and by reputation among those who have studied under him? Does the school or college subscribe to a specific language method, and is this method the one that suits your purpose? If you are partial to a language lab procedure, does the school have a well-equipped lab that you can use? If you prefer the written-language approach, is its library well stocked with books in the language you propose to study? Does the school offer extracurricular activities bearing on the language or area in which you are interested, such as a Maison Française, where conversation in French is available every afternoon, or a Casa Italiana, where lectures on cultural topics are frequently given in Italian, or a Casa de las Españas, where they arrange excursions into the Spanish-speaking section of the city where you live?

Even if you are a high school student, and your choice is necessarily restricted to what is available in the school you must attend, you may find that one of the four or five languages offered holds out better side benefits than the others, such as more efficient teachers, more interesting group activities, better library facilities. Your choice of a language may be dictated by other considerations, as will be brought out in the second part of this book. But if such considerations are not operative, the ones mentioned here may be worth thinking about. Do not view the language you are required to select as a mere requirement for graduation. Regard it rather as an adventure in world exploration, and as a second string to the bow you will have to use later on, in the adult world, to shoot your way to success.

Coming back to the schools and colleges, there is one feature I would strongly urge for all of them, without exception—a general language survey course of one semester or one year, prior to the actual selection of a specific language, to familiarize the students with the language situation throughout the world, the chief languages spoken, their location, the extent of their speaking populations and economic potentialities, along with a sampling of those which the school offers.

The "General Language" courses offered by many high schools in the past, and later generally discarded because they were found to be of little advantage, differed from what I envisage in several important respects. They were usually administered by Departments of English, and tended to be courses in the history of the English language and in English etymology rather than to present the broad worldwide features of a geolinguistic nature that I advocate. They stressed the theoretical rather than the practical aspects of language, and devoted too little time and attention to the foreign segment of language. Only the last few sessions would be given over to a demonstration of Latin, French, Spanish, German, and Italian, and that without the proper introduction to present the present-day uses of those languages.

The type of geolinguistic course I have in mind would serve various highly useful purposes. It would stimulate interest in both geography and history, two fields in which American students are notoriously weak, as well as in language itself. It would serve as a prognosis test of what might be expected of the student in the way of interest and proficiency once he enters a regular language course. It would give him much-needed information about the world we live in, and develop his sense of balance and proportion with regard to his own language and the languages of other groups.

The broadening and brightening of world horizons, in this day of fast and widespread travel and shrinking national barriers, is a worthy objective for our institutions of learning—perhaps among the worthiest.

9

How Good Are Our Recordings?

Is Repetition Worth While?—What Is Available?—The Voice of the Speaker—How Many and What Kind of Speakers to Use—What to Put into a Recorded Course—Special Recordings for Special Purposes—What the Record Can and Cannot Give You—The Recording and You

LANGUAGE recordings have a long and honorable history. Among the oldest on the market are Linguaphone and Cortinaphone, which have been in use for many decades.

The original idea behind language recordings was precisely the one that interests us most: a device whereby a learner who for one reason or another is precluded the possibility of attending regular language classes with living teachers may nevertheless acquire the spoken language by listening to and imitating recorded living speakers of the language.

Prior to the Second World War, recordings available on the market were of a fairly uniform type. They consisted of a fairly large number of discs (up to 20) which were double-faced, but fast-playing, and were therefore rather high in price ($50–$75 was an average cost for a set). They were, of course, accompanied by descriptive material which invariably contained the text of the recording, and often by a fairly comprehensive grammar of the language. The record was played straight through, without interruption for reflection or repetition. The student merely ran his eye over the written text at the same time that his ear listened to the speaker's voice. He could, of course, stop the record and repeat what he had just heard, but that was not recommended procedure, as it tended to damage the record. His assimilation of the spoken features of the language was rather of the osmosis variety, duplicating real life conditions, where you are exposed to the language's speakers speaking at more or less normal speed, and there is little you can do to slow them up or make them repeat.

At the time of the war there came a major breakthrough in recording methodology. The linguistic scientists in charge of the Army's specialized language program (men like Henry Lee Smith, now of the University of Buffalo, and Milton Cowan, now of Cornell) were intensely practical linguists as well as descriptive theorists, and they realized that the element of repetition was essential in the learning process. Since they had over twenty languages to cover in connection with the Army's needs, and since the long-playing record had been finally developed, they hit upon the expedient of having their native speakers give out their lesson not in one long, connected passage, but in very short installments, later run together into longer passages, with blank spaces on the recording that would give the learner time for on-the-spot repetition. "Where is a restaurant?" would be given in English. Then would come *"Où est ——,"* followed by a "pause of silence" on the record; it was during this pause of silence that the learner was supposed to repeat to the best of his ability *"Où est ——."* The process would be repeated. Next would come the full sentence *"Où est un restaurant?"* Again a pause of silence for repetition. Again the voice of the native asking for the location of a restaurant. Again a pause for the student's repetition.

This procedure was, at first glance, enormously wasteful of good recording space, and it made the old-timers wince. But it was also enormously effective for the purpose desired. It would have to be a poorly equipped student indeed who could not say *"Où est un restaurant?"* with fair approximation to a native accent after all this rigmarole.

The new system was quickly adopted by all major language recording houses. The original Army recordings, in twenty or more languages, became commercially available to the general public through Henry Holt & Company. They were still, however, in the $50–$75 price range. Also, while some of them, in the more sought-after languages, were highly profitable, others, in languages of strategic importance but of little interest to the average civilian (Thai, Burmese, Korean, etc.) ran at a big loss on the civilian market. Fortunately, the Army had paid most of the costs of production in advance.

As the interest in learning through recordings grew, more and more commercial houses got into the picture. Also, partly by reason of the competition, partly because of technical advances and lower production costs, prices came down. Today it is possible to purchase an acceptable set of language records for $10, or even less. They may not be quite so comprehensive as the $50–$100 sets, but a good deal can be learned from them. Their recorded native speakers are uniformly authentic and can be trusted, though some of them show side deficiencies that will be discussed below.

As samples of what is available in the various price ranges, Linguaphone, which is one of the oldest concerns in the field, offers comprehensive courses in the following languages: European Spanish, Western Hemisphere Spanish, French, Italian, Portuguese, German, English, Swedish, Norwegian, Dutch, Afrikaans, Russian, Polish, Czech, modern Greek, Esperanto, Finnish, Irish, Icelandic, Chinese, Persian, Hindustani, Arabic, Hebrew. Briefer and less expensive are courses in Japanese, Bengali, Malay, Swahili, Luganda, Hausa, and Efik. With its recorded courses and their accompanying booklet material, Linguaphone offers its purchasers a Free Inquiry Service which amounts to a correspondence course, with correction of exercises based on the lessons, and personalized advice as to their needs and how to meet them. Holt, Rinehart & Winston, which inherited Henry Holt & Company's Army recordings, has available very comprehensive sets in Arabic, Burmese, Chinese, Danish, Dutch, Finnish, French, German, Greek, Hindustani, Hungarian, Italian, Japanese, Korean, Malay-Indonesian, Norwegian, Portuguese, Russian, Serbo-Croatian, Spanish, Thai, and Turkish. In addition, there are magnetic tape recordings in French, German, Spanish, Italian, Russian, and Norwegian which are available on loan for duplication or sale for individual use; duplication on tapes is permitted from a single magnetic tape set for schools using the Holt textbooks. Living Language, an arm of Crown Publishers, has available at moderate prices recordings in Spanish, French, German, Russian, Italian, Hebrew, and Japanese, and by the time this book appears will probably have Chinese and Greek as well. Dover has, at even more moderate prices, single records containing over 800 phrases for each of these languages: French, Spanish, Italian, German, Russian, Japanese, Portuguese, Greek, and Hebrew.

Language recordings form part of all language labs in universities, colleges, and even high schools that subscribe to the theory of a lan-

guage lab. They are largely supplemented by tape and wire recordings that serve the same purpose and function the same way, and
have the added advantage of being erasable and usable over and over
again for different purposes. All these mechanical aids play very large
roles in institutions that have gone over to the aural-oral method.
Their future in institutions of learning seems thoroughly established.

The other great function of the language recording is to serve the
individual learner who for one reason or another is unable or unwilling to join a regular course with regular hours and a regular program. Here the fortunes of the language recording have been much
more fluctuating, for a number of reasons.

To begin with, the language recording can give you only what it
has. It cannot be questioned or solve problems for you, like the living
teacher. All it can do is to repeat, monotonously, ad infinitum, what
is inscribed on it. True, it does not tire, it does not hesitate. But
many persons like the personal touch, the warm exchange that
ideally goes on between learner and teacher, or even among the
learners themselves. Like a computer, the language record is a robot,
a piece of efficient machinery, unendowed with the breath of life.
Psychologically, this can be bad with some learners.

Next comes the question of the speaker or speakers. The mere
fact that they are natives, usually fairly cultured natives, does not
suffice. They should have clear, audible, even ringing voices. A
drawling, indistinct monotone can be characteristic of a native speaker
of a language, too. Consider the quality of the voices of most of our
radio and TV announcers, and compare them with the voices of
some of the guests who occasionally appear on their programs. The
former speak clearly, incisively, so that it is no effort at all to grasp
everything they say. The latter often mumble, and force us to strain
our ears. Yet both are native speakers, and so are we. It was characteristic of a few early recordings, made in haste for Army use, that
the speakers were not at all distinct, however native. Many had
what one would be tempted to label "uninteresting" voices. Just as
some lecturers drone on and on until they finally put you to sleep, so
would they. To a great extent this has been corrected in recent times,
but I still recall an experience where a group of language people,
I among them, were given a demonstration of recordings by some

Army experts, who started with French. This went over well, until it occurred to a skeptic to remark that we all knew French; how about a language we didn't know? The experts obliged with a recording of Turkish. The speaker had a mumbling voice from which the sounds could not be unscrambled, and since the printed booklets were not available (they would at least have given us some idea what to expect in the way of sounds), the experiment was a dismal failure. It needn't have been, if the Turkish speaker had been better selected.

Another occasional drawback of recordings lies in poor direction and timing. The native speaker knows his own language, and he is unconsciously in a hurry to get through with his assignment. Unless he is carefully watched and directed, he may hurry on from phrase to phrase, from sentence to sentence, and not allow his unseen audience time enough for proper grasping and repetition of what he says. This happened to me with a very widely advertised Hebrew recording. The publishers had wanted to send me French and Spanish, but I objected that I knew French and Spanish too well to be a good judge of the effectiveness of what they had to offer. So they sent me a language of which I know very little. The speaker was clear and vibrant enough, but he already knew Hebrew, and no one had told him that his audience did not. There was not enough time in the pauses of silence for either sound grasping or thorough repetition. If I, with my language ear and linguistic preparation, could not use those recordings to advantage, how could anyone else, unless he already had a fairly firm grip on the language?

Many recordings make it a point to include at least two speakers, preferably of different sexes. This breaks the monotony of listening to the same voice, and also precludes getting used to one person's pronunciation to the exclusion of everyone else's.

As for the materials that go into a recorded course, they are as varied as what goes into grammar books. Some are aimed at specific markets. Producers of recordings for school and college use generally pay a good deal of attention to the curriculum and mode of presentation of the institutions, and try to base their content on them. For individual use, there is far greater variety. Some recordings are spoken tourist phrase books, and give all those expressions which the average tourist is likely to want in the course of his travels. Others base themselves on literature, and give long passages from well-known authors. Still others try to base themselves on real-life situations, taking in turn the family group, the classroom, the store, the railroad station, etc. Some try to give you a connected story, and even make room for different characters, usually the members of a family who go together on a trip to the land where the language is spoken, and there have conversational interchanges both among themselves and with the natives. This permits both dramatization and family use, and records have been known to be sold for group family instruction, with dad, mom, and the children all playing their respective roles by imitating the imaginary characters on the record.

There is no question that the recorded course, properly chosen in accordance with one's requirements, supplies the best method of as-similating at least in part the spoken language to those who cannot follow regular language courses. Properly constructed, and properly used, it can be highly effective. There is, however, one big drawback which can be thrown squarely into the lap of the learner. The record can talk to you, but it can't argue with you. Above all, it cannot hold you in line. You have to do that yourself.

If you have registered for a course in a school of adult education, you know that it meets three times a week at a stated hour. Not only do you realize that you have a fixed commitment, but you also realize that you omit any of the stated sessions at your own risk and peril. The class will go on whether you are there or not, and the next time you come in you may find yourself out of your depth. The fact that you have already invested your money in the course acts as a power-ful magnet. Only a serious emergency, or real illness, or impossible weather conditions, will make you miss a class.

The record is far too easygoing and relaxing for your own good. You can make a date with a record, and say "I'll be with you every Tuesday and Friday, seven to eight P.M." Then your best friend calls up and suggests that you go bowling. If you had a class, you'd say no. But with a record, what difference does it make if you take it on Wednesday instead of Tuesday? You can always pick up where you left off. Then something else comes up on Wednesday. Pretty soon your dates with your records grow more and more infrequent, more and more irregular. Ultimately the records rest comfortably and undisturbed in your record cabinet, and your learning French by recordings is over, until some time in the future when you will be less busy and have more free time at your disposal.

Note also that a record is not something you can slip into your overcoat pocket and carry with you for use on the bus, as is a book. It calls not only for time, but for absolutely free time, and for the necessary equipment. Someday a genius will create a set of language records that will work like a transistor pocket radio, and that you can transport with you and use at will, anywhere. But it hasn't happened yet.

The concern that produces the recordings knows that what we have described above can very easily happen, but it doesn't care. It has already sold you a set of records, and its responsibility is over. It will tell you in glowing terms of all the things you can do with its product, but it will not warn you that one of the main ingredients is your own will power. For this you cannot blame the company. Yet it is curious to see how the point finally gets around to the consumer, and damages the industry.

Spurred by a tremendously costly campaign of publicity, certain sets of language recordings sold by the hundreds of thousands five or six years ago. Everybody wanted to learn languages by this inexpensive, simple process. Then came the disappointments, occasioned not so much by the records themselves as by the lack of will power of the purchasers. The word got around that you didn't learn languages with recordings any more than you learned them in two-year high school courses. The fact that in both cases the real burden of the fault lay with the consumers rather than with the producers was overlooked. (If high school and college "consumers" demanded minimum four-year courses, they would get far better results. too.)

The net result has been a sharp falling off both in sales and in interest in recordings for individual use, though they hold up fairly well as adjuncts for regular academic courses, where there is supervision and a measure of compulsion. This is highly unfortunate, because a good set of recordings is still one of the best ways to learn much of the spoken language, if it is used properly.

Today, there is not anything like the same scramble on the part of publishers to get into what looked like a highly profitable field. Many of them have had very unpleasant experiences. Specialized firms that produce recordings and tapes for institutional use are still doing well, and a children's market for recordings has developed. The latter works out better than the adult market, because the child is normally supervised and told what to do. Also, the same advantages that accrue to a child in learning to speak naturally with living people are operative with recordings, provided someone stands over the child and makes him keep his appointments with the records instead of running off to watch TV or play baseball.

Language recordings for specific purposes, including language instruction in high school and college courses, can take varied forms. For the casual, individual learner, one important question he must ask himself before he pays his money and takes his choice is: "Do I really have the time to go through with this? Above all, do I have the inclination? Am I man enough to stick to it, and treat the recorded course as I would treat a course in University Extension? If the recordings are of the family group type, can I get my family to cooperate, and turn the operation into a collective project?"

As a prospective purchaser of a set of language records, you have the right to a free demonstration. Try the recordings out in a listening booth, or order them on approval. Beyond telling you that you will learn the language, does the recording contain material that suits your purpose? Does it teach you to say and understand the things you want to say and understand? Does it give you the necessary pauses for repetition? Is the voice of the speaker crystal-clear, or do you have to strain your ears to catch the sounds he is producing? Is there more than one speaker?

I have directed recordings in French for McKay, in French, Russian, and American English for Folkways, in Italian for Funk & Wagnalls. In all of these recordings I have attempted to embody the principles outlined above. I have also served as a native speaker of both English and Italian on various recordings where the method of presentation was set by others. Despite the drawbacks I have outlined, I consider a good language recording as a powerful aid in language learning, though I like to see it combined with other features, such as a good written-language grammar. But I can never sufficiently stress that such effectiveness as a recording may have depends very largely on the will power (and won't power) of the individual learner and his real desire to learn. More than any other language-learning device, the record puts the learner squarely on his own.

IO

Can You Learn a Language
by Living in the Country That Speaks It?

*The Foreign Residence—Guided and Unguided Tours—Mingling
with and Mimicking the Natives—Training the Ear and the Eye
—Insulating Yourself from English Speakers—Reading Local
Newspapers and Magazines—Building Up a Vocabulary and
Phrase Stock—It's Up to You*

NEXT to being born and raised in the country whose language you
want to speak, residing in it is, in theory at least, the best way of
learning its language. Starry-eyed people often ask you: "How long
would I have to reside in Spain in order to learn Spanish?"

This reminds me of the story of the ancient Greek sage who was
met on the public highway by a stranger who asked him: "How long
will it take me to get to Athens?" "Get going!" replied the sage. The
puzzled stranger repeated his question, but got the same answer. He
then shrugged his shoulders and went on his way, thinking that all
Athenians were either mad or boors. But he had not proceeded
twenty steps when the sage called out after him: "It will take you
about two hours to get to the city." Even more puzzled, the stranger
turned back and asked the sage: "Why didn't you tell me that when
I first asked you?" "I had to see how fast you walk before I could
give you the right answer," replied the sage.

Residence and travel in a foreign land can be one of the most
effective ways to learn its language. It can also be the best way of
making it impossible for you to learn it.

If you insist on speaking and being spoken to in the foreign tongue,
you will learn it fast. If you take the path of least resistance, lapse
into English because it's easier on you, allow the foreign speakers to
practice their English on you, which they are often very anxious
to do, and, worst of all, if you isolate yourself from the native population and become part of an American-British colony, you'll never
learn anything: not the language, not the thoughts and viewpoints

and attitudes, not even the basic customs and institutions of the land that is your host.

More and more colleges now have as part of their language curriculum what they call a junior year abroad. Here the students of a particular language go to the country of their choice, under the supervision of one of their own professors, attend regular courses in the country's universities, given in the country's language, of which they have already acquired more than a smattering, and often are billeted with private families of which they become temporary members. At the same time, they are encouraged to mingle with the natives on every possible occasion, to attend their feasts and celebrations, to shop by themselves, to live in every way as though they were at home, save that their living is done in the foreign country and in the foreign language.

This procedure can be, and generally is, highly effective, particularly at the advanced level. The trouble with it is that not everybody can afford it. On a lower level, there are all kinds of substitutes: tours, guided or unguided, of various durations, to the country whose language you want to learn; getting yourself assigned to the country, either by an employing firm or by a grant, for specific purposes. Even excursions to foreign quarters in your own locality can be of help.

There are special arrangements whereby you can be the guide, if duly qualified, like the ones run by the American Institute for Foreign Study or the Foreign Language League, semiofficial, nonprofit associations of high school teachers and students, which appoint regular teachers as chaperons and guides for student groups of high school vintage who wish to study abroad. These tours include intensive conversational courses at Audio-Visual Centers of regular European universities, preceded and followed by all sorts of travel itineraries in the country of your choice. The cost is held down to below $1,000 for students, while if you are a teacher-chaperon your full expenses are paid, and you get a small stipend besides.

Variants on the theme of foreign residence, guided or unguided, are numerous. There is, for example, an extremely popular adult education school in Denmark, where they will teach you almost anything under the sun—in Danish. Before they let you in and permit you to round out your education, they advise you to do some studying of Danish on records, both before you leave America and on shipboard. Then they board you with two Danish families, a month at a time. When they finally admit you, you are already a fairly fluent speaker of Danish, and they give you the final polish. On the French Riviera there is, or was, a Foreign Service Institute branch where future diplomats learn French under ideal conditions, with a house staff that speaks nothing but French and class instruction up to twelve hours a day. These might be styled guided residences.

There are also unguided ones. A lady with a little time and money and a desire to learn Spanish went down to Guatemala and boarded with a local family. Her account of her experiences is both instructive and exhilarating. At first everything came to her in a jumble of staccato sounds. Then she began to isolate and recognize a few words and phrases: *"¿Cómo no?"*, *"¡Ya, ya!"*, *"un ratito."* The last, which means "a little while," she misinterpreted at first as having to do with a little rat. But this was quickly cleared up. Among her first shopping experiences was that of going into a store, asking (so she thought) for soap, and being told they didn't *want* any. She had used *quiere* ("do you want?") instead of *quiero* ("I want)." Next she asked for a bomb instead of an electric bulb (*bomba, bombilla*). *"Creo que sí"* ("I think so") at first struck her ear as "crocuses," which was all the more surprising because they don't grow in Guatemala. Other word borders remained undefined for a time, so that she would come out with the tail end of one word and the initial syllable of the next, thinking that was a word. They tried to use English to her, but she, having been forewarned, would have none of it. Everything cleared up eventually, and on her return to the States she was even able to reassure a Puerto Rican who had asked for change for a ten-dollar bill in a supermarket and was justifiably alarmed when the cashier rang up "No sale" on the cash register, which is excellent Spanish for "It isn't going to come out."

There are many ways of playing the learning game abroad if you are really minded to learn. One is exchanging not formal lessons but conversations, with a native speaker who wants to inflict his English on you. "One day we'll talk your language, the next day mine." Another device that can be used to good advantage is for two people who speak each other's language in less than perfect fashion to converse, each speaking the other's tongue; when stuck, one can always interject a word in his own language, and probably be understood.

The conversation may be slowed up a bit, but that is no tragedy. A third method is for each of the speakers to use his own tongue, asking for explanations when he does not readily understand the other.

The system that is most advantageous to the language learner, however, is to insist, if he is in a position to do so, that only the foreign language be used. This is the big advantage that immigrants to the United States enjoyed in their language learning. No one felt that it was necessary to defer to them; everybody spoke English to them, and expected them to reply in the same tongue. They learned fast.

The American tourist or resident abroad does not enjoy this advantage. Everyone wants to defer to him, save perhaps in France. Yet it is amazing to what extent the same people who use English far better than you can use their language appreciate any attempt on your part to speak a few words in their tongue. Any Portuguese will brighten up if you start the interchange with *"Bons dias!"* In pre-Communist Hungary, the elevator operator at the Szent Gellért Hotel would smile broad approval when I called out the number of my floor in Magyar: *"Három."* The big exception are the French. They have the same feeling that everyone should speak French, and reasonably good French at that, that animates Americans in their instinct that everyone should speak English. A few tourist phrases spoken with an American accent will generally get you nowhere in France. But a really good command of the language opens the door to every Frenchman's heart.

If you begin your foreign residence with some previous knowledge of the country's language, the thing to do is to consort with the natives, preferably those who don't speak any English, and insulate yourself as much as possible from your fellow Americans. This is hard at first. But the rewards are enormous. The jumble clears up, and more and more words and phrases begin to emerge from it, words and phrases that you can both recognize and use. It is difficult for an adult to relinquish his inhibitions, and his fear that he will sound foolish, or, at the very least, uncouth. But don't let that deter you. Very, very seldom will people laugh at you. If they do, laugh with them. Mimic everything they say and do, even to the intonation and the gestures, for these, too, are important in the acquisition of a language.

In my Lisbon hotel I spoke what was at first very imperfect oral Portuguese to everyone I came in contact with. This included both those of the hotel staff who could speak English better than I could speak Portuguese, such as the hotel clerk, the manager, and the head-waiter, and those who could speak no English at all, such as the bell-boy, the doorman, and the chambermaid. It worked like a charm. In a very few weeks I was able to converse fluently, and even lecture, in the spoken Portuguese which on crossing the border I had realized I could not understand. A little study out of a grammar or phrase book at the same time that you are training your ear and tongue is of great help. So is the reading of local newspapers and magazines, in-stead of relying for your news and reading matter on the Paris edition of the *Herald Tribune.* So is a little conscious attention devoted to the many written signs which face you at every step.

I have known Americans who after years of residence in a foreign land were utterly incapable of speaking its language. They had done all the wrong things: insulated themselves from the native population and consorted exclusively with American cliques, or with natives who spoke flawless English. When faced with natives who spoke no Eng-lish (and these, strange as it may seem, are a clear majority in every country, superficial impressions to the contrary), they had insisted on making themselves understood by speaking English more loudly and slowly, and accompanying it with sign language, which occasionally works on a very limited scale. They had done all their reading in English, and had never bothered even glancing at a local newspaper. They had acquired the meaning of a few indispensable signs, such as "Women," "Men," "Push," "Pull," by the total-picture-reading method rather than by spelling out the word and trying to pronounce it. A few of them nevertheless wondered why some of the language hadn't rubbed off on them. It would have been a miracle if it had.

I have even come across a few foreign immigrants to the United States who had managed in the course of many years to learn no English by using the same methodology. It was a bit more difficult in their case, but it could be done. The editor of a New York Italian-language weekly, a highly cultured man who wrote excellent poetry in Italian, once told me: "I have never learned any English, nor have I felt any need or desire to learn it. I live and work in an Italian sec-tion, where everyone speaks Italian—the shopkeepers, the renting agent, all my advertisers and writers, even the policeman on the beat and the postman who brings me the mail. Why should I bother to learn English when I can live perfectly without it?" His experience, of course, was more unique than rare. He had no children, which probably saved him from exposure to English in the bosom of his own family. But rare as was his accomplishment, it was hardly praiseworthy. If nothing else, he should have shown enough deference to the laws of hospitality to take some interest in the language of the country that was playing host to him and enabling him to earn a reasonably comfortable living. I did not hesitate to tell him so.

Neither do I hesitate to tell Americans who reside abroad that they should make a decided effort to acquire at least some part of the language of the country in which they find themselves. What they miss in failing to make the effort is altogether to their own detriment.

Residence abroad can be the very best means of acquiring a language at the adult stage; or it can be a total or almost total loss, depending on you. It takes courage and a spirit of adventure to enter the market place, mingle with the natives, listen to them, mimic them, ultimately speak with them. Inhibitions are of absolutely no use in language learning. The way to understand is to start listening. The way to speak is to start speaking. In so doing, you are far from making yourself ridiculous. You are displaying your intelligence. You make yourself truly ridiculous if you don't do it.

II

Can You Learn a Language All by Yourself?

I Can Teach You, but I Cannot "Learn" You—The Value of Persistence—Distractions and How to Get Around Them—How to Use Books and Recordings on Your Own—Unlearning and Relearning a Language—Learning Two or More Languages at Once

THIS chapter, with the three that follow, are in a sense the crux of the whole book. If you are studying a language under guidance, whether the guidance be of the institutional or the private variety, you must to a considerable degree submit to a methodology and program that have been worked out by others. The others are no doubt "experts," either in the field of linguistics or that of education, but that does not prevent them from differing radically, often violently, about how best to impart languages. Perhaps their basic fault lies in their tacit assumption that all learners have the same native equipment, disposition, reactions, and motivation, which is not at all the case. One man's meat can be another man's poison, in language learning as in almost everything else. Some people learn best through the ear, others through the eye. Some are quick, others slow learners. Some want primarily the spoken, others the written language. But the methodology, curriculum, and program of a school, college, or university must of necessity strike a balance and try to achieve a cross section and a compromise. The alternative would be a tutorial system of individual instruction, which is not practical for those institutions. And even with a tutorial system, the tutor would have his own ideas as to what is best, and impose them on the learner.

But if you are learning by yourself, you are squarely on your own, and you are free to develop and apply the method that best suits your type of mind and your needs. You can select your own textbooks and recordings, space your periods of instruction to suit your own convenience, proceed at your own pace. This freedom of action can be turned to advantage, and can largely make up for the disadvantages of being unguided.

In all types of instruction, guided and unguided alike, one big principle has to be kept in mind. You can lead a horse to water, but you can't make him drink. A classroom instructor, a private tutor, I, through the pages of this book, can teach you; but we cannot "learn" you. Learning is something you must do for yourself. You have to have motivation, of one kind or another, from the lowly one of accumulating credits toward graduation to the lofty one of mastering like a native, in all its aspects, the tongue you are studying. If you're not interested to the point of wanting to do something about it, it will be better to drop the language-learning project and turn your attention to something else, in which you are interested. It will be far more profitable all around.

We owe the Russians something for the Sputnik which aroused official American interest in languages. Though this is not so well known, we owe them another debt, for a contribution their language makes to learning terminology. The verb "to learn," in Russian as in other Slavic languages, does not exist. What you have in its place is *uchit's'a,* the literal, etymological meaning of which is "to teach oneself" (it may be added that in Slavic the reflexive verb is regularly used to express the passive, so that the verb might also translate "to be taught"; but this is a secondary development). The basic idea seems to be that you "teach yourself" to do something, and this is precisely the idea we are trying to impress you with.

As in everything else, in language learning there is no substitute for persistence, stick-at-itiveness, guts. If you resolve to learn a language, you must grit your teeth and stick at it. At the time of the war, when the Army language courses began, with their terrific concentration of time and effort, some critics remarked that a smattering of a language could be acquired by far less drastic procedures. The Army replied that it was not interested in smatterings. The proposition could well be transferred to resolutions to learn languages. A halfway resolve is of no interest, and generally leads nowhere, representing only a waste of time on the part of the would-be halfway learner and anyone who happens to be connected with him in his halfhearted attempt.

As in everything else, there are distractions. These the Army Language Schools try to eliminate by freeing their students from all other duties, and filling up with language activities most of their waking hours. This procedure is generally impractical in any surroundings other than the Army schools themselves. Also, it lends itself to monotony, boredom, tension, and occasional nervous breakdowns. It is not recommended for the individual learner.

There are, however, many ways of getting around distractions. If you are learning by yourself, try to keep fixed hours for your language study, insofar as possible, by budgeting your time availabilities in advance. Do not permit side activities to break in upon your appointed schedule save under emergency conditions. Treat your records and textbooks as you would treat a regular class assignment. Do not let your sense of freedom lead to irresponsibility. Try to arrange, insofar as possible, not to be disturbed while your lesson is in progress. Request the members of your family, or those around you, to respect your privacy for the hour or two that your lesson lasts. Have surprise visitors and telephone calls deferred. You would not normally allow people to break into the classroom where you are studying with a message to the effect that "Mr. So-and-so is here to see you" or "Mrs. Brooks is on the phone." Why let them do it to you in your own home when you are engaged in something you consider important? They can be told that you will see them some other time, or call back in an hour.

In addition, utilize odds and ends of time which are normally frittered away. If you do not have the time to go through a full record, or one side of it, it may nevertheless pay you to put on the record for five or ten minutes, listen to its phrases, and repeat them. Treat this sort of experience as you would a brief five-minute chat with an acquaintance you might meet on the street. A few cordial phrases, of the common garden variety, then "Good-by; I'll be seeing you."

Carry a paperback phrase book or small grammar around with you in your pocket. Modern life is such that we sometimes spend what seems like half of it waiting in line; at a theater ticket office, at a supermarket checking out, in the office of a physician, dentist, or public official. In the latter cases, we usually sit down, pick up a magazine from the table, and browse through it, though its contents may be of very little interest to us. If we are standing on line waiting for our turn, we normally have nothing to do but stare into space, wondering impatiently how long it is going to take the people ahead of us to get through with their transactions. Taking out our pocket book and going over a few phrases will not only give us a little practice; it will calm and soothe our nerves and bring down our blood pressure. Waiting periods that seem interminable when we have nothing to do turn out to be surprisingly short when we engage in a purposeful activity.

If the textbook turns out to be too bulky for pocket use, even in paperback form, there is no reason why we cannot carry in our inside coat pocket a few phrases written out in advance, a few irregular verbs of the troublesome, pesky variety, that we are having difficulty in memorizing. This has the added advantage that it won't even draw the attention of the other people on line; they'll think we're just rereading a letter we got this morning.

Fairly extensive trips, on a subway, bus, train, or plane, can be beautifully utilized in the same fashion. It would be an exaggeration to say that we can learn a language on our way to and from work. But we can learn segments of a language, and languages, after all, come in segments.

The Army may not have been officially interested in smatterings at the time of the war, but the individual soldiers found smatterings extremely useful in the course of their peregrinations through foreign countries. The ability to speak and understand a few words, a few phrases, often went all the way from contributing to a GI's comfort to saving his life. In the matter of languages, it is desirable to strive for perfection, but it is quite legitimate to settle for less. Not only is perfection not of this world; not only is it a proven fact that no one possesses even his native tongue in "perfect" fashion (if you did, you would know all of the 600,000 words in the New English Dictionary; do you?); but *any* knowledge of *any* fraction of a language can be put to use as soon as it is acquired. If you knew only how to say "water" or "bread" in a foreign tongue, that one word would carry your meaning across and get you what you wanted. Do not let yourself be at all impressed by those language scholars who imply, even if they don't say it in so many words, that you must not open your mouth in a foreign language until you have mastered all its intricacies. The main function of language is to get meaning across from one person to another. Any type of language, perfect or imperfect, that gets your meaning across to the other party, and his meaning across to you, fulfills the basic function of language.

Do not let yourself be impressed by the oft-repeated and partly true statement that you may acquire a language, but that you will quickly forget it if it isn't constantly practised. What the proponents of this theory forget is that once you have learned something, it comes back to you far more quickly and readily than if you are acquiring it for the first time. The grooves in your mind may become blurred, but they are never completely erased. Consider what happens in the matter of swimming, dancing, driving a car, playing a game. Of course you're rusty when you come back to it after a number of years. But how fast it comes back, once the initial period of unfamiliarity is over! What you have once learned is never really unlearned. The French you learned in high school (if you really learned it) will come back to you, not the minute you land in France, to be sure, but after you have been exposed to French for a week or two. After all, even the Army, with its heavy, barrage-like concentrations of language and its insistence on quasi perfection, feels the need of one- or two-week refresher courses for its language experts when they have been away from the school for two or three years and have had no occasion, during that time, to use the language they learned and overlearned. It all comes back.

The question is often asked: Can you learn two or more languages at once? Do they help each other out, or interfere with each other? To this there is no stock answer. In civilian institutions where language is only part of the program, it is extremely common for the students to take two, three, even four languages at once. Since civilian courses rely largely on the intellective rather than the reflex processes, there is no question that two or more languages at once broaden the horizon, arouse a sense of comparison, and are in the main helpful, though they may lend themselves to occasional (but only occasional) confusion. In intensive, spoken-language programs, such as those of the Army schools, there is no room or time for two languages at once. Concentration is on a single language at a time, though many students repeat the experience, going on to learn a second language when the first is over. (Among my classmates in the Mandarin Chinese class at Monterey, there was one staff sergeant who had previously gone through the full course in Japanese and the full course in Korean). The unspoken philosophy in these institutions seems to be that for their purpose it is best to concentrate on one language at a time.

Perhaps a better criterion is offered by small European countries, where the students are required to learn several languages. In Sweden and Holland, for example, it is customary to learn at once, in both spoken and written form, English, French, and German, along with, of course, the national tongue, and students who go in for Classical studies normally take their Latin and Greek in addition to, not in substitution for, the three modern languages. It seems to do them no harm, and the educated Swedes and Hollanders of my acquaintance all speak excellent English, French, and German.

Judging from this, as well as from my own experience, I should say that it is psychologically and pedagogically not at all impossible to learn at least two, probably more, languages at once. The one big drawback to this procedure is the time element. Americans have been described as people who deliberately, and as a matter of course, bite off more than they can chew, and try to do too many things at once. This may be true. Yet I have not noticed any deficiency in any other field of learning or human activity on the part of the educated Hollanders and Swedes described above. Perhaps they budget their school time better than we do.

Or perhaps we tend to create alibis for ourselves to account for our imperfections in the matter of setting up certain goals and pursuing them. Perhaps the legend that people cannot learn two or more languages at once goes hand in hand with that other, widespread myth that Americans lack a language sense with which other nationals are somehow miraculously endowed.

12

Some Specific Learning Hints

Paying Attention—The Law of Diminishing Returns—Learning Plateaus and How to Get off Them—Inductive or Deductive Learning?—Listening to How Your Language Is Mispronounced—The General Psychology of a Language—Phrases vs. Words—Proverbs, Sayings, and Songs

IF you are taking a regular course in a school, it would be somewhat trite to advise you, at the adult stage, to pay attention. Yet the same principle applies if you are engaged in the self-learning process. It won't do to let your mind wander to other things while you are listening to a recording, or reading a textbook. There must be concentration, even intensity, in your imitation and repetition as in your reading of grammatical rules and examples, or of a page from a foreign novel.

Edgar Dale, an educational psychologist of some renown, tells us that in the learning process we must develop the motivation to learn (he calls this the "want-to"), but also couple it with the methods and materials of learning, the "know-how" and the "know-why." Problems, he goes on to state, should be attacked in depth; if this is done, our usable memory of the subject will be greater, and the enjoyment that comes from really knowing a subject will turn into stronger motivation.

He advises (and I agree) that it is desirable to map the field in advance and note its basic principles and structure. A bird's-eye survey of a language in anticipation of going into it in detail will help. A skeleton outline of a language's grammatical system, shorn of all petty exceptions, is worth having at our fingertips before we really attack the language. Imitative action, he warns us, is mere training; creative interaction is true education. We must learn not only how but why. It would not be amiss if more grammars, particularly for self-learning, started off with the ten- to twenty-page condensation of grammatical structure that appears in my *World's Chief Languages* or the *Getting Along In* tourist manuals.

97

Two psychological factors must be reckoned with in language learning. One is the law of diminishing returns, which means that we cannot expect from an hour's study after we have had a year of the language the same abundant per-hour yield that we get at the outset of our studies. The other is the fact that there are in language learning definite plateaus. We achieve a certain degree of proficiency. Then our progress seems to come to a halt, and for a time there is no discernible improvement, such as there was with every day of the initial stage. With patience and work we get off this plateau and begin our upward climb again. Eventually, advancing from plateau to plateau, we reach what might be called a saturation point, beyond which it is difficult if not impossible to advance. But this is no reason for worry, because the saturation stage means, usually, that we have assimilated as much of the language as we care to know or have use for. Some slight measure of improvement is always possible. But is the game worth the candle? At any rate, once we have reached the saturation point improvement comes to us naturally rather than through deliberate effort. I have probably reached my saturation point in French and Spanish. I speak both with native-speaker accent, and with complete fluency. Occasionally I may be at a loss for a word; but at the point at which I am, I can make suitable substitutions. If the term for "windshield wiper" has slipped my memory, I can say, with the greatest of ease: "That instrument which cleans your windshield when it rains." The station attendant will readily understand what I mean, and the chances are he will give me the exact term himself. The word will then come back to me naturally and without effort on my part. I may occasionally meet an unfamiliar word in my reading. If the context or the etymology doesn't give me the meaning, I may have to look it up. But this can happen to me in the languages to which I am fully native, too. Else why are so many copies of Webster's Dictionary sold in English-speaking countries?

Some linguist once mentioned the futility of language learning for purposes of exalted self-expression. Yet writers like Joseph Conrad are there to show that it may not be altogether futile. It is perfectly true that exalted self-expression is easy for a few, hard for the majority; but this applies to our native tongue as well as to languages we may acquire. There is such a thing as "knowing thyself," and setting the sights at a practical level. Do you want to speak French like a man born and raised in Paris? You may lack the equipment. Do you want to speak German so that a German will understand what you want to say on practical everyday topics? That is not too difficult to achieve, even if you are not a born linguist. You may even want to settle for a limited amount of reading ability, so that you will know that *Gefahr* means "danger," *Vorsicht* "caution," *Herren* "men," and *Damen* "women." Learning to compensate for one's known deficiencies is half the battle. If you are driving a car and the road is unfamiliar, you will go a bit more slowly than you would where you know every inch of the way. If the language is partly unfamiliar, go more slowly, don't let yourself in for conversational exchanges beyond your depth, and don't be afraid to let people know that you *are* a foreigner, and entitled to some consideration in the matter of rapidity of speech and repetition of what you haven't understood. "Please speak more slowly" and "Please repeat" are two phrases that have high priority among the hundred or so clichés I advocate.

Much can be learned about another language from the way its native speaker mispronounces or otherwise mishandles ours. All foreign speakers' mispronunciations are due to substitution of sounds and sound groups current in their language for somewhat similar sounds and sound groups that appear in ours. This in turn is due to taking the path of least resistance, otherwise known as sheer laziness. The Russian who says "manyi" instead of "many" is using one of two possible approximations in his language for the *-ny* combination in English. Neither coincides precisely with the English, and he is choosing the lesser of two evils. But it's an evil nevertheless. He should listen to and imitate my "many" until it becomes second nature to him. It is bad for him that he doesn't do it, but it is good for me, because his mispronunciation gives me the clue (if any were needed) to the precise way in which that syllable should be pronounced in Russian. The German speaker who says *fount* and *bik* for "found" and "big" gives me warning that his language does not permit voiced consonants in final position, no matter how much they may appear in writing. The Japanese waiter who says "This meat is too few" informs me that his language does not make a clear-cut distinction between paucity of quantity and paucity of number. The Czech who writes "I thank you from bottom of my heart" notifies me that there is no word for "the" in his language.

A critic once chided me for offering students literal translations, often highly picturesque, of foreign words and expressions. Yet such literal translations are powerful memory aids, since they tie the word to a mental picture. Who is going to forget the word for "cotton" in German once he learns that *Baumwolle* is literally "tree-wool," or the word for "olive oil" in Roumanian when he hears that *unt de lemn* has the literal meaning of "grease from wood?" The Japanese "throat has grown dry," the Russian "I want to drink," for "I'm thirsty" lend themselves to easy memorization. So does Arabic "Oh, the peace!" for "Too bad!" So does Chinese "You well not well?" for "How are you?" Memorization of ten thousand or so words (the minimum one needs to converse intelligently) is a long and dreary process; it surely can't be wrong to liven it up with a few picturesque word-for-word translations, which occasionally also serve to illustrate national points of view, as when the Arab says "Smooth and level" when he welcomes you to his home (we, of course, sometimes "roll out the red carpet," which is also ideally made "smooth and level"), or the Spaniard says "This is your house."

One of Italy's greatest language teachers and popularizers was P. S. Rivetta, now deceased. He once published a set of general language-learning rules. A few are worth summarizing here, with occasional comments:

1. Proceed from the general to the particular, not the other way round; get a view of the forest before you start examining the trees. (This coincides exactly with both Edgar Dale's advice and mine.)

2. Get the phonetic structure of the language, imitating not only the sounds but also the intonation and cadence. Listen to foreign radio stations.

3. Listen to the way the speaker of the language you want to learn mispronounces yours. Get a line on different degrees of muscular tension (French, for instance, is spoken with considerable tension of the vocal organs, while English is comparatively lax). Watch also for the placing of the voice (chest, head, etc.; speakers of Slavic languages emit far less air through the nose when they speak than we do).

4. After getting acquainted with the language's basic grammar, investigate some of the syntactical examples, so as to gain some grasp on the psychology of the language and its speakers.

5. Link the content of the foreign phrase to its mental concept rather than to its English translation; if possible, link it to a picturable object or action.

6. Language starts with thought, and thought does not belong to any language in particular, but is common to the speakers of all languages. The trick is to link the thought concept not with your own language but with the language you are learning.

7. Try, as far as possible, to think in the foreign language, even when not speaking out loud. Your foreign-language thinking will soon expand.

8. Learn phrases rather than isolated words. (Here I differ somewhat; the isolated word may sometimes serve a special purpose, and in highly inflected languages too many phrases may be needed to give you the word in all its possible forms.)

9. Make up your own private dictionary of words and expressions you are interested in.

10. Learn idioms at the start, not at the finish. Note also the currency and frequency of occurrence of such idioms. Some idioms are antiquated, and not worth learning. This goes also for proverbs and popular sayings, some of which are on everybody's lips, while others are purely literary.

11. Note the psychological content and intent of apparently equivalent expressions (English "please leave"; "go away"; "get out"; "scram").

12. Languages are not necessarily logical. "School of law" could be in Italian *scuola di legge,* which is the literal translation of the English expression, and might even be understood. But that's not the way the Italians say it; they use *facoltà di diritto,* "faculty of right" ("right" is here used in the sense of "justice").

13. As you learn a point of grammar, try to memorize it in condensed form.

14. Don't be sloppy. Learn every phrase you take up in complete form, with the correct spelling, the right pronunciation and intonation, possibly even the gesture that goes with it.

Rivetta mentions, among his language-learning devices, foreign radio programs. These are easy to get in Europe, a little more difficult in the United States, where they require a short-wave set. On the other hand, many of our larger cities have local radio stations that "speak your language" and offer excellent programs in a great number of languages. People living in the New York metropolitan area, for instance, will encounter no difficulty whatsoever in selecting on their radios local programs in Italian, Spanish, Yiddish, German, Polish, Hungarian, modern Greek, and many other tongues. On a lesser scale, this is also true of other American cities.

If you are musically inclined, you will find that the singing of songs in the language you are interested in supplies excellent exercise in pronunciation, as well as a convenient way of memorizing both words and phrases. This device is one of the favorites of foreign language clubs in the schools and colleges. There is no reason for not using it in your home if you are at all vocally qualified. It doesn't have to be grand opera. Popular songs will work just as effectively; in fact, more so, because while the language of opera is often stilted and antiquated, that of the latest song hits is invariably popular and current.

13

How Do You Learn to Speak and Understand?

The Four Language Skills—The Mental Translation Process and What It Means to You—Redundancy and Clues—Speaking by Imitation—Intonation and Syllabification—Slow-Motion Speech, Its Advantages and Disadvantages—Memorization and Declamation —The Real-Life Situation—The Jumble That Clears Up

OF the four language skills, largely unrelated among themselves, speaking, understanding, reading, and writing, the most difficult by far is the second. In part, this is due to the fact that it calls for greater totality, amounting almost to perfection. One can string together, after a little study, an acceptable sequence of words, and utter them in such a fashion that the native will grasp the general meaning. Reading and writing are arts in which you have time and aids at your disposal; you can read or write slowly, with a dictionary by your elbow. But the spoken word, particularly of a native using his own language, at his own rate of speed, is fleeting. You either catch it on the wing or you don't. If you don't, you are a failure.

You may on occasion have time to translate mentally your own proposed utterance from your own language to the one you are trying to speak, though the procedure is not recommended, on practical grounds; the native's words and thoughts will be miles away by the time your translation is completed. What you never have time to do is to translate his utterance mentally into your language. Before you can translate it, you must perceive it in its proper sound pattern, anyway, and that you seldom do if you are not already familiar with that sound pattern.

Consider what happens in your own language. You never have real difficulty in formulating and expressing your own thoughts. But how often do you fail to grasp what is said to you? There may be too much extraneous noise around; the speaker may mumble, or speak too softly; or you may be unfamiliar with part of what he is saying, even though he is saying it in your common language. "How do you spell that?" is a frequently asked question. It is asked most frequently in connection with family names and place names, but it may be asked of common nouns, verbs, and adjectives as well.

"Redundancy" is a term used by communications experts to signify that complex of clues by which you identify the utterance you hear and give it its proper meaning, and more specifically to refer to the fact that usually those clues are far more than you need. In ordinary speech, between two people speaking the same language, what is actually, physically heard is often half or less than half of what is said. The balance is supplied by various inaudible clues: lip movement, facial expressions, gestures, your knowledge of the situation that is being discussed, and, above all, your long-acquired, ingrained knowledge of the context, your quasi-instinctive expectancy of certain things to accompany and follow certain other things, because long experience has taught you that they always come together. On a telephone conversation where the connection is not too good, what you may actually hear is: "How . . . Mother. . . . ing?" Knowing the person you're speaking to, the situation, and the context, you translate this partial message into "How is your Mother feeling?" and confidently answer: "Pretty well, thanks." You think you have heard all of what the other party is saying. You have *heard* only half; the rest you have supplied yourself.

This beautiful redundancy, or superfluity of language clues, occurs only under given conditions, as outlined above. If you are speaking a language with which you are only partly familiar, there is a drastic cutting down of redundancy. You strain the ear for every possible clue, and still you may not have enough. The flow of speech goes on at too fast a clip for you to pause and reflect and piece your clues together. You are lost. You have not understood the speaker. Linguistically, you have failed.

In this matter of clues, as we have stated, everything goes. From the standpoint of the ear, it is not only the actual language sounds that supply you with clues. It is also what the linguists call "suprasegmental phonemes" or "suprasegmental features": the intonation, the pitch, the pauses and breaks between words and syllables, between phrases and sentences, the stress and the emphasis. All of these are significant clues, and contribute to your grasping the purport of the message. That is why they are important in learning a foreign language, in which they may differ from the ones you are used to. That is why you are told to imitate not merely the bare sounds, but the intonation, stress, pitch, pauses of the native speaker; partly so that you may imitate them to the best of your ability, and thereby sound more or less like a native speaker yourself; but even more important, so that you may recognize them when you hear them, know what they mean, and use them as clues to understanding.

The same goes for visual clues, if you are in a position to see the person you are speaking to. Again, his gestures, his posture, his facial expression, his eyes, his hands, his movements, are significant in connection with what he is saying, because they naturally accompany his utterance. Again, imitate them to the best of your ability or willingness to go through motions that may seem exaggerated or ridiculous; but at least learn to recognize them for what they mean.

All this business of recognizing and pigeonholing clues has to be done on split-second timing in ordinary conversation. You do it instinctively in your own language, because you have had interminable training, all your life, in unconsciously interpreting gestures, looks, tones of voice. Can you get to the point where you do it instinctively in another language? A good deal of it sounds and looks exaggerated or ridiculous simply because it doesn't fall in with your preconceived notions of how gestures and looks and tones should go. Can you let your inhibitions go? That's where the child has a big advantage over you. He has no inhibitions. In fact, he thinks it's fun to mimic everything he sees and hears.

In this matter of redundant clues, some languages work out better than others, depending on how clear their sound scheme impresses you (this is subjective, and hinges on your own previous language habits) and on the relationship between their spoken and their written form, which you have probably learned first (this is objective; some written language systems come much closer than others to the ideal sound-for-symbol, symbol-for-sound correspondence). To illustrate: I once received a letter from Finland, written entirely in Finnish, a language of which I have only a faint structural knowledge plus a dozen spoken phrases. It would have taken hours to translate with a grammar and a dictionary. Instead, I called up a colleague who is a native Finn. "I am going to read you this letter over the phone," I said. "Please translate it for me, sentence by sentence, as I read it to you." I proceeded to read each sentence, clearly, but not too slowly, and as I read he gave me the English translation. I never once had to pause, repeat, or spell out a word. I am practically a native speaker of French, but I could never have done this in French. At the very least, I would have had to repeat some sentence containing homophonic words (words that sound alike but have different meanings and spellings, like *right, write, rite, wright* in English), or spell proper names, or place names. True, to do what I did in Finnish, I had to know the Finnish sound scheme; but that is extremely simple, and its relation to the written system is covered by the shortest and easiest set of ground rules of almost any language on record. You can learn to *read* Finnish correctly, and with a reasonably fair accent, in half an hour, though you won't understand a word of what you're reading.

Understanding depends not only upon your catching and properly interpreting the sounds and suprasegmental features produced by the speaker. It also depends upon your knowing the meaning of the words he speaks. Here I take issue with some linguists who advocate the acquisition of a very limited vocabulary during the initial period of learning. It is of little use to be able to identify sounds and grammatical patterns if you can't identify the words. At the most, I may be able to make out that the speaker is voicing a request for vital information about something. But what? Vocabulary building, from the very outset, is extremely important. Suppose I say to you: "You can bot some oscar from your cobber." You may think I'm using double-talk. I'm not. I am using English in its Australian colloquial variety, and the phrase, rendered into the sort of equivalent American English you are used to, would read: "You can wangle some dough from your sidekick." It's your language, but the meaning does not get across to you, not because you don't recognize the sounds or the grammatical constructions, but because you don't know the words. The same can happen to you in Russian and Chinese if you don't know the words.

You build up a vocabulary the hard way, by memorizing. A few memory aids have already been mentioned: picturesque literal translations, where they appear; etymology, if you are an expert at breaking down words into their component parts (but etymology is no sport for amateurs); cognates, if they appear (English *cat* and French *chat;* English *verdant* and Spanish *verde;* but too often you get what linguists call "deceptive cognates," like English *lust* and German *Lust,* which means harmless "pleasure"; or English *gift* and German *Gift,* which means "poison"). Then there are languages like Chinese, where there are no etymologies (at least accessible to you), and few if any cognates. Here you are thrown back on the memory pure and simple. It helps mightily to bring writing to the aid of visual and aural memory and write down several times the word you want to remember; this introduces a third type of memory, the kinesthetic; that is, recollection of the movements your hand goes through as it writes the word. Kinesthetic memory, which plays a big role in mechanical activities such as driving a car, works subconsciously for language, but it does work. That is why one of the favorite forms of punishment for misbehaving in school, back in the days when they believed in punishment, was making you write out the vocabulary of the day's Latin lesson ten times; they figured the vocabulary would stick in your mind better that way, which it did, and so they killed two birds with one stone.

In the matter of understanding, you must be alert, wide-awake, quick to seize any and all clues. It is difficult and tiring at first. Yet, as the lady who went to Guatemala testifies, the jumble eventually clears up if you stick at it long enough.

Learning to speak is, of course, best achieved by direct imitation of words, phrases, and sentences pronounced by a native speaker, whether live or on a record. Too much should not be expected of you at first. The right kind of instructor, or recording, will at first break up long utterances into manageable units (the shorter the better), which are then run together and repeated until you are able to pronounce the entire sentence without stumbling and at normal speed. *"Je vais vous voir ce soir, et nous irons ensemble au cinéma"* ("I'm going to see you tonight, and we'll go together to the movies") will at first run: *"Je vais"* (you repeat; then the speaker repeats; then you repeat again); *"vous voir"* (same procedure as above); *"ce soir"; "et nous irons ensemble"; "au cinéma."* The next time, what you get is: *"Je vais vous voir ce soir"* (repetitions); *"et nous irons ensemble au cinéma"* (repetitions). Lastly, you get and repeat the whole compound sentence, and by this time you can really do it. It is important that each unit, however brief, be spoken at normal speaking speed, because that is what you eventually are going to be faced with in real life.

The only permissible exception to this rule is to break up words and utterances into syllables to teach you proper spoken-language syllabification in the language you are learning. Most people have the impression that syllabification is merely a matter of dividing your written words "properly" (that is, in accordance with Webster's prescriptions) at the end of a line if you don't have space enough to finish them. Actually, syllabification is far more than that. It applies primarily to speech, and is concerned with the almost imperceptible pauses between breath groups that the speaker of a language unconsciously makes, and that set the tone, so to speak, for that particular language.

English is partial to syllables that end in consonant sounds; when you say *general,* you are breaking it up into *gen-er-al.* The consonant at the end of the breath group means the vowel `will be clear if stressed, shortened and slurred if unstressed (note that the vowels of the last two syllables of *general* would have the same indistinct sound if they were spelled with any vowel letter). In Romance languages, the syllable generally ends in a vowel, which means that the unstressed vowels are much more clear and definite than in English (Spanish *ge-ne-ral,* French *gé-né-ral,* Italian *ge-ne-ra-le*). Since it is the unconscious tendency on the part of the English speaker to divide up the word in the fashion to which he is accustomed, this would mean that his pronunciation of Spanish *general* would come out as *gen-er-al,* with slurred and indistinct vowels in the last two syllables instead of clear and full ones. It is therefore a good practice to force the learner to syllabify his words and phrases properly, in accordance with the phonetic structure of the language he is studying, pronouncing at first syllable by syllable, then gradually speeding up his utterance until he finally achieves normal speaking speed, but with proper syllabic division and authentic sounds.

Constant repetition, of living models as of recordings, can become boresome and monotonous, and eventually lead to loss of interest. To break this ennui, there are many devices. One is the memorization of a conversational passage, preferably with two or more learners, of whom each takes a role. Another is the memorization and singing of songs. A third is the memorization and recitation of poetry. But if you take songs and poetry, select passages with an emotional content that appeals to you, so that you can sing and declaim with feeling, as though you really meant it. This tends to get you away from yourself and your self-consciousness, and breaks down your inhibitions. Don't hesitate to use appropriate gestures as you sing or recite. There is a bit of the ham actor in every one of us, and there is no reason why it should not be put to work for learning purposes.

Do not hesitate to inflict your poor language on a native speaker if you can get hold of one. For the most part, he won't mind, and may even enjoy it. Invite corrections, but not at each and every step. Too many interruptions for correction tend to build up self-consciousness and inhibitions. Tell your native to save up all your mistakes until you're through talking, and then throw them at you all at once. But as he throws them at you, don't hesitate to make him repeat, and to repeat yourself, until you are both satisfied.

In classes and among groups of people learning the same language (such as a family group where everybody wants to learn Spanish) there is a procedure which I have found enormously effective, that of the impromptu real-life situation. The best speaker in the group takes the role of a native who has some specific function (hotel clerk, restaurant waiter, gas station attendant, museum guide, storekeeper). In a class, this role naturally falls to the instructor. The others ask him questions, try to elicit information or services out of him, to the best of their ability, floundering for words, using pocket dictionaries or phrase books, consulting with one another in English, as they would in real life. The "native" is quite willing to serve or inform; but he doesn't know a word of English. He is the judge of whether the foreign language of the others is comprehensible to him or not; it doesn't have to be 100 per cent correct, just comprehensible. If he judges it incomprehensible, he shakes his head and asks for a repetition or restatement. Corrections, comments, discussion, if any, come at the end of the performance, though the "native" is allowed to repeat, correctly, what one of the others has said incorrectly but comprehensibly. It is amazing what fast progress can be made with this device, however much puristic teachers may frown upon it by reason of its unconventional and, above all, "incorrect" features.

But remember that language is only a tool for the transfer of thought from one individual to another. If this transfer is completed, does it make any real difference if the method is contrary to the dictates of perfectionism? Once inhibitions are thoroughly broken down, and the speaking-and-understanding habit thoroughly established, all sorts of refinements can be made, until the language finally comes out correctly. But without an initial start, it will never come out. More students than I care to think about have been made thoroughly tongue-tied and afraid to open their mouths by teachers who were too ready with their corrections, and who insisted upon perfection from the outset.

Practical language learners are men like the New York taxi driver who services the piers where the big liners dock, and who boasts of having learned to say a few things in many languages, so that when he lands as his fare a girl just over from Italy he is able to say, to her delighted astonishment: *"Ah, signorina! Come sta? Sta bene? Dove vuol andare?";* or the ship steward who claims he needs only a few stock phrases in each of the languages spoken by his passengers, has written them all down, memorized them, and learned to speak them with perfect pronunciation, so that he is able to say upon receiving a complaint: *"Lo investigaremos en seguida,"* or *"Señor, déjese usted de molestar a la señora con sus atenciones."*

In brief, you learn to speak by opening your mouth and speaking, not by sitting, brooding, and thinking about it. You learn to understand by listening with all your ears, watching for every possible clue, trying again and again if at first you don't succeed, until you are finally in a position to unscramble every message. And even if you don't succeed at once, note the satisfaction you get when that part of the spoken chain with which you are familiar finally comes along. It stands out crystal-clear from the rest of the jumble, be it a word, a phrase, or a whole sentence. If you stick at it long enough, everything will stand out with similar clarity. In the meantime, be thankful for small favors, and learn to count your blessings. "Today, I have listened for half an hour to the Hungarian program on the radio, and I have been able to pick out five numerals, six nouns, two adjectives, half a dozen assorted verb forms, and three complete utterances: *'Mi a baj?'* ('What's wrong?'); *'Igazán sajnálom'* ('Too bad!'); and *'Hideg van'* ('It's cold'). Tomorrow, the world!"

14

How Do You Learn to Read and Write?

Importance of the Written Language—The Current Written Language of Menus and Signs—Books vs. the Daily Press and the Magazines—The Literary Reader and the Parallel Text—Writing for Kinesthetic Memory—The Correspondence Manual—Problems of Translating—Reading Strange Alphabets

IN the old days, when modern spoken languages were taught by the same method as Latin and Greek, there was a widespread misconception, fostered in part by teachers with a literary bent, that the written language was the "real" language, and that it mattered little, if at all, whether or not you learned to speak and understand. Perhaps the misconception was helped along by the learners themselves, who saw little point in learning spoken tongues that they would probably never be called upon to use. If any thought at all was given to the matter, it was tacitly assumed that once you had learned the "real" language, its spoken aspects would follow naturally, by the simple process of exposing yourself to the language in its native habitat. This is a half-truth, and like all half-truths, more harmful than an outright lie. The result was widespread disappointment in both languages and language learning when the recipients of a two-year high school course in French or German found themselves up against the living reality of the spoken foreign tongue, and realized that they could neither speak nor understand it. This was basically nothing that a few weeks of residence in the foreign land and communion with its speakers couldn't cure, but few had the time or inclination to do what I insisted on doing in Portugal.

Actually, there is no good reason why courses in the written language should not be given their own status, with a clear understanding of their nature, purpose, and function. Some people need certain languages, or are interested in them, only in written form. The study of a written language, with little or no reference to how it's spoken, has one added advantage, which seems extremely difficult to attain in the case of a spoken language course. You can learn many of them at once. In fact, it is better if you do so, because they will reinforce each other far more than they will interfere with each other.

The written language can be of extreme importance and utility. It is not merely a matter of reading literary masterpieces in the original for aesthetic appreciation (something highly legitimate, but which very few people are qualified to do or interested in doing); or even of reading scientific books, papers, and abstracts for purposes of professional information (something of which far more ought to be done; one year after the commotion caused by Sputnik, the head of the Soviet Academy of Sciences told the American space scientists in Washington that American surprise at Sputnik had caused almost equal surprise among the Russian scientists; they had told the world one year in advance what they were planning to do; but they had told it in Russian, in their scientific journals; the latter were received in many American universities and government bureaus, but no one knew how to read them).

Outside of literature and science, there is another undeniable fact, one to which our spoken-language enthusiasts, nurtured on a diet of unwritten American Indian and African Negro languages, find it difficult to resign themselves. In the languages of civilization, the languages that really count, at least for the present, the written language has an importance that rivals that of speech. Not only are there books on all subjects, magazines, reviews, newspapers galore. Not only is there the enormous volume of correspondence, of a business, industrial, professional, personal nature that goes on all the time; not only are there mountains of official documents, forms, questionnaires that officialdom uses and forces us to use. There are also the innumerable signs, some of a vital nature, that appear in stores, in buildings, on roads and highways, in planes, trains, buses, streetcars, subways: "Don't speak to the driver"; "No smoking"; "No trespassing"; "Keep out"; "School—Caution"; "No left turn"; "Push"; "Pull"; "Entrance," "Exit" (or "In," "Out"); "Admission 25 cents"; "Men"; "Women"; "Danger"; "Dead end." There are restaurant menus, price lists, catalogues, advertisements.

These are things we all take for granted, because illiteracy has gone out of fashion in our midst. It has gone out of fashion in other civilized countries, too. Try one little experiment. *With your knowledge of your own American surroundings, laws, and customs,* try going around for one day (perhaps one hour will suffice) paying absolutely no attention to any written sign, yet relying on your general knowledge of what to do and how to do it. You will accumulate a collection of summonses, plus a lot of dirty looks and harsh words. You will be driving your car in a city like New York. You will be trying to park in a certain block. Even though you know that there is a general one-side parking rule at certain hours for purposes of street cleaning, you won't remember whether in this particular block the sign says "No parking 8–11 A.M. Mon. Wed. Fri." or "No parking 11 A.M.–2 P.M. Mon. Wed. Fri." You won't know whether a nice empty spot is covered or not by a sign that says "Taxi stand—no parking" or "Temple entrance—no parking." You will enter an unfamiliar department store, start shopping, and light a cigarette because you are forbidden to read the sign that says "No smoking by order of the Fire Dept." You will board a bus that says "58th St. only" when you want to go to 78th Street, ask the driver, and he'll say: "Lady, can't you read?" You will try to push or pull a building door the wrong way. You will go into the wrong rest room. You'll do lots of other things wrong, but by this time you have the idea. Now put yourself in a Russian city, where the signs are in Cyrillic, and the only thing that is like ours are the numerals. You speak Russian, but you can't read it. Tell me how you'll fare.

It is true that the general tendency today is to combine both types of learning, the auditory and the visual, to teach you how to read and possibly do a little writing, at the same time that they teach you to speak and understand. This is done in most of our schools and colleges (practically all, if you exclude those institutions where they deliberately withhold from you any glimpse of the written language until after six weeks or so of spoken instruction, which is probably a mistake in any but the ideograph-using languages). It is also true that many grammars for school or home use are accompanied by recordings, and many sets of recordings by more or less extensive grammatical outlines, and, in any event, by booklets that contain the text of the recording. All of this shows that we are intelligent enough to correct past errors without falling into the opposite extreme.

Written-language study offers several advantages over spoken-language study. The written language gives you time to reflect, go back for a better understanding of what you have just read, make corrections, use such aids as dictionaries or reference grammars. The written language has more permanence than the spoken (but the possibility of recording the spoken word has made large inroads into that particular advantage). It is more economical to transmit (a letter still costs you less than a phone call, even though it takes more time and effort). Learning the written language requires less bulky equipment, and permits you to utilize odds and ends of time.

On the other hand, it is undeniable that at least 90 per cent of human communication, even in ultracivilized societies, takes place through speech. We must therefore strike a proper balance, based on our inclinations, native equipment, financial and time availabilities, and, above all, needs, aims, and purposes.

The best way to begin learning a written language is through a good, up-to-date grammar, one that does not incline too much to the old, traditional literary approach or to newfangled notions about the supremacy of the spoken and even the vulgar and substandard tongue for purposes of grammatical instruction. The grammar should preferably be broken into small, convenient units rather than long-winded chapters. It should have plenty of reading and exercise material, with key to the exercises if it is meant for self-instruction.

Beyond covering this type of grammar, almost anything goes. There are good readers aplenty, with notes, sometimes exercises, and two-way vocabularies. There are composition books featuring models of all kinds: literary, scientific, commercial.

You learn to read by reading, just as you learn to speak by speaking. The more you read in the foreign language the more you'll learn. By all means supplement your official reading with regular newspapers and magazines in the foreign language. Imported ones are generally available, but there is also in this country a flourishing foreign-language press, which may occasionally lean over in the direction of the "colonial" language (that is to say, the hybrid mixture of foreign language and English loan words from the American environment that old-time immigrants developed in their new homes), but is less and less inclined that way at the present time, by reason of more cultured editors and readers, who know how to keep their languages apart. It will pay you, incidentally, to read the foreign-language press, both imported and local, because of the side information it gives you on customs, viewpoints, and attitudes. During the war, the OSS had a staff of foreign-language press readers, whose job it was to summarize the ideas and attitudes of foreign groups in our midst as reflected in their newspapers, which the government found it worth while knowing about.

There are all sorts of fascinating variants on the language reader theme. One is the dual reader, where facing pages bear a literary text in the foreign language and a good English translation of the same text, so that if you are stuck you can unstick yourself by merely glancing across the page. There are Dutch door readers, with the text in the upper portion and the pertinent notes and vocabulary in the lower. There is even a highly impressive device called Euroclock, printed in alternate lines in French, English, Italian, and German, with a reading screen that blocks off three of the languages from view, but permits ready access to any of them by the simple expedient of pushing the screen up or down. This quadruple interlinear translation has been used with success in European countries. Dual readers, along with many grammars and dictionaries, have the advantage of appearing in paperback, so that they may be easily carried and used anywhere, and for any period of time.

Get yourself a good two-way dictionary, and don't be afraid to use it in your reading. You'll need it in your writing anyway. On the other hand, don't get into the habit of running to it at every other word. Unless you have reason to desire absolute precision, try to achieve a global picture of the meaning of a sentence you read, guessing at a few words if they are not crucial to your understanding. Later, you may want to check your guess, particularly if you run into that word again. But disturb your reading flow as little as is practicable.

Bringing your kinesthetic memory into play by writing out repeatedly those words or phrases you wish to memorize serves the learning of the written language as much as it does the spoken, and is a highly recommended procedure. So is making out your own private vocabulary. So is having a list of words, or grammatical forms, written out and placed where you can readily refer to it. In Portugal I had a list of high-frequency irregular verb forms on one corner of my reading desk. Glancing at them several times a day helped fix them in my mind.

Corresponding in the foreign language develops your writing ability, particularly if your correspondent corrects your letters and sends them back. This principle is used to good advantage in the pen-pal relationships established among high school students of different countries.

The correspondence school methodology mentioned earlier is in some ways a glorified and commercialized form of pen-pal relationship, with all the receiving done by you save for what concerns money. Guided study at a distance, regardless of the fact that recordings are sometimes employed, is necessarily of the reading-writing rather than the speaking-understanding variety.

The ability to translate in writing is something that the traditional methodology doted on. Translation exercises were one of its mainstays. Only occasionally were the exercises of the spoken variety, even more seldom extemporaneous. These exercises fostered the ability to translate from one language into another, which forms the basis of an established and fairly lucrative profession. One can become a translator of literary, scientific, business, or diplomatic material, and the techniques and abilities involved differ considerably from one to the other.

In the case of the literary translation, the translator should ideally be himself an accomplished literary writer in the language into which he translates. At the same time, he must have a very firm reading grasp on the language from which he translates. His ideal process is to read a brief section of the text from which he is translating, put it aside, and rewrite it in the other language. The idea is not to give a literal rendering, or anything even remotely approximating a literal rendering, but to render every nuance of the author's thought, adapting it to the forms, both linguistic and psychological, of the receiving language. This means that, while lots of translating of literary works goes on, few of the translators are really equipped for their job, which is one reason why many people study a language merely to get at its literature in the original. A truly good literary translation is a literary masterpiece in its own right. But there are few.

It is otherwise with the commercial or scientific translation. Here literalness is almost of the essence, and what is wanted is not literary nuances but a faithful rendition of precise terms and meanings. The translator of this sort of material often works with impressive specialized lexicons which contain the technical terminology of the two languages, equated in no uncertain terms and with no room for doubt. This kind of translator must have an approximately equal command of both languages (which need not at all be of the creative variety), and have in addition a specialized knowledge of the subject matter and its terminology, or at least access to unerring lexicons.

In the case of diplomatic translation, as in UN circles, there is need for precision, but the terminology is not quite so complicated. A tour de force in the early days of UN was the translation into English of the Albanian constitution, achieved by one of UN's master translators from scratch, with only five days of previous study of Albanian. While this feat was impressive, it was not quite so impossible as the press described it. The translator had started by going through an Albanian grammar and getting a structural knowledge of the language, or improving on the one he perhaps already had. After that, a good Albanian-English dictionary was all he needed. I have done as much with languages like Czech and Serbo-Croatian, of which I can speak only a few words. You must know thoroughly the language you are translating into, but a basic structural knowledge, plus a good dictionary, of the language you are translating from suffices.

In connection with learning to read and write, a point must be made which will be discussed more fully in the second part of this work. Americans are normally paralyzed with fear at the sight of a language which uses a different alphabet from the Roman to which they are accustomed, and in which a majority of the world's chief languages appears. Yet alphabets such as the Greek or Cyrillic, or even the Hebrew or Arabic, are not too difficult to learn, with a little persistence and exercise. You will never read them as readily as you do your own, and your reading of Russian or Greek may be somewhat slowed down by the alphabet. But this is merely a matter of practice. If you had as much training in reading Cyrillic as you have had in reading Roman, you would use it just as fluently. Conversely, don't be too ashamed of reading it slowly. After a year of studying Russian, you are in approximately the same position with respect to the alphabet as is a Russian child of seven or eight, who has just learned to read and still stumbles and hesitates over the longer words.

The situation is altogether different in the case of languages using an ideographic system, such as Chinese and Japanese. Here the link is not between symbol and sound, however imperfect the link may be, but between symbol and thought. Memorizing four thousand ideographic characters with their meanings, which is the minimum for even a scanty reading knowledge, represents several years' work. You may therefore be excused for taking your Chinese and Japanese in transcription, if you want those languages primarily for spoken use. It is nevertheless not a bad idea to familiarize yourself with a hundred or so of the most common characters. If you start doing that, you may discover that appetite comes with eating.

PART II

What Languages to Learn

15

Which Language Shall I Study?

Relative Importance of Languages—Number of Speakers, Area, and Distribution—Economic and Political Importance—Cultural Background—The Big Six

NEXT to the question "How do I go about learning a language?", the most widespread request for information takes the form "Which language or languages should I try to learn?"

The most logical and direct answer is "The one you need"; but the question is seldom asked by people who are aware of needing a given language.

The man whose firm assigns him to a post in Argentina knows he is going to need Spanish. The Foreign Service specialist who is working on our relations with the Soviet Union knows he is going to need Russian. The missionary who has been given the task of spreading the Gospel in northern Nigeria knows he is going to need at least a smattering of Hausa. French is far more widespread than Finnish; but if you are going to reside in Helsinki for the next two years you will do better to learn Finnish than French.

So this chapter and the next are dedicated to the people who still don't know what the future holds in store for them in the way of foreign contacts, or who haven't yet made up their minds what foreign contacts they want to aim for. High school and college students, whose future careers have not yet crystallized, are among our very special clients for this part of the book.

Theoretically and structurally, all languages are on a par, no matter how extensive or puny, civilized or barbarous, their speaking group may be. To the descriptive linguist all languages are, and should be, alike; they all possess a sound scheme, a grammatical structure, and a stock of words or expressions that take care of their speakers' present needs and can be expanded at will.

Beyond this, equality ceases, as it does among human beings as soon as you depart from their physiological structure. Some languages

have a long, proud history of achievement in the arts of civilization
(these, by the way, are not at all restricted to our Western type);
others have no recorded past. Some are widespread, distributed
throughout the globe, encountered almost everywhere you turn;
others are highly localized and generally unknown outside their
own restricted areas. Some have enormous speaking populations,
amounting in a few cases, like Chinese and English, to one fifth or one
tenth of all the people on earth; others have speaking populations
that are only a small fraction of one per cent of the world's total population, which makes them no less essential if you happen to be in their
speaking area, but makes your chances of needing them not too likely.
Some can be, and are, very easily used as substitute languages, in
the sense that if you meet a Czech and he speaks no English, you can
ask him whether he speaks German or French with some likelihood
of drawing yes for an answer. You could also ask him whether you
could talk to him in Swahili, provided you knew Swahili; but the
chances of his replying in the affirmative would be one in a million.
Some have tremendous political, military, economic, scientific significance, to the point of being among the official UN languages, or
being the language that you can use as a substitute tongue in Viet
Nam or North Africa, or a language in which a large volume of international business is transacted, or the language in which one fourth
of all the world's scientific reports appear; others have none of these
advantages, or next to none.

Under the circumstances, the person who wants to learn some languages but is uncertain where his choice should fall ought to do a
little investigating to determine which languages are most likely to be
of service to him. He may find out all the facts, and still bet the wrong
way, because human affairs often take ironical twists. It is a commonplace that the man who took Spanish in high school because he had
a hunch he would do business in Latin America later finds himself
placed at the head of his firm's agency in France or Germany or
Japan; that the man who studied Russian in anticipation of a Foreign
Service career is later assigned to Indonesia or Ghana; that the future
scientist who took three years of German later discovers that his particular field of specialization happens to be an Italian specialty. But
for this there is no help. These are the chances we have to take.

Spurred by strategic considerations in connection with a war that was sooner or later bound to come to an end, a great many people were forced into the study of languages that under peacetime conditions had little if any practical use. A very large contingent of Navy cadets receiving their training at one of our large universities during the war were given a thoroughgoing course in Melanesian Pidgin English, although it didn't take a military strategist to know that only a fraction of them would ever see service in the area where Pidgin is current, and that the hours spent on Pidgin would be a total loss for all the others, who might have largely profited from being given a smattering of ten or twelve important world tongues.

Even today there is a deplorable tendency in some linguistic circles to overrate, for popular consumption, the importance of some obscure languages that have no present practical value outside their own limited areas. That this is caused by the descriptivistic habit of viewing all languages as on an absolute par is beside the point. Scientific description and practical utility both have their places; but they should be kept separate.

Three general considerations may be offered at this point, before we go further in depth into the somewhat thorny question of what languages to learn. Out of a total world population estimated at over two and a half billion, fully one billion, or two fifths of the total, speak seven languages: English, French, Spanish, Portuguese, Italian, German, Russian. These seven languages (seven out of about three thousand) are all of the Indo-European family, and demonstrably related to one another. They are, justifiedly, the modern languages most widely studied in American high schools and colleges.

The UN, which represents an absolute majority of all the world's constituted nations, has only five official languages, in which any delegate may deliver an address. They are English, French, Spanish, Russian and Chinese. These five languages are spoken by an absolute majority of the world's total population (about one and a half billion out of two and a half billion). Of these five languages, two may be described as "unofficially superofficial" (a paradox in terms, perhaps), to the extent that all directional signs in the UN building appear in them, and the majority of public addresses are made in them. They are English and French.

The Universal Postal Union, which supervises the handling of all exchanges of postal matter across national borders, issues international money orders and other official documents in seven languages. They are English, German, Arabic, Chinese, Spanish, French, and Russian. These languages are spoken by well over two thirds of the world's total population (about 1.6 billion out of 2.5 billion).

These are not value judgments, reflecting individual preferences or prejudices. They are verifiable facts and statistics. They set the tone for this chapter and the one that follows.

There are in spoken use throughout the world today some three thousand languages, exclusive of dialects. Of these, only slightly over one hundred have speaking populations of one million or more, and need be seriously considered by the language learner, save for very definite and specific purposes. The full list of these languages with their speaking populations and other relevant information appears elsewhere (see S. Muller, *The World's Living Languages,* Ungar, New York, 1964; M. Pei, *Invitation to Linguistics,* Doubleday, New York, 1965; M. Pei, *Language for Everybody,* Devin-Adair, New York, 1956). Suffice it to say that even this restricted list includes, side by side with well-known and highly significant tongues such as Polish, Turkish, Dutch, Czech, modern Greek, Norwegian, and Hungarian, other languages of little practical interest, such as the Bicol of the Philippines, the Aymará and Guaraní of South America, the Umbundu and Mandingo of Africa, the Frisian of the North Sea coast, the Khmer of Cambodia.

The truly big languages, whose speaking population and area entitles them to first-class practical rank, are only thirteen in number —those mentioned above (Chinese, English, Spanish, Russian, German, French, Italian, Portuguese, Arabic) plus the Hindustani or Hindi-Urdu of India and Pakistan, the Bengali of the same area, Japanese, and, with certain qualifications, the Indonesian-Malay of the Republic of Indonesia, Malaysia, and surrounding areas. All of these have speaking populations that exceed fifty million.

Even so, they are not all numerically on a par. As against Chinese with its 700 million, and English with 350 million, Italian has only about 60 million. Only Chinese, English, Hindu-Urdu, Spanish, and Russian go well beyond 100 million. Indonesian, though official in a nation of 100 million, can at the present time be said to be firmly in the grasp of only about 20 million, while the unofficial Malay (official, however, in Malaysia) from which it sprang is far more extensively spoken and understood.

Russian is official over one sixth of the earth's land surface. English, extending over most of North America, all of Australia, and numerous other far-flung regions, has almost as much space under its direct control. But Bengali, despite its 85 million speakers, holds only a restricted area in northeastern India and East Pakistan.

But speaking population and area tell only part of the story. There is also the question of distribution, which means that you will encounter the language over and over again, in various localities, as you travel over the globe. Here English, French, Arabic, Portuguese, Spanish hold the top places. Russian, despite its area, Chinese, despite its mass of speakers, and to an even greater degree Indonesian-Malay, Japanese, German, Italian, Hindu-Urdu, are languages of scanty distribution, though some of their speakers, notably those of German and Italian, may be encountered, on an unofficial basis, almost anywhere. It may be remarked that the distributional factor is to a considerable degree the fruit of remote or recent colonialism, and although colonialism is in the process of disappearing, its linguistic results often tend to linger on.

The factors of economic and political-military importance are rather easy to determine objectively, though they are subject to drastic and sudden changes. At the present time, the languages whose speakers hold a high economic, industrial, and commercial position are English, French, German, Spanish, Russian, Japanese, Italian, Portuguese. There are strong future economic potentialities in Chinese, Arabic, Hindi-Urdu, Indonesian, but they are far from fully developed. It may further be remarked that some other languages, whose speaking populations, areas, and distribution are relatively low, stand fairly high in the economic scale, often outstripping some of the numerical and areal giants. Dutch, Swedish, Danish, for example, are the vehicles of flourishing economies; but their speakers in the business world are usually able to handle English, French and/or German in highly satisfactory fashion.

On the political-military front, the scene is dominated by the English of the U.S.A. and the British Commonwealth and the Russian of the U.S.S.R. But nations like China, France, Germany, Italy, Japan, India, the Arab states, even Indonesia, cannot be expected forever to take back seats.

Least objective to determine is the cultural factor, particularly for what regards past contributions to world civilization and artistic and literary output. But even here a few objective yardsticks are supplied by scientific output, literacy figures, books, newspapers and magazines, radio and TV stations. Here the nations that speak English, French, German, Russian are in the forefront, followed closely by those that speak Japanese, Italian, Spanish, Portuguese, much more remotely by those whose languages are Arabic, Chinese, Indonesian, Hindi-Urdu, Bengali.

All these factors must be considered by the man who is in doubt as to which language or languages to study. Also, they must be placed in juxtaposition with his own immediate or anticipated needs, if these can at all be determined. The languages that combine all the factors that spell out practical importance (though not all in the same order) are English, French, Spanish; to a slightly lower degree in some divisions, German, Russian, Italian. These happen to be precisely the modern languages most widely studied in our high schools, colleges, and universities, and the languages most sought after by individual learners, as we shall see in the next chapter. Our educational institutions may not reflect the changing needs of the people they serve with lightning-like speed. But by and large, and with the time lag that it is natural to expect, they follow those needs rather closely. In this there is a lesson to the individual learner, and at least a partial answer to his question "What languages shall I study?"

16

Which Languages Are Being Studied? Why?

Historical Survey—Situation in U.S. Elementary and High Schools, Colleges, and Universities—What Private Language Schools and Recorded Courses Show—Motivation for Choice in the Past and in the Present—The Situation Abroad

LANGUAGE study in the American colonies that were later to become the United States began, almost as soon as the first settlers landed, in the tradition set by the European Renaissance. Latin, Greek, and Hebrew were the three languages of scholarship, and some of our Massachusetts Plymouth Colony leaders were Biblical scholars who could at least read all three of them. The early days of both Harvard and Yale saw even commencement addresses delivered in the three great Classical tongues.

The modern languages were making far more modest headway, being imparted mostly to children of groups that spoke them. This was the case with the French taught by missionaries and nuns in Canada and Maine, the German taught in Pennsylvania, the Spanish taught in Florida and the Southwest.

The year 1735, when Harvard permitted the substitution of French for Hebrew (but not for Greek or Latin), marked a milestone. A Philadelphia academy imparted French and German as early as the middle of the eighteenth century, and in 1779 the College of William and Mary set up the first American professorship of modern languages.

During the early nineteenth century the high school and college tradition held on firmly to Latin and Greek, and only two modern tongues, French and German, found a firm foothold in the American educational system. German began to outstrip French around 1850, at the time of the big German immigration to our shores. It held, roughly, a two-to-one lead over its competitor until the outbreak of the First World War. Both modern languages, however, were far outstripped by Latin, which had over 50 per cent of the total student body of both high schools and colleges.

It is of some interest that in the late nineteenth and early twentieth centuries up to 85 per cent of our high school students, and practically 100 per cent of college students, studied at least one language. This was in strong contrast to what happens even today, when despite rapidly growing interest in languages only about 35 per cent of all our high school students include a foreign language, Classical or modern, among their studies. Let us not forget, however, that the high school population has grown from about 200,000 in 1890 to some 15 million in 1964. Our regularly constituted language courses today include at least half a million elementary school pupils, nearly five million high school students, and close to one million college and university scholars.

The First World War marked a decided change in America's language picture. At that time our high school population had risen to more than one and a half million, but the percentage of language enrollments had been dropping gradually, while language preferences were in for a big change. The bottom fell out of German's popularity in the course of the war, and Spanish came in to replace it. In 1922 Latin still had an absolute majority (over 700,000 high school students); French, now firmly in the saddle as the leading modern language, had about 400,000; Spanish, the newcomer, had risen to 283,000; and German had sunk to an all-time low of a mere 16,000.

The years that followed the First World War were a period of virulent isolationism. The study of languages generally fell into disrepute. The Second World War brought them back to the fore, by reason of our worldwide military commitments; but after it was over there was a strong tendency to forget them once more. Between 1945 and 1955 our high school population went up to six million, but the students taking even a single language sank to a mere 22 per cent of this total. It was only Sputnik's triumphal appearance in 1957 that finally aroused the American people to the need for languages in a world grown so small that a space satellite could revolve around it in a few hours.

Again, there was a noticeable shift in tastes and choices. By 1949, Spanish, with 450,000 high school students, had outstripped Latin, with 420,000. French, as a result of loss of prestige in the course of the Second World War, had dropped to 255,000, while German was very slowly forging its way back with some 43,000. Things were more evenly balanced in the colleges, where German had about 130,000 students to 150,000 for French and close to 200,000 for Spanish.

But between 1958 and 1963, language enrollments in our high schools more than doubled, increasing at a much faster rate than the high school population itself. In the 1962–63 school year, with a total junior high school and high school population (public, private, and Catholic) of about 15 million, language enrollments had risen to nearly one third of the total. Of our 4,800,000 or so high school language students, slightly less than 36 per cent (1,721,000) were taking Spanish; over 33 per cent (1,605,000) studied French; more than 23 per cent (1,117,000) followed Latin; about 6.5 per cent (315,000) were taking German; and Italian and Russian accounted for slightly less than 1 per cent (30,000) each. (There are about 300 public high schools in the land where Russian is offered, and Italian appears in the public high schools of only eleven of our fifty states). The balance of high school language students (less than 0.5 per cent, or about 20,000) divided itself over a large number of languages of local interest (Norwegian and Swedish in states where there is a heavy Scandinavian population; Polish; Hawaiian and Japanese, mainly in Hawaii; Hebrew, Portuguese, Chinese, modern Greek, Arabic, Ukranian, Slovak, Lithuanian).

Private and religious schools do much better than public schools in the matter of languages. In public schools about 25 per cent of the students take a foreign language, while in private and religious schools over 75 per cent of the students are enrolled for one or more languages other than English. While large public high schools have as many as 60 per cent of their student bodies enrolled in language courses, the far more numerous small ones have an average of only 20 per cent. In fact, no language instruction whatsoever is offered by 20 per cent of American high schools, both large and small. Even where the students are offered a language, 30 per cent take only one year of it and 30 per cent more only two years.

As a special sample of language choice, we have the 1959 figures for all New York City public high schools: Spanish 83,000; French

60,000; Italian, 13,000; German, 6,000; Hebrew, 5,000; Latin, 5,000; Russian, 100; Norwegian, 50; with half a dozen students taking Greek. Portuguese, once offered, was removed from the list because of lack of demand.

The college picture, as might be expected, differs considerably from the high school picture for what concerns language choice. Here we have very approximate 1963 figures showing 302,000 for French; 246,000 for Spanish; 183,000 for German; 34,000 for Russian (now taught in over 600 colleges); 17,000 for Italian (in nearly 300 colleges); less than 20,000 for all other modern languages put together. The ones that range between 5,000 and 500, in descending order, are: Hebrew, Japanese, Chinese, Portuguese, Norwegian, Swedish, Arabic, Polish, modern Greek. Languages that range between 200 and 100 students across the nation are Danish, Dutch, Czech and Slovak, Hindi-Urdu, Indonesian, Korean, Persian, Serbo-Croatian, Turkish, Thai, Swahili. Below 100 are Armenian, Hawaiian, Ukrainian. Below 50 are Bengali, Bulgarian, Burmese, Hausa, Finnish, Lithuanian, Mongol, Roumanian, Ruthenian, Slovenian, Tagalog, Yiddish, Tibetan. Fewer than ten students are claimed by Albanian, Amharic, Telugu, Tamil, Icelandic, Berber, Catalan, Estonian, Manchu, Georgian. It may be added that only sixteen institutions of higher learning throughout the land, including the big Army Language School at Monterey, offer a dozen or more languages each. But there are 76 institutions that offer Portuguese, 67 Chinese, 55 Japanese, 52 Hebrew, 40 Arabic, 38 Polish, 22 Hindi-Urdu, 20 Swedish, 18 Norwegian, and 15 Persian, Serbo-Croatian, Turkish, Czech and Slovak.

Graduate enrollments for advanced degrees, such as the M.A. and Ph.D, for 1960, showed the following figures: French, 1,504; Spanish, 1,272; German, 777; Classics (Latin and Greek), 642; Russian, 300; Hebrew, 118; Italian, 81; Chinese, 44; Arabic, 41; Portuguese, 20; Japanese, 9. Slavic languages outside of Russian had 103; Germanic languages outside of German and English had 15; Romance Philology and Literatures, 340; Germanic Philology and Literatures, 101. All other languages besides those mentioned had 536. The spectacular growth of language study on the graduate level may be gauged from some comparable 1963 figures: French, 10,500; German, 8,000;

Spanish, 7,000; Russian, 2,700; Italian, 650; other modern languages, 3,200.

Lastly, the National Education Association reports that as against 2,193 college graduates prepared for high school teaching of foreign languages in 1950 (a figure that dropped to 1,328 in 1955, down almost 40 per cent), there were 2,178 in 1960, 4,272 in 1963, 5,281 in 1964, 6,486 in 1965. Again, the growth is little less than spectacular, with a nearly 200 per cent increase by 1965 over the 1950 figures. By way of comparison, the increase in prospective teachers of English over the same period was slightly over 70 per cent.

One final angle of the American language-learning picture for what concerns public instruction is supplied by the languages in the elementary schools, which have been growing by leaps and bounds. From an estimated total of fewer than 2,000 students in 1939, they rose to over 200,000 in 1949, 330,000 in 1954, and 700,000, or 7 per cent of all elementary school enrollment, in 1961. The 1954 figures showed 173,000 taking Spanish; 35,000 French; over 2,000 German, with Polish, Italian, and Latin trailing. The 1955 figures (latest detailed ones available to me) showed a total of over 430,000, of whom over 270,000 were in public elementary schools and 160,000 in private (mostly Catholic parochial) schools. The public schools had 222,000 taking Spanish, 49,000 taking French, 3,000 taking German, with such assorted tongues as Italian, Japanese, Latin, Norwegian, Swedish, modern Greek trailing. The parochial schools had 89,000 taking French, 40,000 Polish, 16,000 Italian, 8,000 Lithuanian, 3,000 Slovak, 2,000 Ukrainian, 1,000 Spanish, 1,000 Latin.

These highly encouraging figures, combined with the preceding ones for high schools and colleges, begin to supply an answer to the question: "Why are certain languages more popular than others?" The parochial school picture tells a story of ethnic groups that want their children to learn the mother tongue spoken at home, a thoroughly legitimate and highly praiseworthy desire, but one based on sentiment rather than any form of profit motive. Graduate school enrollments directed at higher degrees tell a story of private scholarly interests in special fields of research, which nevertheless to some extent coincide with the general framework of language preferences.

The latter are perhaps best illustrated by regular college, high school, and elementary school enrollments. Here the picture is basically the same. The languages considered most important and desirable by the overwhelming majority of Americans in the present generation are Spanish, French, Latin, German, Italian, Russian, in the order given, with a fairly large gap between the first three and the last three; a gap, however, that tends to narrow as we go up the educational scale.

Other languages, however great may be their interest from a specialized viewpoint, are best described as occasional and subsidiary. Whatever our linguistic theorists may say concerning the theoretical equality of all languages, the practical language learner sets up a definite hierarchy. This hierarchy, however, is far from everlasting. Over a period of three centuries it has shifted from a Latin-Greek condominium to a Latin-French-German tripartite arrangement, then admitted three more languages, Spanish, Italian, and Russian, while at the same time demoting German from second to fourth place. There is no reason why the existing setup should not change in the future, with new historical conditions, as it has changed in the past.

But before our conclusions crystallize, it may be worth while to take a glance at what happens in the field of private language learning, as illustrated by private adult schools where the curriculum is not set by an administration that has other considerations besides languages on its mind; by sales percentages for recordings and books that are not primarily meant for classroom use, but are purchased by individuals who really want them; and by language choice motivation as expressed by those consumers of regular courses (college and university students) who have both a more definite idea of purpose and a broader range of choice.

In contrast with the six million Americans, more or less, enrolled in regular language courses in the nation's public elementary and high schools, private and parochial preparatory schools, and colleges and universities, even the largest of the fully private language school chains, Berlitz, with twenty-five or more large schools scattered throughout the country and numerous branches abroad, has only a limited number of students at one time.

The Berlitz system offers the following percentage figures for 1964 in its North American Schools: French, 36 per cent; Spanish, 26 per cent; German, 9 per cent; Italian, 5.5 per cent; English to foreigners, 14 per cent; Vietnamese, 3 per cent; about 1.5 per cent each for Russian and Japanese, 1 per cent for Portuguese, fractions of 1 per cent for Greek, Dutch, Korean, Indonesian, Danish, Swedish, Turkish, Arabic, Cambodian, Lao, Serbo-Croatian, Norwegian, Chinese, Hebrew, Hungarian, Czech, Hindi-Urdu, Swahili, Latin, Thai, Malay, Tagalog, Persian. Almost 92 per cent of the Berlitz courses were imparted in the five great high school languages: French, Spanish, German, Italian, English.

Abroad, the picture changes somewhat. In 1963 French claimed almost 50 per cent of Berlitz students, German 21 per cent, Spanish 20 per cent, Italian 8 per cent, Russian 3 per cent.

Again, there is some change in connection with the Berlitz Home Study Course books. In North America during 1964, Spanish sold 25 per cent, German 23 per cent, French 23 per cent, Italian 13 per cent. Runners-up were English for Spanish speakers (5 per cent), Hebrew (4.5 per cent), Russian (4 per cent), Japanese (3 per cent), Portuguese (1 per cent). It is difficult to determine what may cause Spanish and German to run ahead of French in books, while French leads in courses in North America, but it is easy to understand why abroad, particularly on the European continent, German runs ahead of Spanish.

The Language Guild of New York, a private language school that specializes in group instruction for members of industrial organizations as well as individuals, is equipped to do teaching and translation work in 36 languages, and caters to several hundred students each year, lists the demand at about 20 per cent for Spanish, 15 per cent for French, 10 per cent for English to foreigners, 8 per cent each for Italian, Russian, German, and Latin, 2 per cent each for Japanese, Greek, Indonesian, Portuguese, and Swedish, 1 per cent or less for Thai, Turkish, Serbo-Croatian, Gypsy, Dutch, Norwegian, Hindi-Urdu, Gujarati.

In contrast with these individual and industrial needs are a few government-sponsored institutions which reflect the needs of government. Elementary and high school teachers of languages enrolled in language institutes sponsored by the federal government under the

National Defense Education Act distributed themselves as follows: nearly 2,000 in Spanish; about 1,600 in French; almost 600 in German; about 250 in Russian; 45 in Chinese; 25 in Italian. Their choices, however, may to some extent have been dictated by the curricula of their respective school systems.

Assignments of U.S. Military cadets to foreign language groups reflect to a greater degree the specific requirements of the armed forces. Out of some 700 new cadets, 200 were assigned to Spanish, 180 to Russian, 130 to French, 130 to German, 60 to Portuguese. At the U.S. Army Language School in Monterey, at the time I was assigned there in the summer of 1960, the largest department by far, covering about one fourth of all students and instructors, was Russian. Runners-up were Mandarin Chinese and Korean. French, Spanish, German, and Italian were modest departments by comparison. It is probable that present-day figures would show a large expansion of the Vietnamese Department.

The Foreign Service Institute for the training of diplomatic personnel handles many languages, but their three main foreign branches are located in Mexico City, Nice, and Frankfurt, for mass training in Spanish, French, and German, respectively. Over one hundred American published periodicals have their main distribution in foreign countries; they favor the same three languages.

United States military personnel stationed abroad often goes in for language courses, usually of the country in which they are stationed. More of them, until recently, were studying German than any other language, but more of them were stationed in Germany than in any other country until the expansion of operations in Viet Nam.

Sales of recorded language courses, expressed in percentage figures, are highly significant. Among the more comprehensive and higher-priced courses, Funk and Wagnalls carries recordings in only four languages, French, Spanish, German, Italian. No percentage breakdown is available, but the fact that only four languages appear is itself meaningful.

Linguaphone reported a few years ago that fully 50 per cent of its recorded courses sold were Spanish; runners-up were French, German, Japanese, and Russian, in the order given. Holt, on the other hand, shows 50 per cent of its sales in French, 36 per cent in Spanish, 10 per cent in German, with 4 per cent in all other languages combined.

Dover, which specializes in inexpensive $5.95 single records containing over 800 phrases in common use, offers a percentage breakdown of 1964 sales that shows French, with 27 per cent, slightly leading Spanish, with 25 per cent; German has over 19 per cent, Japanese over 9 per cent, Italian over 5 per cent, modern Greek over 7 per cent, Portuguese over 3 per cent, Russian over 2 per cent, Hebrew over 1 per cent; a rather large percentage increase in German and Japanese over the preceding year appears.

Living Language (Crown Publishers), another low-priced recording house, gives the following ratios: 11 for Spanish to 10 for French to 5 for German to 2 for Russian and 2 for Italian to 1 for Hebrew and 1 for Japanese to ½ for Portuguese.

In the matter of book sales, we have, in addition to the Berlitz figures cited above, my own tourist manuals of the Harper & Row "Getting Along in ——" series, with Bantam paperbacks. These books are so constructed that they can serve the purpose of a conversational course as well as that of a tourist phrase book. The popularity of the six languages in which they appear, as reflected in their sales figures, is in the ratio of 9 for Spanish and French, 6 for German and Italian, 5 for Russian, 3 for Portuguese. The publishers firmly rejected outside suggestions for similar manuals in other languages, such as Chinese, feeling that the potential market was not large enough to warrant publication.

Slightly divergent, though showing a similar preponderance for Spanish, French, Italian, and German, are the sales percentages of Dover's "Say It" series. Here German accounts for 23 per cent of one year's sales ending October, 1965, Italian for 15 per cent, French for 12 per cent, Spanish for 11 per cent (a total of 60 per cent for the four favorite languages of the American curriculum). Greek shows up with 6 per cent, Japanese with 5½ per cent, Hebrew with 4 per cent. Norwegian, Portuguese, and Turkish have about 3 per cent each. Yiddish, Swedish, Russian, Polish, Dutch run to about 2½ per cent, Danish to 2 per cent, Esperanto to 1 per cent.

Again, the indications we get from private schools, recordings, and books are to the effect that the favorite American modern languages are Spanish, French, German, Italian, and Russian, in that order. This order generally holds save where specific factors of a military, educational, commercial, or other nature prevail.

Specific motivations for language choice are, of course, of all kinds. The military needs of the armed forces do not at all coincide with civilian needs; hence it is not at all surprising to find Russian, Chinese, and Korean at the head of the list in Monterey, while the French, Spanish, German, and Italian that loom so large in civilian institutions take back seats. Something similar applies to various government bureaus, such as wartime's Censorship Office, which employed thousands of readers during World War II, the foreign radio monitoring service of the State Department, the FBI, OWI, the wartime OSS, now turned into the CIA, and other highly specialized units. From time to time pleas are voiced in government circles for a larger number of students of "critical" languages, such as Telugu, Thai, Burmese, Mongol, Vietnamese, and Uzbek. They generally go unheeded, as will be noted from the list of such languages studied in the various colleges which appears on pages 130–1. For this there is a perfectly comprehensible reason. A man cannot be expected to put in long years studying a language for which there is no commercial or educational demand, unless he can be guaranteed employment as an expert in that language, which is precisely the practice followed by our rivals the Soviets. As a result, they are seldom hard put to it to find the expert they seek for a special assignment.

While opportunities for using various languages in various occupational fields abound, it is usually quite difficult for the individual to determine his needs in advance. Schools like Berlitz and the Language Guild are kept busy imparting crash programs in languages to personnel about to be sent abroad by such international concerns as Socony Vacuum, General Motors, Remington Rand, and the Deere Company. Receptionists and secretaries are often hired on the basis of their linguistic abilities. In a city like New York nurses, policemen, firemen, teachers, and other city employees find it advantageous to know other languages than English. Two nurses with linguistic attainments produced, some years ago, phrase books with medical questions and answers in Spanish, Italian, French, German, Chinese, and Japanese. These phrases include explanations of common medical examinations and treatments, lists of foods for special diets, techniques for handling small children, parts of the body, and such other expressions in common use as numerals and the days of the week. Two interesting experiments were tried in connection with the "Help Wanted" ads of the Sunday *New York Times*. One yielded 35 ads calling for a knowledge of Spanish, 9 for French, 5 for Italian, 3 for German, and 1 apiece for Dutch, Hebrew, and Yiddish. The other gave 440 ads calling for Spanish, 147 for French, 108 for German, 38 for Italian.

A survey of specific motivations among college students taking unusual languages (outside of Spanish, French, German, Italian, Russian, Latin) gave the following results: out of 6,106 students in public institutions polled, 1,453 expected to use the language of their choice in teaching; 622 wanted it for purposes of travel; 569 were impelled by family and national tradition; 516 expected to use the language in some branch of government service; 400 in research and writing; 270 in business; 245 for cultural purposes; 221 for missionary work; 1,810 had other assorted motivations or were impelled by no definite plan.

The Language Guild reports as motivations for its students, in decreasing order: travel and touring; business (oil is particularly important in the case of Arabic and Indonesian); Peace Corps and other government service; preparation for college teaching (especially strong in the case of Russian); family reasons.

Some final reasonable conclusions to be drawn from this mass of statistics would seem to be that fewer Americans still study languages than should; that while many of them are impelled by specific motives, others (probably the majority of high school and even many college students) select languages at random, or on the basis of supposed ease (this may in some part account for Spanish preferences); that for the time being the people of the United States are firmly committed to a list of five modern and one classical language (Spanish, French, German, Italian, Russian, Latin); and that other languages do not offer too much of a market, save in special instances; that if we want more study of other tongues, it will have to receive special moti-

vation that will be valid from the point of view of the individual and
his economic needs.

It is of interest to compare this national picture with what happens
in other lands. As against our secondary school language course that
seldom runs beyond one or two years, other nations have courses
ranging from four to ten years, and often extending from elementary
school to the university. This, rather than a lack of language ability
on the part of Americans, may account for the higher linguistic
achievement of foreigners. The study of foreign languages is generally
compulsory in other educational systems; it is still largely optional
with us. Some countries do not hesitate to inflict from three to five
languages on their students (this is the case with the Netherlands and
the Scandinavian nations), with no apparent detriment to their performance in other subjects. Languages are generally started earlier in
life abroad than they are here.

In the U.S.S.R., all high school students without exception must
take at least five years of English, German, or French (their choice,
by the way, is 45 per cent English, 35 per cent German, 20 per cent
French; this is in notable contrast with what used to happen in
Czarist Russia, where every educated person knew French, and members of the aristocracy spoke French better than they did Russian).
College students in the Soviet Union are generally required to take up,
in addition, an Asian or African language.

In France, where about 8 per cent of the population claims to know
English, our language is easily the winner in secondary schools, with
at least 60 per cent of the students taking it. German is the runner-up,
with about 20 per cent. Spanish, Italian, and Russian trail behind.
Again there is a shift from the early decades of this century, when
German had 50 per cent, English 40 per cent of the students.

French still leads English in many countries, notably those that
speak another Romance tongue. In Italy there are at least four students of all grades taking French for every one taking English. In
Spain, Portugal, and most countries of Latin America French is still
ahead of English. Spanish, which with us is a first choice, usually
trails French, English, German, and even Italian and Russian in
countries outside the Western Hemisphere.

The languages that generally stand out as being deemed worthy of extensive study in countries to which they are not native are about the same everywhere, though their order may vary. They are English, French, German, Spanish, Italian, Russian, and, in the Classical division, Latin. This picture is unfair to other great languages, particularly Portuguese, Chinese, Arabic, Japanese, and Hindi-Urdu, but is nevertheless the existing state of affairs. History shows us, however, that the language preference picture, like all human pictures, is subject to change, sometimes of a sudden and drastic nature.

17

What Languages Go Together? In What Ways?

The Problem of Language Transfer—Common Endings and Cognates—The Dangers of Etymology—The Special Idioms of Each Language—The Learned and the Popular Words—The Farther Up You Go the Easier It Gets

PEOPLE are often chided for living too much in the past. It is perhaps just as much of a mistake to live too much in the future. In the matter of languages, there are plenty of linguists to warn us that we pay too much attention to traditional grammar, as embodied in the grammatical structure of the Classical languages, particularly Latin. These same linguists would like us to pay undue attention to the grammatical structure of other languages, whose period of predominance is yet to come, or may not come at all.

Observant readers will have noticed from what was said in the preceding chapter that the languages most in vogue among American language learners because considered of the greatest practical use (French, Spanish, German, Italian, Russian, Latin, along with English) are all languages that originated in Europe. Some readers may also be aware that they all belong to one family of languages, the Indo-European, which happens to be the largest, with an absolute majority of the world's population speaking languages of various branches that stem from its trunk. Three others among the world's current languages in the over-fifty-million class, Portuguese, Hindi-Urdu, and Bengali, and another of the great Classical languages, Greek, are also of the Indo-European family. The other four of the Big Thirteen of the language world (Chinese, Arabic, Japanese, Indonesian-Malay) not only are not Indo-European but belong each to a different family. Chinese is Sino-Tibetan, and has as minor relatives Thai, Burmese, and Tibetan. Arabic, which is accompanied by another great Classical language, Hebrew, is Semitic. Japanese is in a family by itself, with a doubtful link to Korean. Indonesian-Malay belongs to the far-flung Malayo-Polynesian family, which includes among its lesser members the official Tagalog of the Philippines, the Malagasy of Madagascar, the Maori of New Zealand, Tahitian, and our own Hawaiian, along with most of the other tongues of the Republics of Indonesia and Malaysia (Javanese, Madurese, Dayak, Balinese, etc.).

Therefore, the language choices of the United States and of the Western world generally are based not only on practical self-interest and utilitarianism but also on what might be styled a family feeling, which in turn has some additional utilitarian features of its own, because languages of the same family must in some ways resemble one another and be easier to learn for people whose native tongue belongs to the same group.

As a matter of fact, the languages of the Indo-European group hold many features in common, though these may not be evident at first glance. The semi-concealed similarities are greatest in the matter of grammatical structure and in certain basic portions of the vocabulary (numerals, names of family relationship, certain common nouns, adjectives, and verbs). They are smallest (indeed, almost non-existent) in the matter of sounds and sound structure. But do not expect too much help from this similarity of origin. The languages have traveled a long way in different directions since the days when they were all one big happy family living together.

Some, however, stayed closer together and had intimate relationships to a far greater degree than others. This is particularly true of three of the Indo-European branches, the Greek, the Italic (to which Latin belongs), and the Germanic. The Germanic branch includes both English and German (Dutch and Scandinavian fit in here, too). The Latin of the Italic branch gave rise to the Romance languages (French, Spanish, Italian, Portuguese, Romanian). Greek did not give rise to any widespread modern group, but has been influencing Latin and its descendants, as well as English and other Germanic languages, since the days of antiquity.

English speakers are singularly fortunate in having a language which, though fundamentally Germanic, has received through the centuries following the Norman Conquest a tremendous superstructure of French, itself a language derived from Latin, and of Latin and Greek. The end result is that wherever the English speaker turns in seeking out his favorite languages he will find copious connections—

kindred words, kindred grammatical structures, recognizable acquaintances. This emphatically is not the case when he turns to the other big languages, Chinese, Japanese, Arabic, Indonesian-Malay. These languages have, especially in modern times, taken in a large number of loan words from the languages of the West, and have in turn contributed many words of their own to our Western languages (*tea, kimono, magazine, orang-utan* are four single samples of what we have taken from each of these non-Indo-European sources). But our borrowings from them, like their borrowings from us, are relatively scanty, as compared with the tremendous masses of words where English and German, or English and French, or English and Latin, or English and Greek show a connection that is evident even to the casual onlooker. Also, we cannot recognize in them the similarities of grammatical structure and word order that we are often able to perceive in such tongues as Spanish, Italian, German, even Russian.

Let it be emphasized at this point that this matter of seeking and finding similarities and links concerns primarily the written language, which gives you time and the opportunity to look for them and think about them. The spoken language comes too fast for rationalization and etymological research. Even there, however, the English speaker who hears the Spanish *atención,* or the Italian *messaggio,* or the German *Wasser,* or the Russian *professor,* is likely to understand that one word even if he understands nothing else in the sentence. Needless to say, the same advantages that accrue from this family relationship to English speakers studying French, Spanish, German, or Russian also accrue, in reverse, to French, Spanish, German, and Russian speakers trying to learn English.

Perhaps all this constitutes a sort of aristocratic club of languages, a restricted fraternity to which admission is by Indo-European origin. Perhaps this is deplorable in principle, and may someday be changed by some sort of linguistic desegregation procedure. But for the time being it is an established fact and must be reckoned with. In fact, it is so firmly established that speakers of non-Indo-European languages, where they have the possibility of studying another language than their own, almost invariably select one of our own choices. Despite geographical proximity to China, and ancient cultural links, far more English than Chinese is studied in Japanese schools and colleges. The Arabic speakers of North Africa and the

Hebrew speakers of Israel prefer learning English and French to learning each other's kindred Semitic tongues. Despite their common Indian tradition, the Tamil and Telugu speakers of southern India prefer learning and using English to learning and using Hindi. The Russians have their numerous specialists studying all sorts of Asian and African tongues, as we should be doing in our national interest; but the compulsory language choice in Soviet high schools is between English, French, and German. Our own college enrollment figures are quite eloquent; as against more than three quarters of a million students enrolled in courses that deal with Spanish, French, Latin, German, Italian, and Russian, we have fewer than 20,000 for all other languages put together.

Let us therefore, at least for a time, stop worrying about the question of language discrimination, even while we take constructive steps to remedy it, and concentrate on taking advantage of the very real advantages that the similarity of origin and structure of the Big Six of the American curriculum bestows upon us.

There definitely is such a thing as language transfer, though not all people know how to make it work, and a few experts even refuse to believe in it. There are possible tables of equivalent endings and equivalent spellings for words of the same origin and the same type that run across the board. As a single example, take the very frequent ending -*ation* that we find in *nation*. It is of Latin origin and has in Latin the form -*atio* in the nominative case (-*ation*- followed by a case ending in other case forms: *natio, nationis, nationi, nationem, natione,* etc.). In French and German it will appear as -*ation,* but French pronounces it -ah-SYŎ, German -ah-TSYOHN. In Spanish it is -*ación* (ah-THYOHN or ah-SYOHN, according to your choice of a Castilian or Latin-American pronunciation). In Italian it is -*azione* (-ah-TSYOH-nay). In Russian it takes the form -*atsya* (-AH-tsyuh) in the nominative case. Portuguese, in case you are interested, gives it to you as -*ação* (-uh-SĂU), with a regular shift to -*ações* (-uh-SŎYSH) in the plural. It is perfectly true that -*ation* words are for the most part of a learned nature; but this does not preclude their very frequent appearance in all Western languages, and is also a guarantee that they will not, as a rule, undergo too drastic a change of meaning from one language to another. Or take the fairly frequent -*age* that we find in *voyage, message,* etc. While this goes back to a Latin *-aticum* suffix, it drastically changed both its form and its meaning as Latin turned into Romance. It will be found to appear in pretty much the same words in French, Spanish, Italian, Portuguese, seldom in German and Russian. But even if restricted to the Romance languages alone, it is worth knowing what happens to it. The French equivalent forms end in *-age* (-AHZH), the Spanish in *-aje* (-AH-hay), the Portuguese in *-ajem* (-AH-zhãy), the Italian in *-aggio* (-AHJ-joh). Seldom do these words shift their basic meaning from one language to another. Our *-meter* words (*thermometer, barometer*) come from Greek *metron,* "anything that serves as a measure." Latin borrows the Greek word as *metrum.* It goes on to German as *-meter* (*Thermometer*), to French as *-mètre* (*thermomètre*), to Spanish, Portuguese, and Italian as *-metro* (*termómetro, termometro*), to Russian as *-metr* (*termometr*). Note, however, that while German and French, like English, use in their spelling the original Greek *th* of *thermos,* but, unlike English, pronounce it as a plain *t,* Italian, Spanish, Portuguese, and Russian even spell it with *t.* You may, in fact, set it down as a universal rule that where Greek, Latin, English, German, and French use *th, ph,* and *y* in their spelling of original Greek words, Italian, Spanish, and Portuguese will regularly replace these spellings with *t, f,* and *i.*

These points may seem of minor importance in language learning, particularly of the spoken variety. Yet they are memory aids that ought not to be scorned. They will simplify at least written-language understanding, permit you to add to your vocabulary by taking an educated guess, even if you don't know the word in the language you are trying to speak or write, and, of course, prove two things: the strong link that binds together the Western languages that have grown up in a common culture, and the fact that the higher up you go in subject matter the easier the foreign language becomes, because the learned vocabulary tends to be more and more the same. My father, in our early days in this country, used to wonder why he had so much more trouble with the English of the sporting page than with that of a scientific or literary treatise. I couldn't give him the explanation then, but I could now, if he were here to get it. Big differences among languages of the same family come in the common, everyday vocabulary; they are largely smoothed out in the more rarified tongue of science, literature, and philosophy, where the Latin and Greek roots not only predominate, but extend across the board. There was a movement at the Massachusetts Institute of Technology some years ago to standardize the language of science still further, by requiring common endings for common concepts even in the few cases where they do not exist, such as the Italian *-uro* for the English *-ide* in binary chemical compounds (*solfuro-sulphide, ioduro-iodide*). One of our more popular constructed languages, Interlingua, designed primarily for use at scientific congresses, is based squarely on the principle of vocabulary elements common to the majority of the Western world.

It is also submitted that this sort of international etymologizing can be lots of fun, and make for diversion and relief from the drudgery of mere imitation and repetition of basic pattern phrases. For purposes of true language learning, however, it must not be overdone.

To begin with, the etymological process, while it may be of considerable help in acquiring the written form of a language, will never by itself lead to spoken-language mastery. The spoken language moves far too fast for etymology to catch up with it.

Secondly, etymology can be a hindrance instead of a help in any type of language learning, unless it is applied with caution and under expert guidance. There are far too many false cognates, as has been seen, words like *Gift* in German and *gift* in English, *rente* in French and *rent* in English, *Knabe* and *Knecht* in German and *knight* and *knave* in English. There are far too many words that look exactly alike in two or more languages, but have different origins, different pronunciations, different meanings, like the *sale* that to us is the act of selling, but in Italian means "salt," in French "dirty," in Spanish "he is going out." Other words are disguised beyond recognition. German *Pflanze* and *Pferd* are both borrowed from Latin (*planta, paraveredus*). Both have English cognates in *plant* and *palfrey*. But would you be able to figure that out without help? English takes *radiator* and *illiterate* from Latin; one would naturally suppose that the same words would work out in Italian, which is the most Latin of the Romance languages. But if you made the necessary sound-and-spelling shifts, and tried to use *radiatore* and *illetterato* you would not hit the mark. Italian, for reasons of its own, prefers two Greek words, *termosifone* and *analfabeta* (if we used them in English, they would appear as *thermosiphon* and *analphabet*). Italian borrowed the concept of "call girl" from English, but used its own imagery to render "call"; it came out not as *ragazza-chiamata* or *ragazza da chiamata*, but as *ragazza squillo; squillo* can be the blare of a bugle as well as the ringing of a phone. We speak of *wholesale* and *retail*, using Germanic roots for the first, Latin-French for the second (*re-tailler*, "to cut up again"); we might expect a Latin-based language like Italian to use the same form for "retail"; not at all; Italian prefers *al minuto* ("minute style") as the opposite of *all'ingrosso* ("in big style"); *al dettaglio* is sometimes used, but that would correspond etymologically to *detail* rather than to *retail*. The fact of the matter is that languages are both illogical and supremely independent. They coincide only where it suits them, not where it suits you.

It is fashionable in some quarters to claim that English is terse as compared with other languages, notably the Romance. Also, that it is extremely precise. This may be generally true, but observe the terseness of Italian expressions such as *salvo contrordini* ("save in case the order is countermanded") or *salvo complicazioni* ("unless complications set in"); note also the extreme precision of a traffic sign such as *Veicoli a passo d'uomo* ("Vehicles at the pace of a man" or "Drive no faster than a man can walk").

We must learn in our language study to put up with the fact that each language is a law unto itself, not accountable for its choices to the speakers of any other language; that a large part of the expressions in common use in each language are idioms, not directly translatable or etymologizable, and that these must be memorized the hard way; for the spoken tongues, we must above all remember that each language has its own sound scheme, or, better yet, phonemic structure, which means not only sounds that have different points of articulation from the ones we are used to, but sets of oppositions between sounds that become significant to the meaning and understanding, as where an Italian double consonant carries a different meaning for the word where it appears from the corresponding single consonant, everything else being the same (*cade,* "he falls"; *cadde,* "he fell").

In spite of all this, the language learner will be wise to take advantage of all the similarities that languages of the same family afford him. He will do well to remember, for instance, that if a verb is strong in English (*speak, spoke, spoken,* or *sing, sang, sung,* as against *walk, walked, walked,* or *love, loved, loved*), it is extremely likely to be strong, or irregular, not only in German, but in Dutch and the Scandinavian tongues as well, if it appears at all in those languages, and expect in advance to find the irregularity. In studying the Romance languages, he will be wise to remember that the verbs are likely to fall into the same conjugational class in French as they do in Spanish or Italian, and that the scheme of tenses will generally be the same, though the tenses may show some individual differences of use; also, that if a noun is masculine in French, it has at least nine out of ten chances of being similarly masculine in Spanish or Italian; also, that the word order you use in Spanish will, by and large, work out satisfactorily for French and Italian as well.

There is definitely such a thing as taking your Romance languages together. For what concerns vocabulary, but not grammatical structure, Latin can be added to the Romance group. The best comparison for German is with English, though English goes over to the Latin-Romance side of the vocabulary far more often than does German. For what concerns grammatical structure, there is a strong link between the Classical languages (Greek and Latin) and modern Russian, with German occupying an intermediate position between the highly inflected structure of the Classical and Slavic tongues and the more analytical structure of Romance and particularly of English.

Spoken languages are best learned in isolation, as there is little or no reconciling their conflicting sound patterns, or using one as an aid to another save in limited areas of vocabulary and grammar, and as speech works too fast for rational mental comparisons. For what concerns grammatical structure, vocabulary, and the written language generally, language comparison can be of considerable service, and is a recommended practice.

18

How Should One Handle the Romance Languages?

Individually or en bloc?—*Is There a Carry-Over?—Common Elements that Are Transferable—Possibilities of Confusion—How to Use One Romance Language to Speakers of Another*

COLLECTIVELY, this is the most important group of languages for the average learner. Together, the Romance languages account for something over 400 million of the earth's population of nearly three billion, roughly one person out of seven. Their speaking area includes practically all of the American continent south of the Rio Grande, most of Southern Europe, and, in the form of secondary languages (colonial or cultural), vast tracts of Africa, Asia, and Oceania. Furthermore, the speakers are, at least for the present, among those with whom we find it most profitable and desirable to communicate, whether for economic, political-military, or purely cultural reasons.

On a spoken-language level, the Romance languages, like all languages, are perhaps best taken individually. But there are many other levels on which they can be studied to good advantage en bloc, or at least two or three at a time. Their written-language similarities are self-evident, as is their descent from a common ancestor, Latin. From any angle save that of straight colloquial speech, be it philological and historical, or literary and philosophical, or even structurally descriptive (at least for what concerns morphology, syntax, and vocabulary), they lend themselves superbly to comparative study. If you are already acquainted with one of them, or with the Latin from which they all sprang, there is no earthly reason why you should not utilize your knowledge of one to broaden your knowledge of another.

While common, immediate descent from Latin is one of the outstanding characteristics of French, Spanish, and Italian, as well as of Portuguese and Romanian, it must be stressed that the Latin which is their immediate ancestor is not quite the Classical Latin taught in our high schools and colleges, but rather a more popular brand of Latin, replete with slang and colloquialisms and deviations from the norms of Classical grammar. This Vulgar Latin was current among the masses of the western Roman Empire even when the Empire was in its most flourishing period. After the Empire's fall it degenerated, from the Classical standpoint, even while maintaining some semblance of unity due to a combination of the old Imperial tradition and the new universality of the all-important Christian Church of the West, whose vehicle of communication, conversion, and religious propaganda it was.

This semblance of unity was maintained, if all the available evidence at our disposal is to be trusted, down to the eighth century of our era, when it was finally snapped by the Moorish invasion of the Iberian Peninsula, the attempted language reforms of Pepin and Charlemagne in France, which had a contrary effect to the one they were meant to have (to bring back some measure of Classical Latin standards to the written and spoken tongue), and, in the ninth century, by the final fragmentation of Charlemagne's former empire.

But the new Romance languages, of which the first recorded manifestations appear in ninth-century France and tenth-century Spain and Italy, are far from indicating a complete break in the links of the chain binding together the Western descendants of Latin. Relations of all kinds, religious, military, cultural, commercial, were preserved among the new nations arising on what is now French, Spanish, Italian, and Portuguese soil. These relations were maintained at all times in the centuries that followed, and are still maintained today. The one big exception is Romanian, which was completely cut off from its Western relatives around the fifth century. It thereafter developed in a Byzantine Greek, Slavic, and Turkish environment, and it shows in its structure and vocabulary the effects of the long separation from its Western kinsfolk (full communications between Romanian and the Western Romance tongues were not really reestablished until the dawn of the nineteenth century).

The other languages, each of which is in its own right a member of the "Big Thirteen Club" of languages, constantly borrowed from, lent to, and otherwise influenced one another. Their grammatical and lexical similarities, therefore, are based not only on their common Latin heritage but also on their unbroken and intimate cultural contacts.

All these languages show a basically similar structure for articles, nouns, adjectives, adverbs, pronouns, and verbs, with common and very perceptible divergences from the structure of the Latin from which they sprang.

Latin had no article, definite or indefinite. The Western Romance languages all have definite articles, used before the noun, and stemming from the Latin demonstrative adjective-pronoun *ille,* which modified its use and meaning so that it got to mean "the" instead of "that." At the same time, the Latin numeral *unus,* while continuing to be used as a numeral in the sense of "one," took on also the functions of "a" or "an." For this, there is an exact parallel in Germanic, and particularly in English; our article *the* comes from *that,* and our *a* and *an* are unstressed forms of *one.*

The three grammatical genders of Classical Latin (masculine, feminine, neuter) were reduced to two, with neuter nouns generally joining the masculine, less often the feminine, type. Since a good deal of this change occurred in Vulgar Latin, it is natural that most nouns that are masculine (or feminine) in one Romance tongue should be of the same gender in the others, and this fact is worth remembering.

The distinction of singular and plural appearing in Latin remained. What emphatically did not remain was the system of Latin cases marked by separate endings. French went through an intermediate stage with two separate case forms (but only for masculine nouns), a nominative; and an oblique, which united the functions of the Latin genitive, dative, accusative, and ablative. It was not until the fourteenth century that these two forms merged. But Spanish, Italian, and Portuguese show the almost universal merger of all Latin case forms into a single form from the very outset of their written documents. The numerous Latin declensional types were also largely merged, so that where Latin had five separate declensions plus many exceptional types, Spanish, Italian, and Portuguese today have only a masculine type, a feminine type, and a type that may be of either gender. French, going a little further, has merged even the third into the other two types. Basically, today, Italian has masculine nouns ending in -*o* with a plural in -*i,* feminine nouns ending in -*a* with a plural in -*e,* and nouns of either gender ending in -*e* with a plural in -*i.* Spanish and Portuguese have masculine nouns ending in -*o* with a plural in -*os;* feminine nouns ending in -*a* with a plural in *-as;* and nouns of either gender ending in *-e* or consonant with a plural in *-es.* French has merely a masculine noun ending, generally, in consonant (occasionally in *-e*) with plural in *-s;* and a feminine noun ending in *-e* with a plural in *-es* (for spoken French, since the final written *-s* is not pronounced, the distinction between singular and plural is really made by the prefixed article: *le* for masculine singular, *la* for feminine singular, *les* for all plurals).

Syntactically, the obliteration of the Latin case system means that the distinction between subject and object has to be made by position (subject before, object after the verb). Other distinctions, marked in Latin by genitive, dative, accusative, and ablative case endings, are made in Romance by the use of prepositions (*of, to, in, toward, against, with, by, from,* etc.). Some of these, however, were used even in Latin, concurrently with the case endings, as still happens in modern German or Russian.

The adjective scheme closely follows the noun scheme. French has basically a single type of adjective, with masculine singular ending in consonant, feminine singular in *-e,* masculine plural in *-s,* feminine plural in *-es* (some adjectives have *-e* in both masculine and feminine singular, and *-es* in both plural forms). Spanish and Portuguese have two classes of adjectives, one with endings *-o, -a, -os, -as,* the other with *-e* or consonant for both genders, plural *-es.* Italian likewise has the double adjective class, but the endings are *-o, -a, -i, -e* for the first, *-e,* plural *-i* for the second. There is full agreement of the adjective with its noun, in any position, attributive or predicate, but in view of the different types of both nouns and adjectives in Spanish, Portuguese, and Italian, agreement does not necessarily mean identical endings (Italian *la donna forte,* "the strong woman," *le donne forti,* "the strong women"; Spanish *el muchacho fuerte,* "the strong boy," *los muchachos fuertes,* "the strong boys").

Adjectives generally follow their nouns, but with a few high-frequency exceptions (*le grand homme,* "the great man"; *la bonne jeune fille,* "the good girl" but *les hommes importants,* "the important men"; *les filles intelligentes,* "the intelligent girls").

The comparative and superlative degrees of the adjective are formed by prefixing the word for "more," "the more," to the positive degree of the adjective. ("More" is *plus* in French, *più* in Italian, *más* in Spanish, *mais* in Portuguese, *mai* in Romanian). Actually, there is no distinction in Romance between comparative and superlative if the comparative happens to be preceded by an article; "the better of the (two) boys" and "the best of the (four) boys" would both come out the same way: *le meilleur des deux (quatre) garçons; el mejor de los dos (cuatro) muchachos; il migliore dei due (quattro) ragazzi,* etc. French alone among the Romance languages makes a halfhearted attempt to distinguish, but only when the adjective follows the noun, in which case it gets an extra article (*le garçon le plus intelligent de la classe*). Latin, on the other hand, had an organic comparative in *-ior* (*fortis, fortior*) and an organic superlative in *-issimus* (*fortissimus*), quite like English *-er, -est.* The *-issimus* superlative survives in Italian *-issimo,* Spanish and Portuguese *-ísimo,* but only as an absolute superlative (*la montaña altísima* in Spanish can mean only "the very high mountain," not also "the highest mountain," as *mons altissimus* could mean in Latin).

Adverbs are usually formed from adjectives by adding *-ment* to the feminine singular of the adjective in French, *-mente* in Italian, Spanish, and Portuguese. The origin of this formation is interesting, as Classical Latin formed its adverbs differently (*sane* from *sanus, fortiter* from *fortis*). A tendency arose in Vulgar Latin to describe mental states by the use of a so-called "ablative of manner" construction: *sana mente,* "with a sound mind." The use of this construction gradually spread to other answers to the question "How?" which did not involve mental states. There is a curious parallel in English, where our adverbial *-ly,* earlier *-like,* comes from a noun that meant "body," which, though disappearing from the language as a common noun, occasionally appears in family names (Litchfield, which originally meant "graveyard"), and still appears in the cognate German *Leiche,* "body," "corpse." One could therefore say that while French *sainement* is in origin "with a sound mind," English *soundly* is originally "with a sound body." Perhaps the Germanic languages are more concretely inclined than the Romance.

The case distinctions that went out of style for nouns are still fairly alive for pronouns. One could, without stretching the imagination too much, describe Italian *egli* as nominative, *lo* as accusative, *gli* as dative, and *lui* as ablative (*egli è arrivato,* "he arrived"; *lo vedo,* "I see him"; *gli do il libro,* "I give him the book"; *vado con lui,* "I am going with him"). Generally speaking, direct and indirect object pronouns are placed not after the verb, as in English, but before the verb, as illustrated by the above examples. There are, however, numerous exceptions, which are not the same for all the languages.

In contrast to what happened to the noun, where wholesale simplification and merging of forms took place, the Romance verbs follow with some degree of faithfulness the old and highly complicated Latin scheme. The four main Latin conjugational types (*-āre, -ēre, '-ere, -īre*) generally survive, though Italian has merged the second and third everywhere save in the infinitive (*-áre, -ére, '-ere, -íre*); Spanish and Portuguese have absorbed the third into the second (*-ar, -er, -ir*); and French, having drastically transformed *-āre* into *-er, '-ere* into *-re,* and *-īre* into *-ir,* has relegated the old *-ēre* types, after first changing them to *-oir,* to the role of irregular verbs.

The various Latin tenses live on, with some change of function and with copious additions. Where Latin had six indicative and four subjunctive tenses, the Romance languages have ten of the former, either four or six of the latter. The new tenses include those of the conditional mood, which Latin did not have, and new compound tenses formed by combining past participles with "to have" or "to be" used as auxiliary verbs.

The drastic reduction and simplification of noun forms is in strident contrast with the increased complexity of the Romance verb. Why this discrepancy of treatment, which does not at all lend itself to the theories of those who believe that the speakers grew lazy and tired of their "complicated" noun endings? No one really knows, but the results are crystal-clear. All the complaints that are voiced by columnists and other superficial writers against the complexities of languages like French are invariably directed at the French verb, never at the French noun. It is the over-numerous verb forms, regular and irregular, that call for big exercise of the faculty of memorization on the part of those who are not born to a Romance tongue.

In the matter of syntax and word order, the Romance languages generally hang together, though with interesting differences. In the course of centuries of cohabitation, they have borrowed heavily not only words but also grammatical constructions from one another. Word-for-word translation is far more possible and idiomatically feasible from one Romance language to another than it is from English to any one of them, or to equally Germanic German, for that matter. Indicative of this state of affairs is the fact that when French and Spanish publishers decided to bring out their versions of my *Story of Language,* they translated from the already existing Italian version, not from the English original. Comparative grammars of French, Spanish, and Italian, like that of Oliver Heatwole, are of considerable help in speeding up the acquisition of the grammatical structure of one Romance language by a learner who is already acquainted with another.

When we come to vocabulary, which is by far the most difficult part of a language to acquire, at least in acceptable form, we find that, while there is a sort of basic unity among the Romance tongues, there are also confusing divergences. It is perfectly true that perhaps as many as 75 per cent of the words coincide, at least as to origin and form. No one who knows French *pain* for "bread" will be seriously troubled by Italian *pane,* Spanish *pan,* Portuguese *pão,* Latin *panis,* even Romanian *pâine.* "Life" is *vita* in Latin and Italian, *vida* in Spanish and Portuguese, *vie* in French, *viaţă* in Romanian. "Horse," which was taken from the slightly slangy *caballus* rather than from the elegant Classical *equus,* is *cheval, cavallo, caballo, cavalo, cal.* "To drink," Latin *bibere,* is *boire, bere, beber, bea.* Hundreds or thousands of word lists of this type could be constructed.

The trouble begins with words of modern and even medieval civilization, the sort of thing that started after the Roman imperial links had been broken. Spanish and Portuguese, having been subjected to long Arab domination, have in their repertories numerous Arabic words which did not spread to the other lands (a great many of them did, but almost as often from Sicily, which was also under Saracen rule for over a century, as from the Iberian Peninsula; where Spanish and Portuguese borrowings from Arabic incorporate the Arabic definite article *al,* as in *Alhambra, Alfama, alhaja, almeja, alfaiate,* the borrowings through Sicily did not; that is why we have Italian *cotone,* French *coton,* English *cotton,* as against Spanish *algodón,* and Italian *dogana,* French *douane,* as against Spanish *aduana).* French and Italian borrowed heavily from the Germanic tongues of the Franks and Longobards, respectively; that is why French has words like *haïr* and *choisir* ("to hate," "to choose"), which appear nowhere else in the Romance world, while Italian has *scherzare* and *strale* ("to joke," "arrow"; compare German *scherzen, Strahl).*

But aside from borrowings, the languages, while staying close together, exercised their God-given right of free choice all along the line. The result is a list of words where none, or only two of the four, coincide, and that list is long indeed. Here is a sample:

English	Portuguese	Spanish	French	Italian
apple	maçã	manzana	pomme	mela
to shut	fechar	cerrar	fermer	chiudere
long	comprido	largo	long	lungo
near	perto de	cerca de	près de	vicino a
to spit	cuspir	escupir	cracher	sputare
to dine	jantar	comer	dîner	pranzare
tailor	alfaiate	sastre	tailleur	sarto
slice	fatia	tajada	tranche	fetta
suit	fato (or terno)	traje	complet	vestito
city block	quarteirão	manzana	pâté (de maisons)	isolato
pardon me	desculpe	dispense	pardon	scusi
fan	leque	abanico	éventail	ventaglio
fork	garfo	tenedor	fourchette	forchetta
pocket	algibeira	bolsillo	poche	tasca
rent	aluguel	alquiler	loyer	pigione
pin	alfinete	alfiler	épingle	spilla
ribbon	fita	cinta	ruban	nastro
store	loja	tienda	boutique	negozio
tip	gorjeta	propina	pourboire	mancia
rails	trilho	rieles	rails	rotaie
appetizers	acepipes	entremés	hors-d'oeuvre	antipasto

There are hosts of words that seem to coincide in two or more languages, but actually lend themselves to hopeless confusion. In the list given above, Italian *fermare,* which corresponds etymologically to French *fermer,* ("to close") means "to stop." *Largo,* which means "long" in Spanish, means "wide" in Italian. Portuguese *fato* ("suit") in Italian means "fate"; Brazilian-Portuguese *terno* ("suit of clothes") is in Italian a series of three numbers in a state lottery. Spanish *cinta* ("ribbon") is Italian for "belt." *Subir* is "to go up" in Spanish, "to undergo" in French. *Palestra,* which in Italian means "gym," has in Portuguese the meaning of "lecture." *Burro,* Italian for "butter," means "donkey" in Spanish, as was made startlingly clear to one of my uncles, who, having gone on a South American tour as an opera singer, entered a Buenos Aires restaurant and, relying on the fact that Italian and Spanish are normally mutually comprehensible, asked for *due uova al burro,* "two eggs frieds in butter"; the Argentine waiter looked puzzled, then politely informed him in Spanish that in Argentina, at least, donkeys don't lay eggs.

Preferred usages also play a part. Portuguese uses *comer* as well as *jantar,* but while the latter is specifically "to dine," *comer* is "to eat;" Spanish uses *comer* in both senses. French *pardon* may be used in any of the other languages (in Portuguese it takes the form *perdão*), but the native form is more common. Italian has *bottega* as well as *negozio* for "store" (like French *boutique*), but of the two Spanish words from the same source, *bodega* means specifically a grocery store or a wineshop, *botica* a drugstore. Spanish *tienda,* "store," "shop" in general, translated etymologically into Italian *tenda* would mean "tent."

There are long lists of cliché expressions which may start out the same way, but don't end alike. "From time to time" is in French *de temps en temps,* but in Spanish *de vez en cuando,* in Italian *di quando in quando.* Spanish *tal vez* looks like a literal translation of Italian *talvolta;* but the Spanish expression means "perhaps," the Italian "sometimes." Portuguese *obrigado,* like English "obliged," has the idiomatic meaning of "thank you"; in Spanish, French, or Italian the equivalent *obligado, obligé, obbligato* would only have the literal meaning of "compelled." Spanish ¿ *Qué ocurre?* means "what's happening?" The literal Italian translation *Che occorre?* means "What's needed?" French *défense* means "prohibition" as well as "defense" and you'll see it, followed by *de,* in all sorts of signs where English says "No (spitting, smoking, loitering, etc.)"; not so with the equivalent Spanish, Portuguese, or Italian forms, which mean only "defense"; while Spanish-Portuguese *prohibido* and Italian *proibito* would barely be understood in French, and the Italian alternative *vietato* not at all.

All this is not said to discourage you from comparative study of the Romance languages, which is basically a recommended procedure. It is merely putting you on your guard against expecting too much.

On the spoken-language plane, a French speaker will neither understand nor be understood by the speakers of the other three languages. French has undergone too drastic a sound transformation, and does not at all retain the original Latin rhythm, which the others do. Portuguese, which has also undergone heavy sound change, is partly accessible to a Spanish speaker, largely because of the strong similarities of grammatical structure and vocabulary in the two languages (though even here we are treading on dangerous ground, as will be seen in a later chapter). A Spanish and an Italian speaker can converse for hours with only occasional confusion, by reason of similarity of sound patterns. The Italian speaker cannot normally understand the Portuguese without some period of adjustment, as I can readily testify. On the other hand, the Portuguese speaker has little difficulty understanding the Italian, by reason of the clearer sounds and fuller forms of the latter's language. On my first visit to Portugal, when I had not yet mastered the intricacies of Portuguese pronunciation, I was asked to address a group of Coimbra students. Only about half of them understood French, and even fewer understood English; I did not make the tactical blunder of suggesting that I talk to them in Spanish, which they would have understood but not cared for; my final suggestion that I use my native Italian met with an enthusiastic chorus of approval; I am sure they understood practically every word I spoke.

In studying Latin or any of its descendants, do not hesitate to bring to bear upon your problems any help you may derive from your knowledge of another Roman tongue. This applies to grammatical structure, word order, noun gender, use of tenses, vocabulary. You have a good 75 per cent chance of being right, or, at least, understood.

For what concerns actual speech, there is no harm in trying to use one Romance language to the speakers of another. French, which has very little spoken-language interchange with the others, is nevertheless the foreign tongue a speaker of another Romance tongue is most likely to have a smattering of. By all means try it with Spanish, Portuguese, or Italian speakers if your English fails. Do not hesitate to interchange Spanish, Portuguese, and Italian. The Portuguese may not like to be addressed in Spanish, but they will understand it, and they are of a sweet, forgiving disposition. Spaniards and Italians have no objection whatsoever to each other's languages, and are capable of rolling right along for hours, and even enjoying it.

One more suggestion, in case you are really stuck in a Romance area, but happen to know some Latin. By all means try it, but without the Latin case endings or rules of grammar. Individual, isolated words have the best chance of being understood. After all, it was Dante who claimed that Italian was "Latin without the rules of grammar." And if you encounter a priest or monk in a Romance country, do not hesitate at all to use such Latin as you know, with all the correctness you are capable of. Practically all of them speak it.

19

What Are the Problems in Learning French?

What You Can Do with French—The Acquisition of the Sounds —How Bad Is French Grammar?—Syntax for Clarity—The Common Vocabulary of French and English

LET us begin by telling you what you can do with French. We do not intend to enter into a lengthy disquisition on the historical, cultural, and literary merits of a language that held a place of predominance in the Western world throughout the Middle Ages, and again from the seventeenth century to the First World War, to the point where the Moslem world designated the Christian West as Feringhistan, "the land of the Franks"; where French, the language of the *defeated* nation, was the *sole* diplomatic tongue used at the Congress of Vienna, after the fall of Napoleon; where French was the first modern foreign tongue taught in American institutions of higher learning; and where no nineteenth-century European could consider himself educated without some knowledge of French. But it may be worth while to note that French is even today in a neck-and-neck race with English as the most widely studied tongue among those to whom neither English nor French is native, and that it has a worldwide distribution and possibility of use second, if at all, only to English. The number of native speakers of French does not reach one hundred million, but the list of countries where French is the official or co-official language is impressive. In Europe it includes not only France, but also Belgium, Switzerland, Luxembourg, and Monaco. In the Western Hemisphere, French is official in Haiti and all French Western Hemisphere possessions (French Guiana, St. Pierre, Miquelon, Guadeloupe, etc.), and fully co-official in Canada. In Asia, French is co-official in Laos, practically co-official in Cambodia, North and South Viet Nam, Jordan, Lebanon, Syria. On the African continent, French is the sole official language in the Central African Republic, the Brazzaville Congo, Dahomey, Gabon, Guinea, Ivory Coast, Mali, Mauritania, Niger, Senegal, Togo, Upper Volta; it is co-official in Algeria, Burundi, Cameroon, the Leopoldville Congo, Madagascar (the Malagasy Republic), Ruanda; it is semiofficial in Morocco, Tunisia, the United Arab Republic (Egypt), and fairly widespread in Ethiopia and Ghana. That a good deal of this is the result of past colonialism is beside the point. The linguistic effects of colonialism are going to linger on long, long after colonialism is dead and buried. French is one of the two or three foreign languages most widely studied not only in the schools of the United States but in those of most countries in the world. If your English won't work, the next language to try is almost invariably French. It is sometimes amazing what can be accomplished with French. At one time, shortly after the war, an organization interested in problems of world government invited me to attend a private dinner offered to the Russian journalist, Ilya Ehrenburg, who was at that time visiting the United States. It turned out at the dinner that of the ten people present no one but I could speak either Russian or French, though most of those present could handle German and even Hungarian far better than I; it also turned out that Ehrenburg spoke no English or German, but only his native Russian plus fluent French. Since my French is far more fluent than my Russian, I did all the talking to our Russian guest and translated to the others. There would otherwise have been no communication. The point I am trying to make is that Ehrenburg, a Russian brought up in the old tradition despite his Soviet affiliations, spoke no English or German, but fluent French. If you have nothing specific in mind, and want to learn a language that has the widest chance of worldwide use, French is probably your best bet at the present time.

French is a language of beautiful but difficult sounds, so far as a speaker of English is concerned. One of your main problems in learning French is that of acquiring an acceptable pronunciation and, even more, understanding what a Frenchman says.

For one thing, there is far greater tension of the organs of speech in French than there is in English. Also, the neutral position of the tip of the tongue is down, toward the lower teeth, rather than up, toward the gum ridges, as it is in English, and this means a different coloring (more dental and less alveolar, to use technical terms) for

those sounds which are usually represented in writing by *t, d, n, l, s.*
The "Parisian" *r* is produced by gently vibrating the uvula, as for a
mild clearing of the throat, not, as in English, by cupping the tongue.
English consonant sounds that do not normally occur in French are
the two *th*'s of *thing* and *this,* the *ch* of *church,* the *j* of *John,* the *h*
of *hat,* the *ng* of *king,* the *ts* of *its* and the *dz* of *ads.* There is, on the
other hand, an abundance of the sounds of *sh* and *s* in *pleasure.*
French vowels are precise, clear, and uncomplicated by the many
glides of English (such as the tail ends of *a* in *late, o* in *note*). But
some of them, represented usually in writing by *u, eu, oeu,* are quite
unfamiliar to us, and call for varying degrees of lip rounding plus unfamiliar tongue positions. French written *u* is the *ee* of *feet* pronounced with lips rounded as for *boot;* French *eu* or *oeu* is the *a* of
gate with lip rounding that can be greater or lesser, depending on the
position of the sound in the word. In addition, French has full-bodied
nasal vowels, which call for partial blocking of the passage between
nose and mouth as you pronounce, respectively, the *a* of *father,* the
e of *met,* the *aw* of *law,* the *u* of *cur.* French stress is rather uniformly
distributed over the syllables of a word, but since English has strong
initial stress, the impression an English speaker gets is that French
stresses final pronounced syllables. The tendency in French, as in all
Romance languages, is to make consonant-vowel the ideal syllable,
making syllabic pauses after vowels where possible, and this happens
even in groups of words, so that *il est* ("he is") comes out in speech
as ee-LEH.

French pronunciation can be described roughly, as above, or in
much more precise technical terminology, but descriptions are of little
value unless accompanied by an actual speaker or recording. More
perhaps than any other spoken language, French should be learned
from actual sounds rather than from printed pages; therefore, the best
piece of advice we can give you is: get yourself a native speaker or a
good set of native-speaker recordings; drill and drill; listen, imitate,
and pronounce; above all, attune your ear to the sounds of spoken
French.

For what concerns the learning of French grammatical structure,
there is not too much difficulty until you come to the verbs. Like all

Western Romance languages, French has only two genders, masculine and feminine, which means that you must accustom yourself to reckoning "pencil" as "he" and "pen" as "she." But this is perhaps easier than having three genders which largely fail to coincide with English usage and natural gender, as is the case in German, Latin, or Russian. The French definite and indefinite articles, nouns and adjectives are quite simple. Masculine nouns take the definite article *le* (*l'* if they begin with a vowel or most *h*'s); feminine nouns take *la* (again *l'* before vowel or *h*); all plural nouns take *les*. But remember that *les* comes in two spoken-language shifts; if the next word begins with a consonant, it's "lay" (this is a very bad approximation, but it's the best we can come up with using the traditional spelling of English); if it begins with a vowel, it's still "lay," but the final -*s* goes over to the next word, forms a syllable with it, and is sounded as a *z* (*les livres*, lay LEE-vruh; but *les épées*, lay zay-PAY). The indefinite article is *un* (masculine), *une* (feminine), and again, remember to make the carry-over if the next word starts with a vowel sound (*un livre*, ũh LEE-vruh; but *un homme*, ũh-NAWM; the *h* of *homme* is silent, and you "carry" the *n* right through it to the *o; une femme*, ün FAHM; but *une oreille*, ü-naw-REH-yuh).

Most masculine nouns end in written consonants which are seldom pronounced; most feminine nouns end in written -*e* which is generally not pronounced (unless preceded by a troublesome consonant cluster), but indicates that the preceding consonant should be heard. The plural is generally formed by adding -*s*, but this -*s* is practically never pronounced. This means that the real distinction between singular and plural in speech comes not at the end but at the beginning, and is made by the article (*le livre*, luh LEE-vruh, as against *les livres*, lay LEE-vruh). This peculiarity, due to thoroughly traceable historical causes, makes French stand apart from its sister Romance languages, and causes it to bear a striking, though purely chance, resemblance to the Bantu languages of southern Africa.

A very general description of adjectives and adverbs has already been given in the preceding chapter. In the matter of pronouns, the French subject (or nominative) forms are more important than they are in the other Romance languages, because they are regularly used, not frequently omitted; but this is an advantage to the English speaker, who is also accustomed to using his subject pronouns. One good reason for this setup is that in spoken French, as in both spoken and written English, the endings of the verbs have largely fallen together. In *je parle, tu parles, il parle, ils parlent,* the verb forms all sound exactly alike (PARL); the use of the subject pronoun is therefore necessary for clarity, as it is in English (*I, you, we, they speak*). By way of contrast, Italian, which has *parlo, parli, parla, parlano,* all with clearly pronounced endings, does not need subject pronouns save for emphasis.

Object pronouns, as in the other Romance languages, generally precede the verb (*je le vois, je lui donne le livre:* "I see him," "I give him the book"). The only exception in French is the affirmative imperative (*donnez-moi, prenez-le,* "give me," "take it"; there are additional exceptions in the other languages). There are complicated rules for the sequence of two or more object pronouns (*il me le donne,* "he gives it to me"; *je le lui donne,* "I give it to him").

Possessive adjectives (*mon livre, sa maison, leur soeur,* "my book," "his house," "their sister") precede the noun, are of very frequent occurrence, and should be learned early in the game. Possessive *pronouns* (*cette maison et la mienne,* "this house and mine") are used far less often, and can be postponed. Note, however, that they are preceded by the article, and that both possessive adjectives and possessive pronouns take the same gender and number as the thing possessed.

The demonstrative adjective (*ce livre, cette femme, cet homme, ces livres, ces femmes,* "this [or that] book," "this [or that] woman," "this [or that] man," "these [or those] books," "these [or those] women") is of very frequent occurrence. It means both "this" and "that" and, in the plural, both "these" and "those." You can make a distinction, if necessary, by adding -*ci* or -*là* to the noun (*ce livre-ci, cette femme-là*), but that is far less necessary than most grammars would have you believe. The demonstrative pronouns (*celui de ma soeur, celle-ci, ceux de mon frère, celles-là,* "the one of my sister" [or "my sister's"], "this one," "those of my brother" [or "my brother's"], "those") are far less often used.

Most frequently used interrogative pronouns are *qui* ("who?", "whom?"), *que* or *qu'est-ce que* ("what?" used as the object; use *qu'est-ce qui* if "what?" is the subject); *lequel* (with variants for gender and number, *laquelle, lesquels, lesquelles*), "which?", "which one?", "which ones?"; the corresponding interrogative adjective "which?" before a noun is *quel, quelle, quels, quelles.* Most frequently used relative pronouns are *qui* ("who," "which," "that," but only as subject or after prepositions); *que* (object of a verb); *dont* ("whose," "of which").

Verbs form the real crux of the language. We refer you to the preceding chapter for what concerns the survival of Latin conjugations and tenses in the Romance languages generally. Note specifically for French:

(a) The regular use of the subject pronoun described above.

(b) Negative forms: *ne* before the verb, *pas* after it (after the auxiliary but before the past participle in compound tenses: *je ne le vois pas,* "I don't see him"; *je ne l'ai pas vu,* "I haven't seen him").

(c) Interrogative forms: you may turn any statement into a question by prefixing *est-ce que* (*est-ce qu'il parle français?* "Does he speak French?"; *est-ce que votre frère a parlé?* "Did your brother speak?"). If your subject is a pronoun, you may also invert (*avez-vous parlé?* "Did you speak?"). If your subject is a noun, you may put the noun first, then invert, using a pronoun (*vos amis, ont-ils parlé?* "Did your friends speak?").

(d) Compound tenses, formed, as in English, with "to have," but in the case of some high-frequency verbs (*come, go, go up, go down, come in, go out, fall, stay, die, be born*) formed with "to be" (*il est allé,* "he went"; *je suis né,* "I was born").

(e) The past participle agrees with the subject if you are using "to be," with the *preceding direct* object if you are using "to have" (*elle est venue,* "she came"; *ils sont morts,* "they died"; *je les ai vus,* "I saw them"; *les femmes que j'ai vues,* "the women I saw"). But this rule affects the spoken language very little, as the participle forms generally sounds alike, even with the addition of *-e, -s* or *-es.* This means, consolingly, that native Frenchmen as well as you can make mistakes in writing.

(f) In the matter of tenses, you cannot do in modern French what you can do in English (also in Spanish, Portuguese and Italian), and say "I am writing." All you can say is "I write."

(g) The imperfect tense, as in the other Romance languages, is used for "I was writing," "I used to write" (*j'écrivais*). For "I wrote,"

"I have written," use the past indefinite, which is what we would call the present perfect (*j'ai écrit*). Do not try, in ordinary language, to use the tense that looks like our "I wrote" (*j'écrivis*); it is literary and oratorical, not colloquial.

(h) For the future ("I shall write"), French very often substitutes, like English, "I am going to write" (*je vais écrire*). You are at perfect liberty to do the same, and it's much easier on you once you have learned the present tense of the verb that means "to go, to be going."

(i) Don't worry too much about the French subjunctive, unless you are scheduled for a written exam. It often looks and sounds like the indicative, though not quite as much as it does in English, and if you make a mistake you'll be readily understood. You have to worry a little more about it in the other Romance languages, where indicative and subjunctive forms regularly show audible differences.

(j) The verb tenses to concentrate on are: present, imperfect, present perfect (or past indefinite), imperative, and, of course, infinitive, and past participle; to a lesser degree, future and conditional. Pluperfect, past anterior, future perfect, all subjunctives, can be left for much later.

(k) One half-satisfactory way of avoiding the past indefinite, if you have forgotten what the participle looks like, but remember the infinitive, is to use the construction *venir de,* "to have just" (*je viens de parler,* "I have just spoken," instead of *j'ai parlé,* "I have spoken"). This means learning the present tense of *venir,* "to come"; but you need it anyway.

(l) Some irregular verbs must be memorized at the outset, at least in the tenses named in (j), as they are among the highest-frequency forms in the language. The verbs you need the most are irregular (*to be, to have, to go, to come, to want, to be able, to know, to put, to take, to do, to make, to keep, to see,* etc.). Learn them very early in the game. Read them, write them, recite them out loud, over and over and over again, until you have them firmly in your grip.

(m) The passive is formed as in English (*je suis puni,* "I am punished"). Since you are using *to be,* remember to make the past participle agree with the subject (*la femme a été vue,* "the woman has been seen"). French generally gets away from the passive by using *on* ("one," "somebody") with the active (*on l'a vu,* "one has seen him," "he has been seen"; *ici on parle français,* "here one speaks French," ""French is spoken here").

Syntactically, French is one of the easiest languages, with a word order which normally makes sense to the English speaker, though it is far less elastic than that of its sister Romance tongues. For one thing, the language is strait-jacketed into fixed, unchanging rules of position, which may not be varied at the whim of the writer or speaker. In part, this is due to the French Academy; but to an even greater degree, it is due to the usage of sixteenth- and seventeenth-century writers and grammarians, who believed in logic and clarity. The result is that when international treaties are drawn up in various versions, the French text is always declared official for what concerns precise interpretation. A by-product is that while French presents more difficulties at the outset, mainly by reason of its sound scheme and spelling, than do some other languages, it becomes easier, not harder, as you proceed in your studies.

By reason of the Norman Conquest, French vocabulary comes perhaps closer to English than do the vocabularies of Italian, Spanish, and Portuguese. But the spread in pronunciation is greater, and while written French *nation* is perfectly clear to you, the spoken French word may go unrecognized. In French, more than in any other of the major languages, you must train yourself in listening, imitating, repeating after a native speaker, if you want spoken-language mastery (you may, of course, perfectly well acquire written French for reading and literary purposes without going through these paces). In French, more than in other languages, you must strain your ears, and train yourself to listen for clues and fit sounds into their context. As a single example: *s'en, cent, sans, sang,* sound exactly alike in isolation (SĀH). But listen to them in context: *il s'en est allé,* "he went away"; *prêtez-moi cent dollars,* "lend me a hundred dollars"; *il est sorti sans parler,* "he went out without speaking"; *il a versé son sang pour la France,* "he shed his blood for France." Compare with English "Will you *write* the letter?"; "This isn't *right!*"; He is a *playwright*"; "The Mass was said in the Roman *rite.*" See what we mean?

20

How Do You Learn Italian?

*Italian for Business or for Culture?—The Easy Sounds—Floren-
tine or Roman Standard?—The Tough Grammatical Forms—
Problems of Word Order—The Standard Language and the Dialects*

AMONG the four Western Romance languages, Italian is the one
having the smallest speaking population and area. For the former, the
50 million or so inhabitants of the Italian peninsula and islands are
joined by less than one million people in southern Switzerland, plus
perhaps 10 million Italian speakers abroad, mostly in North and
South America, plus a remnant of colonial speakers in Libya,
Somalia, Eritrea, Ethiopia, and the Dodecanese, plus an undetermined
number of people who have acquired Italian. All these may or may
not bring up the total to 70 or 75 million. The areas where Italian is
official are even more restricted—the Italian Republic and Switzerland. On the other hand, the 20 to 25 million Italian speakers who
do not live on Italian or Swiss soil are widely distributed, and one
may hear the language spoken almost anywhere—in large areas of
the United States, Canada, Argentina, Brazil, Uruguay; in many
countries of Europe to which Italians have migrated, notably France,
Germany, and Belgium; in Yugoslavia, Albania, and Greece; even in
far-off Australia and South Africa, which have lately played hosts to
numerous Italian entrants.

The economic, political, and military importance of Italian, while
sound enough, is not of the very first rank. It is in the cultural, artistic
and scientific fields that Italian is most useful to the learner. The
Italian Middle Ages and Renaissance conferred upon Italy an absolute predominance in the fields of art, painting and sculpture, while
in more recent centuries Italy has gained what amounts to first place
in the field of music and singing, particularly of the operatic variety,
as well as in many branches of science, illustrated by the names of
Galileo, Leonardo da Vinci, Torricelli, and Volta at an earlier period,

Marconi and Fermi more recently. In the fields of abstract thought, religion, philosophy, and literature, the Italian contributions have been second to none, with an unbroken stream that runs from Leo the Great and Thomas Aquinas, St. Benedict and St. Francis of Assisi, Dante and Petrarch and Boccaccio, through Ariosto and Tasso, down to Manzoni, Carducci, Foscolo, d'Annunzio, Deledda, Ungaretti, and Quasimodo. Hence Italian is today, as it has always been, a language that makes a special appeal to the intellectuals who are more concerned with the infinite manifestations of the human spirit than with military power or economic supremacy. Italian is strongly recommended to those who aim at a career in any of the arts rather than in the business world.

Italian offers, among the Romance languages, certain decided advantages. It is the language that remains closest to the ancestral Latin, of which it is the most direct descendant, so that one who has studied Latin will probably find it the easiest to assimilate. It is also the language with the most aesthetically pleasing sound scheme, a tongue of sonorous vowels and clear-cut consonants, with few of the phonetic difficulties that beset languages like French and Portuguese.

As against these advantages, there are certain drawbacks. Despite its restricted area, Italian is the language probably most fraught with dialects, some of which diverge to a startling degree from the national standard. It is true that in these days of widespread literacy and mechanical means of imposing a prestige pronunciation (radio, TV, spoken films) the dialects are beating a slow retreat before the standard language, as is the case with our own American English; but they are still far from dead. Also, the grammatical structure of Italian, while quite close to that of the other Romance languages, bunches its main complexities at what to the learner must be the very outset.

In the matter of phonology, Italian presents seven vowel sounds, all clear and uncomplicated by glides, save of a legitimate variety, which the spelling will inform you of. There is, however, the matter of the double value of stressed *e* and *o* (open and closed), which can on occasion confuse the meaning (*pesca,* with the open *e* of *met,* means "peach"; *pesca,* with the closed *e* of the first element of *a* in *gate,* means "fishing"). The precise, easily phonated consonants present the feature of occurring single or doubled, which phonetically means prolonged. This difference is quite audible, and almost invariably such as to cause confusion if it is disregarded, as is the normal tendency for an English speaker (*fato,* "fate"; *fatto,* "done"; *eco,* "echo"; *ecco,* "here is"; etc., all the way down the line). The syllabic structure of Italian, even more than that of French, lends itself to the consonant-vowel pattern, and the English speaker should train himself to syllabify his words carefully, then run up the speed until he is speaking at normal rate, but with the proper syllabic division. The imitation of native speakers and records is, of course, recommended, but it is not so crucial as it is in French.

Occasional divergences of pronunciation arise between Tuscan, and particularly Florentine, which is supposed to be the standard language, and the more cultivated variety of Roman, which is the language of the capital. There is a saying *Lingua toscana in bocca romana,* "a Tuscan tongue in a Roman mouth," but it is possible that this slogan was first put into circulation by the Romans. One feature of pronunciation in which Tuscan differs not only from Roman but from almost all the rest of Italy applies to the sound of written *g* before *e* or *i,* which Tuscan pronounces like the *s* of *pleasure,* and practically everyone else like the *j* of *John.* There is some divergence between Roman and Tuscan in the degree of openness of *e* and *o* in some words: *nome,* "name," NAW-may, NOH-may; *gloria,* "glory," GLAW-ryah, GLOH-ryah; *posto,* "placed," PAWS-toh, POHS-toh; *lettera,* "letter," LAYT-tay-rah, LEHT-tay-rah. The Roman speaker tends to unvoice all *s*'s between vowels, the Tuscan only some of them (*rosa,* RAW-sah, RAW-zah; *casa,* KAH-sah, KAH-zah). Outside of the *g* before front vowels, the differences are barely perceptible to the untrained ear, and linguists tend to minimize them. The real purport of the slogan seems to be that the Tuscans speak more grammatically than the Romans, but the Roman pronunciation falls more pleasantly on the ear. It may be added that when it comes to lower-class speakers, both Florentines and Romans use local dialects which diverge to some extent from the literary language common to the upper classes of both.

A few spelling problems arise. An *h* inserted in writing after *c, g, sc,* indicates velar value before *e* and *i* (*chi, preghi, scheletro,* pronounced KEE, PREH-ghee, SKAY-lay-troh; were the *h* not there, the indicated pronunciation would be CHEE, PREH-jee, SHAY-lay-troh). An inserted *i* between the same consonants and a following *a, o,* or *u* indicates a palatal instead of a velar pronunciation (*ciò, Giacomo, sciopero,* pronounced CHAW, JAH-koh-moh, SHAW-pay-roh). Italian does not indicate by a written accent mark where the stress falls, save in final position (*città*). This can be highly confusing to English speakers. Both Italian and Spanish pronounce RAH-pee-doh, but Spanish gives you a break and spells it *rápido,* Italian spells it *rapido* and tricks you into thinking it's rah-PEE-doh, because English speakers have a mistaken notion that all Italian words are stressed on the penult, which is decidedly not the case. It will therefore be worth while to learn words with their proper stress.

One of the big difficulties of Italian grammar comes right at the outset, with the definite article. As against the four forms of French, Spanish, and Portuguese, Italian has seven, in what might be called euphonic distribution. *Lo* sounds better than *il* before the *sp-* of *specchio* or the *z-* (pronounced *ts-*) of *zio;* therefore it's *il libro, il pane,* but *lo specchio, lo zio,* though the nouns are all masculine singular. *La* is the normal feminine singular, but *l'* is used, as in French, before all singular nouns of either gender beginning with a vowel; so we have *l'amico, l'amica,* but *la donna.* In the plural, it is normally *i* for masculines and *le* for feminines; but *gli* is used instead of *i* before vowels, *s* plus consonant, or *z;* this means *i libri,* but *gli uomini, gli specchi, gli zii.*

To make matters worse, Italian, far more than either French or Spanish, combines the definite article into one word with preceding prepositions. This means that "from the" may be *dal, dalla, dallo, dall', dai, dagli, dalle,* depending not only on gender and number but also on what the next word starts with. Since Italian does this with the six most common prepositions (*a,* "to"; *di,* "of"; *da,* "from, by"; *in,* "in"; *con,* "with"; *su,* "on"), lots of drilling is needed before the learner gets to use the right form in anything like spontaneous fashion. Of course, no irreparable harm will be done if a mistake occurs in this department. It is much more tragic not to make the distinction between single and double consonants, because that can really interfere with the meaning.

For nouns, adjectives, and adverbs, the reader is referred to pp. 150–2. Nothing too unusual happens there, but Italian has, in addition to its two regular classes of nouns, a third class, where the singular is masculine and ends in -*o,* the plural is feminine and ends in -*a* (*il ciglio, le ciglia,* "eyelash"; *il labbro, le labbra,* "lip"). This is a throwback to old Latin second-declension neuters, where the singular ended in -*um* and merged easily with the masculine when the time came to merge, but the plural ended in -*a,* which reminded the speakers of the common feminine ending (*cilium, cilia; labium, labia*). Fortunately, there are not too many of these nouns, though some of them are of frequent occurrence, and a few of them show bewildering double plurals, which carry different meanings (*il muro,* "the wall"; plural *i muri,* "the walls [of a house]," but also *le mura,* "the walls [of a city]").

The Italian subject pronouns are seldom used, save for emphasis. But the third person feminine singular *lei* ("she") can be capitalized and used with a third singular verb as a polite singular "you," whether the person addressed is masculine or feminine.

Object pronouns, such as *mi, ti, ci, vi,* shift to *me, te, ce, ve,* if another object pronoun follows (*mi dà,* "he gives me"; *me lo dà,* "he gives it to me"). In the third person, the direct object forms are *lo, la, li, le,* the indirect object forms are *gli, le,* and, in the plural for both genders, *loro,* which enjoys the special prerogative of always following the verb, while the others normally precede (*lo do loro,* "I give it to them"). Italian has more exceptions than French to the rule that object pronouns come before the verb. Not only the imperative affirmative, but also the infinitive and the gerund may attach the pronoun (*vederlo, parlargli,* "to see him," "to speak to him"; *vedendolo, parlandogli,* "seeing him," "speaking to him"). To make the learner happier, the position is optional if the infinitive or gerund has a governing verb (*voglio vederlo* or *lo voglio vedere,* "I want to see him"; *sto parlandogli* or *gli sto parlando,* "I am speaking to him"). As a final complication, the familiar singular imperative is replaced in the negative by the infinitive (*prendilo,* "take it"; but *non lo prendere,* "don't take it").

Italian uses the same forms for the possessive adjectives and the possessive pronouns, but complicates their use by having them preceded by the article, save under special circumstances (*il mio libro,* "my book," but *mio fratello,* "my brother"; however, *i miei fratelli,* "my brothers"). Italian also merges demonstrative adjective and demonstrative pronoun (basically, *questo* means "this" and *quello* means "that"), but again complicates the picture by giving *quello* seven forms similar to those of the definite article when it is used as an adjective, but only four regular forms when it is used as a pronoun. Chief interrogative pronouns are *chi* for "who?" or "whom?"; *che* (but also *cosa,* or *che cosa*) for "what?"; *quale* for "which?", "which one?" The chief relative pronoun is *che,* which does service for "who," "whom" "which," "that" (*cui* or forms of *il quale* are used after prepositions).

The Italian verb still shows the four basic conjugations of Latin, but with a merger of the second and third, and the setting up of what amounts to a new conjugation with its *-isco* verbs (originally Latin inceptives). Since the personal endings are quite distinct, subject pronouns are rather infrequently used. There are many high-frequency irregular verbs, as in all Romance languages, and these should be learned first at the cost of memorizing them the hard way (particularly recommended are *essere,* "to be," *avere,* "to have," *sapere,* "to know, know how," *andare,* "to go," *dare,* "to give," *dire,* to say, tell," *fare,* "to do, make," *venire,* "to come," *volere,* "to want").

Special points to remember in connection with the Italian verb are:

(a) *-iamo* is universal as a first plural present ending; *-i* is likewise universal in the second singular present indicative.

(b) The stress is normally recessive in the third plural (*párlano, véngono*).

(c) The past definite (or *passato remoto,* or simple past) is frequently used in Italian, concurrently with the past indefinite (or *passato prossimo,* or present perfect), in contrast with what happens in French. In verbs that are irregular in this tense, the irregularity will appear only in the first singular, third singular, and third plural, while the other three persons will normally be quite regular, as though they came from the stem of the infinitive.

(d) As in the other Romance tongues, the conditional always follows any irregularity that may appear in the future.

(e) Compound tenses are formed far more often with "to be" than they are in French. Even "to be" is conjugated with "to be" (*sono stato,* "I have been," literally "I am been"). It is almost safe to assert that any intransitive verb (one that cannot take a direct object) is in Italian conjugated with "to be" (*sono riuscito;* French *j'ai réussi,* "I have succeeded").

(f) The participle used with "to be" agrees with the subject (*le ragazze sono andate via,* "the girls went away"). The past participle used with "to have" *may* agree with the direct object, but *must* do so only if the direct object is a *personal* pronoun that precedes the verb (*li ho visti,* "I saw them"; but *i libri che ho visti* or *visto,* "the books that I saw").

(g) Unlike French, but like Spanish, Portuguese, and English, Italian has a fully operative progressive conjugation (*sto parlando,* "I am speaking"). The verb used, however, is *stare,* not *essere* (by itself, *stare* means "to stand, to be [in a certain position, location or condition]"). The point in all three Romance languages is that, while the English progressive may at any time be translated by the Italian, Spanish, or Portuguese progressive, these languages do not use the progressive as much as we do. "He is doing" is just as often *fa* as *sta facendo.*

(h) The Italian passive is formed, as in English and the other Romance languages, by using "to be" with the past participle; but no Romance language is as fond of the passive construction as we are. The favorite French replacement, as we have seen, is *on* with the active. The favorite Italian, Spanish, and Portuguese replacement is the reflexive ("Italian is spoken here": *ici on parle italien; qui si parla italiano; aquí se habla italiano; aqui fala-se italiano;* the reflexive, by the way, takes as its auxiliary "to be," as in French, not "to have," as in English, Spanish, or Portuguese). Italian has, however, another replacement that does not appear in the other Romance languages, and that is often used when there is a real action rather than a general state of affairs: *venire,* "to come," with the past participle (*venne ucciso dal suo avversario,* "he was killed by his opponent," literally, "he came killed"; note the difference between *la casa è costruita in marmo,* "the house is built of marble," and *la casa viene costruita in marmo,* "the house is being built of marble").

(i) The subjunctive is fully alive and kicking in Italian, as in Spanish and Portuguese, not half dead, as in English. It has four tenses, clearly distinguishable endings, and fairly precise rules for its use. You will be perfectly understood if you use an indicative for a subjunctive, but your ignorance will show.

Italian syntax is of the elastic, permissive variety. In no other Romance language are there as many alternative constructions to choose from. Verbs that in other languages definitely compel you to use the subjunctive may in Italian often be construed either way. This elasticity is delightful to the native, and makes for fine literary nuances, but can often be bewildering to the foreign learner, who would prefer ironbound rules. One of Italy's best grammars of Italian for Italians, after trying to account rationally for certain involved alternative constructions, gives up and says: "The creative speaker or writer will know instinctively what to use." This is not too much comfort, however, to one who approaches the language from the outside. Nevertheless, foreign students of Italian are inclined to forgive the language, as one is inclined to forgive a capricious but beautiful woman.

The Italian vocabulary, more than any other, is close to the original Latin, with relatively few changes of sound and even fewer changes of spelling. This is perhaps why medieval Italians referred to their language not as Italian but simply *il Volgare,* "the popular tongue," and why Dante insisted that it was just Latin without the rules of grammar. This beautiful state of affairs, which applies to the official Tuscan and the central dialects generally, is far from applying to the popular speech forms of the North and South, some of which show sound transformations from Latin that outstrip those of French, while a few are even more conservative than the literary language. Italian, more than any other tongue, has the habit of running off to papa any time it needs a new word, and appropriating it straight from Latin. This it has been in the habit of doing ever since the early Middle Ages, and the result is that the literary language, at least, is replete with what the linguists call "learned" borrowings, the inkhorn terms, or aureate words, of sixteenth-, seventeenth- and eighteenth-century English. But in Italian they are in their proper setting, and sound altogether natural. One of the latest manifestations of this tendency is Gadda's recently translated book *That Ugly Mess on Merulana Street.* What Gadda needs, or thinks he needs, and can't find in the Italian dictionary, he coins for himself out of his Latin-Greek background, and his creations sound altogether plausible, at least in the original.

Italian, in conclusion, calls for perhaps less vocal exertion of the imitation-repetition type and more initial grammar drill than any other Romance tongue. As a language, it is definitely on the intellectual rather than the material side, and it is no wonder that it made the tremendous appeal it did to English writers, from Chaucer to Shakespeare and beyond. In the century of mechanization, it has fallen somewhat behind, but it is still a tongue divinely suited for an aristocracy of artistic, musical, literary, religious, philosophical, and even scientific thinkers.

2 I

Can You Learn Spanish and Portuguese at Once?

Extent and History of the Hispanic Tongues—The Written Languages—Conflicting Orthographies—The Eye Is the Enemy of the Ear in Portuguese—A Point-by-Point Comparison—An Archaic and a Modern Grammar

SPANISH is the foreign language American learners believe in most, as evidenced by high school and college registration figures. By the same token, Portuguese is the major language they believe in least, or of whose existence they are most unaware. Worse yet, they show by unerring signs that they want to stay that way. One person out of ten, roughly, knows that Portuguese, not Spanish, is the language of Brazil. Even those who know shrug their shoulders and figure Portuguese is only a dialect of Spanish, and that if you speak the one to the speakers of the other you'll be understood.

To a certain extent, they are right. Portuguese speakers generally manage, with some difficulty, to understand what is said to them in Spanish. But they don't like it. Also, your Spanish ear will help you little, if at all, in understanding spoken Portuguese. But more of this later.

These two great languages together hold practically full sway over the entire Western Hemisphere once you go south of El Paso or Key West. Spanish is the official tongue of an impressive number of nations: in North and Central America, Mexico, Guatemala, Nicaragua, Honduras, El Salvador, Costa Rica, Panama; in the Antilles, Cuba, the Dominican Republic, Puerto Rico; on the South American continent, Colombia, Venezuela, Ecuador, Peru (here Spanish alone is official, but 31 per cent of the population speaks nothing but Quechua), Bolivia, Paraguay (here Guaraní is co-official with Spanish), Uruguay, Chile, Argentina. In addition, Spanish is the language of Spain and the Balearic Islands (including the Costa Brava and Mallorca so beloved of American tourists and writers), of a few rather insignificant Spanish colonies in Africa, of the Canary Islands. It is still widespread in the Philippines, though Spanish domination there ceased with the Spanish-American War at the beginning of this century. It is widespread in some of our southwestern and northeastern states, such as New Mexico (where it is co-official with English), Arizona, California, and the entire metropolitan area of New York City (where it has recently been made semiofficial, at least for purposes of voter registration). Recent figures indicate that well over a million Spanish speakers (Puerto Ricans, but also Cubans, Dominicans, and other Latin Americans) live in Greater New York and nearby New Jersey. Miami and Florida generally have of late received a large influx of Cuban exiles. The total number of Spanish speakers is estimated at somewhere in the vicinity of 160 million.

The speaking population and distribution of Portuguese is only slightly less impressive. Outside of Brazil, which by itself contains half the population of South America, and the Portuguese homeland in the Iberian Peninsula, there are Portuguese possessions like Angola, Mozambique, and Portuguese Guinea in Africa, the Azores, Madeira and other Atlantic islands, even Portuguese Timor and Macao in Asia, along with Indian coastal cities like Goa, Damau and Diu, which now form part of India. The total number of Portuguese speakers is about 100 million.

The two languages developed and grew up in close contact in the Iberian Peninsula, but while official Spanish is basically a development of medieval Castilian, Portuguese comes from another medieval dialect of the peninsula, Galician, which is still spoken in the region of Vigo, Coruña, and Santiago de Compostela. The two dialects were both current in the part of Spain that escaped the Moorish conquest, and both were used at the medieval courts. As the Reconquest unfolded, Portuguese differentiated itself from Galician and became the official tongue of the western part of the peninsula, while Castilian, crowding out other medieval dialects such as Leonese and Aragonese, became official everywhere else. The Andalusian of the south, from which most Spanish American varieties seem to have taken their main traits, is an outgrowth of Castilian mingled with the mysterious, largely unwritten Mozarabic of the Christian populations that lived on under the Moors until they were liberated by their fellow Christians from the north.

Spanish today, in its spoken forms, is a language almost as fraught with dialects as is English. In addition to the Castilian and Andalusian of Spain, there are Mexican, Antillean, Colombian, Central South American, and Argentinian-Chilean versions. But the written version is basically the same, and it has been so scientifically regularized by the Spanish Academy that it presents fewer difficulties to the outsider than any other Romance language, at least at the outset. Also, it is among the Romance languages the one that presents the greatest coincidence between speech and writing. It is a moot question among linguists whether these features of initial ease or the undisputed commercial, political, and literary merits of Spanish contribute most to its popularity in American high schools and colleges.

Portuguese, in its written form, presents greater similarities to Spanish than to any of the other Romance tongues. This similarity extends to grammatical forms, syntax, and to a considerable degree, vocabulary. It does not at all extend to sound schemes. Spanish is a language of clear, uncomplicated sounds (only five full-fledged vowel sounds, and consonant sounds for most of which there is a reasonable approximation in English; exceptions are *b* or *v* between vowels, which indicate a bilabial, not a dentolabial *v*-sound; the slightly trilled *r* and strongly trilled *rr;* the *g* before *e* and *i* and the *j,* pronounced as a strongly articulated unvoiced velar spirant, like the *ch* of Scottish *loch*). But Portuguese shows extensive differences between stressed and unstressed vowels, pronouncing the first clearly, to the point of drawling them, while the latter are slurred and indistinct. In addition, Portuguese nasalizes vowels not only where nasalization is indicated by a *til* over the vowel (*ã, õ*), or by a following *m* in the same syllable (*em, um*), but even where there is no indication in orthography or justification in etymology (*muito,* pronounced MõoY-too). Portuguese rejects the common Spanish diphthongs *ie* and *ue,* but has two frequent ones of its own (*ou, ei*). It still has the sounds of *sh* and *s* in *pleasure,* which Spanish merged into the unvoiced velar spirant *j* at a relatively recent date (at the time when Cervantes wrote *Don Quijote,* it was still spelled *Quixote* and pronounced kee-SHOH-tay, as indicated by English *quixotic* and French and Italian *Quichotte, Chisciotte*). Portuguese still has the sound of English *z,* which Spanish changed to the unvoiced *s* of *house* (*casa* is good written Spanish and written Portuguese, but Spanish pronounces it

KAH-sah, Portuguese KAH-zuh). Both languages have the sounds of *ni* in *onion* and *lli* in *million,* but Spanish uses the spellings *ñ* and *ll,* Portuguese *nh* and *lh;* furthermore, they seldom appear in the same words. A final *s* in Spanish can go all the way from the strong apical sound of Castilian, which is practically a hiss, to the evanescent *h* of the Antilles (*lah casah* for *las casas*); in Portuguese a final *s* can come out as *sh, s* of *pleasure,* or *z,* depending on what follows.

In the matter of spoken-language accentuation, the two languages generally go together. In writing, both subscribe to a convention that words ending in vowels, *s,* or *n* (*m* in Portuguese) are regularly stressed on the penult; otherwise, stress is on the final; and any deviation is marked by an acute accent. The same accent mark is also used when you want to break up what would otherwise be a diphthong. But trouble arises as to what constitutes a diphthong, which from the Spanish point of view is any *a, e,* or *o* preceded or followed by *i* or *u.* But the Portuguese don't believe this. The result is that you get Spanish *frío* and *agua* vs. Portuguese *frio* and *água.* Portuguese also uses acute and circumflex accent marks (occasionally even grave) to indicate open or closed pronunciation of vowels, which Spanish never does.

All this can be slightly bewildering in writing, as you switch from one language to the other. It is infinitely more bewildering in speech. Lastly, Portuguese, in its historical development from Latin, got into the habit of dropping *n*'s and *l*'s between vowels, with the result that a word like Spanish *generales* takes in Portuguese the form *geraes,* and the well-known *luna* of Latin, Italian, and Spanish becomes *lua.* In conclusion, while Spanish and Portuguese speakers, living in close contact, have developed a partial comprehension of each other's languages, you, as an English-speaking learner, have not, and it is altogether hopeless for you to try to understand one exclusively through the medium of the other. The best advice that can be given for the spoken languages is, as usual, to learn them separately and in isolation, from native speakers or recordings.

This is not altogether necessary for the written languages. The grammatical structures are similar, though Portuguese shows in spots a remarkable archaism, using medieval forms that Spanish has long since discarded, while Spanish shows a simplification of grammatical forms which is in part artificially and almost scientifically contrived. The general structure of articles, nouns, adjectives, and adverbs has already been described (see pp. 150–2). But while Spanish has the definite articles *el, la, los, las,* and combines them with preceding prepositions only sparingly (*al, del*), Portuguese has *o, a, os, as,* and makes almost as many combinations as Italian ("of the," for example, is *do, da, dos, das;* "to the" is *ao, à, aos, às;* "in the" is *no, na, nos, nas*). In fact, Portuguese goes Italian one better in certain other respects, such as indefinite articles and demonstrative adjectives ("in a" is *num, numa;* "of that" is *daquêle*). While both languages have the customary three noun classes, with the same endings (*-o, -os* for masculines, *-a, -as* for feminines, *-e* or consonant, *-es* for nouns of either gender), the Portuguese fondness for nasals and tendency to drop *n* and *l* between vowels lead to numerous irregular forms (*nação,* plural *nações, espanhol,* plural *espanhois,* where Spanish has *nación, naciones, español, españoles*).

In the matter of subject pronouns, Spanish behaves largely like Italian, omitting them save for emphasis; but Portuguese retains a medieval rule, which the other languages once had, that you cannot start the sentence with an unstressed object pronoun; therefore, where Spanish says *me conoce* ("he knows me"), Portuguese has to say either *conhece-me* or *êle me conhece.* This in turn leads to greater elasticity in Portuguese in the matter of object pronouns, which in Spanish, as in Italian, is firmly set before the verb, save in the affirmative imperative, infinitive, and gerund.

Spanish, like French, has different forms for the possessive adjective and the possessive pronoun (*mi libro,* but *su libro y el mío*). Portuguese, like Italian, uses the same forms in both connections, and often uses the article even with the adjective (*o meu relojo,* "my watch," vs. Spanish *mi reloj*). But Spanish and Portuguese go together with Classical Latin in using the same forms for "their," "theirs" that are used for "his," "her," "hers," "its" (French and Italian developed late Vulgar forms from Latin *illorum,* "of them": *leur, leurs, loro*).

Both languages use the same forms for demonstrative adjectives and demonstrative pronouns, though Spanish makes a halfhearted attempt at distinguishing between them by writing unneeded accents over the pronouns (*este libro,* but *mi libro y éste*). Both languages make a threefold distinction of distance, like Middle English *this, that* (near you) and *yon* (removed from both speaker and person addressed; Spanish *este, ese, aquel;* Portuguese *êste, êsse, aquêle*). Both languages use similar relative and interrogative pronouns ("who," "whom," "which," "that," *que;* "whom" after prepositions, Spanish *quien,* Portuguese *quem;* "whose," Spanish *cuyo,* Portuguese *cujo;* "who?", "whom?", Spanish *¿quién?, ¿a quién?,* Portuguese *quem?;* "which?", "which one?", Spanish *¿cuál?,* Portuguese *qual?;* "which ones?" Spanish *¿cuáles?,* Portuguese *quais?*)

A couple of minor orthographic differences are illustrated above. Spanish, in questions and exclamations, uses an inverted question or exclamation mark at the beginning of the written utterance, and uses an unneeded accent mark to differentiate the interrogative or exclamatory use from the relative. Portuguese uses neither of these convenient devices, which are like signal flags. Therefore, "who spoke?" is in Spanish *¿Quién habló?,* in Portuguese *Quem falou?*

Spanish uses the preposition *a* not only before indirect object nouns but also before direct object nouns which are both definite and personal; this Portuguese does not do. Therefore, "I see my brother" is in Spanish *veo a mi hermano;* in Portuguese *vejo(o)meu irmão.*

In the matter of verbs, both languages have the same system of three conjugations, having transferred the Latin third to the Latin second (*-ar, -er, -ir*). Both have similar forms and a similar scheme of tenses. But there are a few startling differences:

(a) Spanish is like English in invariably using "to have" as an active auxiliary. So is Portuguese. But whereas the verb "to have" used as an auxiliary in Spanish is *haber* (*tener,* which also means "to have," is used largely to indicate possession), Portuguese uses *ter* in both functions. Therefore, "I have spoken" is *he hablado* in Spanish, but *tenho falado* in Portuguese. It will be recalled that French and, particularly, Italian often use "to be" as an auxiliary for active intransitive verbs. Spanish and Portuguese never do. This means that "I have gone" is *je suis allé* in French, *sono andato* in Italian, but *he ido* in Spanish, *tenho ido* in Portuguese.

(b) Like Italian, but unlike French, Spanish and Portuguese use conversationally both the simple past ("I loved") and the compound past ("I have loved"). Spanish, in fact, even joins English in preferring the first to the second, saying *comí esta mañana,* just as English says "I ate this morning" rather than "I have eaten." Here French would use exclusively "I have eaten," and Italian would prefer it by far, save in certain dialect areas, like Sicily.

(c) "To be," which is *ser* or *estar* in both languages, is used as an auxiliary only for the passive. The past participle used with *ser* or *estar* agrees with the subject. In all other forms, including the reflexive, both Spanish and Portuguese use "to have" (though one is *haber,* the other *ter*), and the past participle never changes from its base masculine singular form. So "the women I have seen" is in French *les femmes que j'ai vues,* in Italian *le donne che ho viste* (or *visto*), but in Spanish *las mujeres que he visto,* in Portuguese *as mulheres que tenho visto.*

(d) Unlike what happens with the two verbs that mean "to have" (*haber, tener* in Spanish; *haber, ter* in Portuguese), both languages use both their verbs "to be" (*ser, estar*) the same way. *Ser* is used if a predicate noun follows or if the quality indicated by the following predicate adjective is viewed as permanent or inherent. *Estar* indicates a quality viewed as temporary, and is also used, as in Italian, for location and state of health. French, which has merged the two verbs, has only *être.* "He is a doctor" is *il est médecin* in French, *è medico* in Italian, *es médico* in Spanish, *é médico* in Portuguese. "He is tired" is *il est fatigué, è stanco,* but *está cansado.* "He is in Rome" is *il est à Rome, è* (or *sta*) *a Roma, está en* (*em*) *Roma.* Spanish, Portuguese, and Italian use *estar* (*stare*) with the gerund to form a progressive conjugation similar to that of English, "he is speaking": *sta parlando, está hablando, está falando* (but Portuguese uses alternatively *está a falar*); French does not: *il parle.*

(e) Portuguese has a "personal" infinitive, and retains two archaic subjunctive tenses which Spanish once had but later discarded, future and future perfect. This confers upon Portuguese a certain freedom of action which is absent in the other tongues. "I left after they had spoken," which has to be translated more or less literally in French, Italian, and Spanish, can be in Portuguese *parti depois de terem falado,* literally, "I left after to-have-they spoken." The two extra subjunctive tenses give Portuguese the possibility of distinguishing between "I fear he is coming (right at this moment)" and "I fear he will come (tomorrow)," or between "if he were leaving (right now), we would know it" and "if he were to leave (tomorrow), we would know it."

The true difficulty of the Iberian languages, and particularly of Spanish, where it is in strong contrast with initial ease of pronunciation and basic grammar, lies in the involved syntax of the literary language. The rules of word order can be delightfully vague, and left to the discretion of the creative writer or speaker. It frequently happens that the subject is where you least expect it, at the very end of a five-line sentence. Subordinate clauses, even main clauses, can follow a word order which seems illogical to speakers of more strait-jacketed tongues, such as English or French. The translator from Spanish into English must often rearrange not only his words but his entire line of thought, almost as much as if he were translating from Latin. There are delicate shades of emphasis indicated by word order. The title of a Spanish-language film appears as *Vuelven los García,* "The Garcias stage a comeback," to put it into semantically equivalent English. It would be just as grammatically legitimate to say *Los García vuelven;* but it would not carry the movement, the breathless suspense that is betokened by the inversion of subject and verb. *¿Para esto van a servir los adelantos de nuestra civilización?* ("Is all the progress of our civilization going to wind up like this?") But the literally translated word order says: "For this are going to serve the advances of our civilization?" The semantic stress is on *para esto,* and that is placed first, as it would have been in Latin, not last, as in English. This explains why the very same American students who find Spanish so easy in the first year often find it extremely difficult in its higher reaches, while those who overcame the greater initial difficulties of French find relatively smooth going in the later years of a language where the syntax and style are comparatively fixed.

In the matter of vocabulary, it is of course true that Spanish and Portuguese, having grown up together on the Iberian Peninsula, with common influences that start with the ancient Iberians and go on to the Romans, the Visigoths, and the Moors, have more in common than either has with Italian or French. But anyone who thinks there is free lexical transfer from one language to the other is in for strange surprises. Not only are there words where either language, for arbitrary reasons, joins Italian, or even French, rather than its Iberian partner; it is also a question of each of the two exercising its right of free choice. Spanish *ventana* and Portuguese *janela* for "window" are both of Latin origin; but one has to do with the wind, the other with Rome's two-headed god of doorways, Janus, who also gives us January, facing back on the old year and forward on the new at the same time. *Aduana* and *alfândega,* "customhouse," are both Arabic; but one has to do with the *diwwan,* or divan, the symbol of the sultan's power, the other with the storehouse, where goods are taken for inspection. The same goes for "ill" (*enfermo, doente,* both Latin, one related to our *infirm,* the other to our *dolent*); "yesterday," (*ayer, ontem*); "office" (*despacho, escritório*), "bottle" (*botella, garrafa*), "to forget" (*olvidar, esquecer*); "knife" (*cuchillo, faca*), "lettuce" (*lechuga, alface*). And this could go on and on and on. My friend and colleague Professor Alexander Prista, a little nettled by the remark of a student that if you knew *written* Spanish you knew written Portuguese, however much the spoken languages might differ, once composed a highly plausible two-page letter in the two languages where each and every word, with the exception of a few indispensable prepositions, like *a, de* and *para,* differed completely in the two languages.

There is also the matter of idioms and clichés, which can be subtly different, like the delightful *estou a experimentar* (literally, "I'm experimenting"; actually, "I'm trying") of the Lisbon operator who was trying to get me a connection; or the *Pode darme as horas?,* "Can you give me the hours?", which stumped me momentarily, even after I had gained fairly fluent command of Portuguese, because I was accustomed to the more usual *Que horas são?* for "What time is it?" Best of all, after I had become quite fluent in the language, was a beggar's query. In transcription it sounded like this: PAWD DAHR-muh-ũh shtõw-ZEE-nyoo? The first three words were clear enough: "Can you give me a ——?" But what kind of money did he want? I wormed it out of him. A coin, corresponding to the English farthing, or our mill, was slangily called *testão* ("big forehead") because it used to bear on one side the imprint of an *infante* of Portugal who had a high and prominent forehead (note, by the way, that *testa* means "forehead" in Portuguese, "head" in Italian). To this form, the Lisbonese, with their love of diminutives, had tacked on the ending

-inho, making it *testãozinho,* "little big forehead." Then came initial apheresis, with loss of the first syllable; what was left, *'stãozinho,* was what I had heard. In Spain, they might have called an equivalent coin *perro chico,* "little dog." It is not enough to know the language. One must also know the customs, the historical background, and, above all, the popular local slang forms. Otherwise, you remain a foreigner. But this is not too bad, so long as you can understand (more or less) and be understood.

The final verdict on Spanish and Portuguese at once is no for the spoken languages, yes (with qualifications) for the written. Possession of both will give you access to practically one person out of ten throughout the world, and both Spanish and Portuguese speakers are people well worth knowing.

22

How Can You Learn German?

Common Origin of German and English—Where They Diverged —The Word Stock and Where It Differs—German Grammatical Forms and Word Order—The Special Problems of German for an English Speaker

AMONG the foreign tongues popular in America, the one which is in many ways closest to our own is seldom rated the easiest to learn. For this there are excellent historical reasons.

English and German are not merely both members of the big Indo-European family. They are not merely both members of the Germanic or Teutonic branch of that family. They even belong to the same sub-branch, the West Germanic (as set apart from the North Germanic or Scandinavian, and from the East Germanic, represented by Gothic, which is extinct). Back in the days of King Alfred, there was undoubtedly as much linguistic transfer from Anglo-Saxon to Old High German as there is today from Italian to Spanish.

But then history got in the way. Old High German, the mountain dialects of Switzerland, Austria, Bavaria, and what today is southern Germany, was undergoing a slow transformation of its own whereby the *t* of *water* and *better* was turning into the *ss* of *Wasser* and *besser,* the *d* and *p* of *dapper* into the *t* and *pf* of *tapfer,* while nothing of the sort was occurring in the seacoast German dialects from which Anglo-Saxon had sprung, or in Anglo-Saxon itself. But this in itself would probably not have broken spoken-language communication between the High and the Low West Germanic sub-sub-branches. The big changes came over English while it was still Old English or Anglo-Saxon.

For one thing, there came to Alfred's England great Danish invasions, which he adroitly turned into permanent settlements involving a merger (what we would today style integration) of Saxons and Danes. The languages merged, too. The Danes were Scandinavians, and spoke a North Germanic tongue close enough to West Germanic

186

Anglo-Saxon to blend with it rather easily, different enough to impart to it a highly distinctive flavor. The merger meant for Anglo-Saxon giving up large numbers of West Germanic words closely linked to the words of Old High German, words like *niman* (German *nehmen*), *snithan* (German *schneiden;* but we still speak of a *snide* or cutting remark); *heo* or *hie* (German *sie*); *wolcan* (German *Wolke;* but we still make the *welkin* ring); *sindon* (German *sind*), and replacing them with Scandinavian *take, cut, they, sky, are.* Other English borrowings from Scandinavian which do not appear in German include *die, leg, knife, trust, want, window, ill, low, call, get, same, though, till, both, husband, skin, hit, happy, ugly, wrong.* Still others, where English has retained the Anglo-Saxon form side by side with the imported Scandinavian are *no—nay; rear—raise; from—fro; shirt—skirt; whole—hale; shell—skull.* To what extent Scandinavian may have contributed to the English sound scheme is partly a matter of conjecture; it is a fact, however, that English and the Scandinavian languages, particularly Danish, have in common certain vowel and dipththong sounds which do not appear in German.

Strong as was the Danish influence in weaning English away from its ancestral West Germanic, it does not even begin to compare with what the French-speaking Normans of 1066 did to our language. Innumerable words poured into English from French in the course of the centuries that intervened between the Battle of Hastings and the days of Chaucer. Some of them dealt with the law and the structure of government (*bar, judge, proof, bail, fine, fraud, heir, tax, court, state, crown*). Others had to do with warfare (*siege, host, lance, peace*). Many dealt with cookery (*boil, taste, beef, veal, pork, toast, cream, fruit, stew, fry, plate*); others with religion (*pray, clerk, dean, saint, faith, preach*); still others with courtly living and attire (*duke, count, page, sir, porch, park, chair, gown, dress, boot*). There were some that were concerned with the emotions (*pain, grief, joy, rage*). Others are hard to classify (*pen, air, cost, noise, pair, piece, sound, seem, chief, firm, large, nice, poor, real, safe, sure, change, close, cry, move, please, pass, pay, push, quit, catch, chase, voice*). Of special interest are those words which French itself had borrowed from the Germanic tongue of the Franks and now passed on to English with a Romance veneer that disguised their true origin (*seize, pledge, spy, guard, rank, robe, coat, fur, screen, rob, wait, roast*).

It may have been noticed that the words selected as typical of importation from the French of the Normans are all, without exception, monosyllabic. We have deliberately set out to do this, to counter the common, erroneous impression that all or most monosyllabic words in English are Teutonic.

At a later period, English continued to import words from French (French was the language of the English court, clergy, and nobility for almost four centuries, and during this period far more writing was done on English soil in French than in English). Nothing like this happened on the Continent in German-speaking lands, where the Teutonic element continued to prevail in the vocabulary. Still later, in the age of Chaucer and down to the Elizabethan period, English was a much heavier borrower than German from other Romance languages, notably Italian, as well as from Renaissance Latin and Greek.

For all these reasons, the learner does not find in German the similarities and the help from his native English that he would like to find. Again, languages are strongly individualistic. Even where English and German show the same roots and words, there is no guarantee that they will be similarly used. Beyond words of an utterly literal nature, such as *Brot* and *Wasser, Fleisch* and *Feuer, Vater* and *Bruder, sehen* and *hören, sprechen* and *kommen, gehen* and *leben, kalt* and *warm,* there lies a whole region of slightly more abstract elements that coincide only in part—enough to throw you off the beam. *Land* is "land"; it is also "country," as opposed to "city." *See* can be "lake" as well as "sea." *Stadt* is not "state," but "city." *Wagen* can be "wagon," but also "car," of the railroad or automotive variety. *Rechnung* is "reckoning," but we would hardly ask the restaurant waiter for our reckoning. As often as not, we find far more similarity for English in a Romance than in a Germanic vocabulary.

Again, in the matter of grammar German has retained the old Teutonic setup far more than English has, with the result that while it would have been easy to translate word for word from Anglo-Saxon into Old High German, there is no such easy approach to modern German for a modern English speaker.

All this is not said to discourage the English-speaking learner, but to give him a realistic bird's-eye view of the difficulties he will encounter. On the other hand, there is no reason in the world why he should not take advantage of the very real aids that common origin of the two languages affords him. There is the basic vocabulary similarity, coupled with the easy shifts of consonants from one language to the other when both use the same word. It is not too hard to remember that where English has *d* and *th,* you are justified in expecting German *t* and *d;* that English *t* will generally appear in German as *z* initially, *ss* in other positions; that where English has *y* or *w,* German will often have *g;* that English *v* between vowels will normally correspond to German *b.*

These, of course, are written-language exercises. For spoken German, the customary advice is in order. Imitate and repeat after a native speaker or a set of good records. The sounds of German are not too difficult for an English speaker. Both languages make a distinction between long and short vowels. What the English learner should remember to do is to cut off the glides that so often appear as appendages on English vowel sounds, and to leave the vowel, so to speak, pure. *So* is good English and good German. But English pronounces the *s* unvoiced, and gives the *o* a final glide that makes it rhyme with the *ow* of *low.* German cuts off that glide, and only the "pure" *o*-sound is heard (German also voices the initial *s,* so that it sounds like *z*). German, like French, has front rounded vowels, indicated in writing by umlaut marks (*ü, ö*); shape the lips for *boot, boat,* then try to say *beet, bait.* The only German consonant sounds for which there is no immediate approximation in English are the ones indicated in writing by *ch.* Here German has two different sounds, which depend not on what follows, but on what precedes. If *ch* is preceded by *a, o, u,* the sound is the unvoiced velar spirant of Scottish *loch* (no trouble here; most Americans pronounce the name of Bach quite correctly). If *ch* is preceded by *e, i, ä, ö, ü, äu, eu* or a consonant, the nearest approximation is the *h* of *huge;* the sound is technically described as a palatal unvoiced spirant; the breath is forced with audible friction through an opening consisting of the hard palate and the groove of the tongue. German *r* can be uvular, as in French, or trilled, as in Italian or Spanish. *S* at the beginning of a word or between vowels is usually a *z*-sound; but initially, before *t* and *p,* it is usually a *sh*-sound; in final position, it is always unvoiced, like *-ss* in English *less.* German written *z,* and *ti* before a vowel is *ts.* Written *w* is *v,* written *v* is *f,* written *sch* is *sh,* written *j* is *y;* written *ei* is like *i* in English *mine,* written *ie* is like *i* in English *machine;* written *äu* and *eu* are the *oi* of *toil.* Word-final consonants, even if voiced in writing (*b, d, g*), are unvoiced in speech (*p, t, k*). German orthographic peculiarities include the capitalization of all common nouns; exclamation marks in commands and at the beginning of letters; commas to set off subordinate clauses. German stress, like English, is initial, save for a few prefixes (like English *be-* in *become* or *mis-* in *mistake*), and foreign loan words, which are less numerous in German than in English.

The German grammatical structure is a little more difficult than the Romance for an English speaker, primarily because German grammars perpetuate a half-myth about a German case system. Actually, the case system shows up to best advantage in such forms as articles and demonstrative or possessive adjectives rather than in nouns. But German has other complications. There are three genders, as in English, but they don't at all coincide with ours. Males are generally masculine and females feminine (but with startling exceptions: "woman," "girl," "Miss" are neuter, the last two with the justification that they have diminutive endings, and that all diminutives are grammatically neuter). The real trouble comes with inanimate objects, which can be anything: "fork" is feminine, "spoon" is masculine, "knife" is neuter. Endings occasionally help, but only occasionally. Abstract nouns are generally feminine, and certain endings are almost invariably so: *-heit, -schaft, -ung, -nis;* but *-tum* is generally neuter. Nouns ending in *-e* are often feminine, but there are many exceptions. All in all, the best advice that can be given the learner is to acquire his nouns with their appropriate articles (*der, die* or *das*), which tell the story, and thereafter keep a firm grip on the articles. Plurals fall into several distinct classes: *-e, -er, -en,* some that are unchanged from the singular, others where the only change is the umlauting of the root vowel (like *Bruder,* plural *Brüder*), still others where *-e* or *-er* and umlaut are combined (*Fuss, Füsse*). The only remedy here is to learn the noun in double form, singular and plural. The cases, on the other hand, can be rather neatly pigeonholed, at least for what concerns nouns. The genitive singular of masculines and neuters takes an *-s* (*-es* is usually optional if the noun is monosyllabic); the dative singular of monosyllabic masculine and neuter nouns may likewise take an *-e.* Feminine nouns don't change in the singular. A few masculines in *-e* change to *-en* in genitive, dative, and accusative, but they can be separately learned. In the plural, once you have mastered the nominative form, the only other thing you have to do is to add *-n* in the dative if an *-n* is not already there. This means that in memorizing nouns all you have to do is learn the noun in its nominative singular form with its appropriate article, its genitive singular ending, if any, and its nominative plural form.

But articles, definite and indefinite, show a full-fledged declensional scheme, as do also possessives and demonstratives. Other adjectives go through a threefold incarnation. They are invariable, and show base form, if used as predicate adjectives. If they are attributive, they go through two sets of endings, one "strong," or more distinctive and varied, if there is no preceding word, such as a definite article, or a possessive or demonstrative, which itself has a strong ending; the other "weak," or less complicated, if there is a preceding "strong" word. To illustrate: in *ein guter Mann,* "a good man," *ein* has no distinctive ending; therefore the adjective *gut* must take a strong ending, *-er,* which indicates masculine singular nominative; in *der gute Mann,* "the good man," the article has the distinctive *-er,* so the adjective can relax and take a weak ending; in *der Mann ist gut,* "the man is good," the adjective is predicate, and therefore in base form, with no ending whatsoever. Anglo-Saxon used to have exactly the same sort of arrangement; but English speakers got tired of complexities, and reduced all adjectives to an invariable form in any position.

The comparative and superlative of adjectives are formed, as in English, with *-er* (*-r*) and *-est* (*-st*); but remember that declensional endings must then be appended, as outlined above. "Old" is *alt;* but "an older man" would have to be *ein älterer Mann;* the first *-er-* in *älterer* is the comparative suffix, the second *-er* is the strong nominative masculine singular ending, called for by the fact that *ein* has no distinctive ending of its own. "The older man" would be *der ältere Mann,* with comparative suffix *-er-* and weak declensional *-e* (note also that many adjectives umlaut the root vowel when comparative-superlative suffixes are added; English does the same in "old," "elder," but the practice is not as widespread as in German).

By way of compensation for these complexities, German permits you to use the plain, uninflected adjective as an adverb, so that *schön* may mean both "beautiful" and "beautifully."

Subject pronouns are fully used in German, as in English, despite the fact that verb forms are distinctive. *Du,* "thou," with second person singular verb, is still currently used in German for familiar address. The polite form of address is *sie,* "they," capitalized in writing, and used with the third person plural of the verb, even though "you" is singular. Possessives and demonstratives show strong similarities to their English counterparts, but are fully declined; if used as pronouns, they usually take the definite article, which means weak endings. Most common relative pronoun is *der,* which is declined somewhat similarly to the definite article, and means "who," "whom," "which," "that." Most common interrogative pronouns are *was?,* "what?"; *wer* (*wessen, wem, wen*), "who," "whose," "to whom," "whom." *Welch,* "which," is both interrogative and relative.

German verbs fall, as in English, into two general classes, weak (or regular) and strong (irregular). As a rule, if a verb is weak (or strong) in English, its German counterpart will likewise be weak (or strong). As in English, there are only two simple tenses, present and past; all other tenses are formed with auxiliaries. The German verb has clearly defined personal endings, but appears regularly with a subject pronoun. Several strong verbs undergo a vowel change in the second and third persons singular of the present indicative, along with the general vowel change in the past and past participle. This means that where the English basic forms are three (*speak, spoke, spoken*), German shows four (*sprechen, spricht, sprach, gesprochen*).

The following points of verb use are important:

(a) Like French, but unlike English, Italian, Spanish, and Portuguese, German has no progressive forms: use *er spricht* for both "he speaks" and "he is speaking."

(b) Perfect tenses are formed, as in English, with "to have" (*haben*). But German, like French and Italian, conjugates several verbs with "to be" (*sein*), including, like Italian but unlike French, even "to be" itself: *ich bin gegangen,* "I have gone"; *ich bin gewesen,* "I have been."

(c) *Werden,* basically "to become," is used as an auxiliary for both the future-conditional system and for the passive. But for the future and conditional, it is combined with the infinitive (*ich werde sprechen,* "I shall speak"; *ich würde sprechen,* "I would speak"); for the passive, it is combined with the past participle (*ich werde geliebt,* "I am loved"; *das Wort wurde gesprochen,* "the word was spoken").

(d) The German subjunctive is fully alive, and has six tenses. The rules for its use differ considerably from those that generally apply in Romance. In a sentence such as "He told me that his brother had arrived," Romance would use the indicative in the subordinate clause, but German would use the subjunctive. Subjunctive forms often coincide with their indicative counterparts, but tend to take umlaut wherever possible (*a* to *ä, o* to *ö, u* to *ü;* indicative *ich war,* subjunctive *ich wäre;* English still occasionally does the same: "I was," "I were").

(e) German has several special verbs, called "modal auxiliaries," which are used in somewhat different fashion from other verbs, and must be separately learned.

(f) The German infinitive normally ends in *-en.* The German past participle, if weak, regularly prefixes *ge-* (this is the *y-* of medieval English *yclept,* or Chaucer's *yronne*), and adds *-t* to the stem (*lieben, geliebt*); if strong, it still prefixes *ge-,* but adds *-en,* usually with a change of root vowel (*sprechen, gesprochen*).

(g) Eight prefixes preclude the possibility of prefixing *ge-* to the past participle (*verstehen, verstanden*). All other prefixes are separable from their verbs in simple tenses, and go at the end of the clause, while the participial prefix *ge-* goes between the prefix and the verb (*anfangen,* "to begin"; *ich fange an,* "I am beginning"; *ich fing diese Arbeit an,* "I began this work"; *angefangen,* "begun").

(h) German has what seem to us complicated rules of word order, most of which used to appear also in Anglo-Saxon, but were later relinquished by English, possibly by reason of Norman-French influence. There is, for instance, inversion of subject and verb if the subject does not begin the sentence (*Jetzt bin ich fertig,* "Now I'm ready"). In dependent clauses, the verb usually comes at the end of the clause (*Ich weiss nicht, wo Sie Ihren Hut gekauft haben,* "I don't know where you bought your hat"; *Als ich ihn sah, ging er nach Hause,* "When I saw him, he was going home"). Many other rules of syntax appear, but fortunately they pertain for the most part to the written language, and may be assimilated gradually, from reading practice.

German is the tongue of at least a hundred million people, concentrated for the most part in Central Europe, and extending beyond the borders of East and West Germany, Austria, and Switzerland, where German is official. These people are among the most industrious and scientifically inclined in the world, and they are superlatively people with whom we want to keep in touch. German was the most widely studied modern foreign language during the latter half of the nineteenth century, partly because of its cultural, scientific, and political importance, partly because of the fact that the German element in our national makeup is numerically second only to the British. While other languages, notably Russian, have come forward in recent times in the field of scientific production, German still rates as one of the greatest languages of science in all its branches, and a reading knowledge of the language is often acquired by people who do not expect to use it in spoken form. But in these days of extensive travel, it is well to remember that German is still the dominant language in Central Europe, and that a smattering at least of the spoken tongue for practical purposes is not at all difficult for an English speaker to acquire, as proved by millions of American soldiers stationed on German soil since the Second World War came to a close. In the more elementary colloquial reaches, the basic similarities of English and German have a better chance to operate than in the more rarified upper spheres. Accentuation, syllabification, intonation, basic vocabulary work to our advantage in a language so closely related to ours. It would therefore be my suggestion that even purely cultural learners of German put forth the relatively slight extra effort that is needed for spoken-language exchange.

23

Can You Really Learn Russian?

The Alphabet Hurdle—"Unpronounceable" Sounds—Is the Grammar Really Necessary?—Slavic and Non-Slavic Vocabulary—The Common Background and the Unfamiliar Elements

AS we get further away from our Germanic-Latin-Greek-Romance heritage, things get tougher. In the old days before World War II, the American who studied Russian was such a rarity as to be almost a seven-day wonder. Then came the war, Stalingrad, the atom bomb, Sputnik, and the Intercontinental Ballistic Missile. The Soviet Union became not just another foreign country, but a formidable power to be reckoned with on a basis of approximate equality. Russian today outstrips Italian in the colleges, and is advancing on German. In the high schools it has finally established a successful bridgehead. But it is undeniably difficult to anyone who approaches it from an English-language background.

Here are two separate verdicts voiced by students at two separate institutions. One was: "Studying Russian isn't so hard once you get used to the strange alphabet and the crazy pronunciation." The other ran: "Students of Slavic background seem to have a feeling for the language that the rest of us don't have." This about sums up the difficulties, which are fourfold:

1. There is the alphabet hurdle to be taken, at or near the very outset. Americans are notoriously disinclined to any form of writing but their own version of the Roman alphabet, uncomplicated by diacritics, subscripts, suprascripts, or any other extraneous markings. In fact, we barely stand for the apostrophe.

2. Russian presents a complex of sounds which are largely unfamiliar, both in isolation and in combination. Perhaps it is simply a matter of our having accustomed our ears to the phonetics of such languages as French, German, Spanish, and Italian over a period of several decades of coexistence, while we have not similarly attuned

our national ear to Slavic and, especially, to Russian. At any rate, the pronunciation problems are there, to a far greater degree than in the other languages, with the possible exception of French.

3. The grammatical structure of Russian is definitely and altogether on the ancient Indo-European pattern, far more so than even that of German. It is highly synthetic, while we, in our linguistic development, have favored an analytical approach to the point of establishing marked likenesses to Chinese. Anyone who has studied Latin or Greek will at once note the striking similarity of the Russian grammatical scheme, with its gender-and-case system for nouns and adjectives, which is even more alive and operative than in the Classical tongues. When we get to the verb, Russian, which does not present the great complications of tenses of the Romance languages, nevertheless has a distinction of aspect which it takes long practice to grasp.

4. Lastly, while Russian has borrowed abundantly, especially in recent times, from the Western languages, it has not done so with the free abandon of English, or even of German. The Romance languages of the West, French, Spanish, Portuguese, Italian, not only have a common origin, but have been in intimate contact all through their existence. English and German joined the Western European cultural community in the early Middle Ages, and have been members of the club ever since. English, in addition, came under such a cultural spell from Norman-French that its vocabulary is at least as much Romance as it is Germanic, if we disregard frequency of occurrence of words. But Russian lived in splendid isolation until the time of Peter the Great, building up its own complex vocabulary out of its own Slavic roots. The common Indo-European background that binds these roots to those of Germanic and Romance is far in the past, and difficult for anyone but a trained historical linguist to unscramble (would you, for instance, recognize at a glance the common origin of English *know* and Russian *znat'*, or of English *hundred* and Russian *sto?*). The result is that, while there is a vocabulary relationship that is visible to the naked, untrained, or slightly trained eye, to the tune of perhaps 50 per cent, between English, on the one hand, and German, or French, or Spanish, or Italian, on the other, we are lucky to get as much as 5 to 10 per cent evident relationship for Russian, and this includes both Indo-European common roots (*nos,* English *nose; mor'e,* English *marine; sneg,* English *snow; videt',* English *video, visual*);

Russian borrowings from the West (*flag, professor, doktor, minuta, armiya*); and Western borrowings from Russian (*bistro, borsch, vodka, czar, sputnik*).

All this means that Russian is a more "difficult" language than any of the others discussed so far; not intrinsically, but with reference to the learner's background. A Russian learns to speak, read, and write Russian as easily as an American learns to do the same things in English. Russian is easier than English to a Pole, Yugoslav, or Czech, whose vocabulary and grammatical system largely coincide with those of Russian. But language learning is a subjective, not an objective affair. The question is not how "easy" the language is, but how "easy" it is to *me*.

Taking these avowed difficulties in sequence, we may start with the Cyrillic alphabet of Russian. Basically, it is an outgrowth of the Greek alphabet, from which our own Roman sprang. There are, consequently, intimate links. Secondly, the Cyrillic alphabet is more abundantly supplied with symbols than the Roman (32 symbols in the present Soviet version, as against our 26), which means greater possibilities of sound-for-symbol correspondence, though Russian, by reason of its sound scheme, is far from taking advantage of all those possibilities (Serbian, which uses a slightly different version, does a much better job, but only because its sound scheme permits it).

There is no way of avoiding the alphabet hurdle, unless you wish to remain an illiterate in the language you are learning. English or other transcriptions of Russian are 100 per cent nonofficial. Anything that appears in written form in "real" Russian appears in Cyrillic. Therefore, the only thing to do is to buckle down and learn it. This you do in exactly the same way that you learned to read and write in English: by long, constant training, reading and reading, writing and writing. Printed Cyrillic gives you a distinct break in that all the letters but *a* and *b* have exactly the same form for capitals and small letters, and for the first you have exactly the same forms as in Roman (A, a). But remember that Russian also comes in cursive, and here the forms differ somewhat from the printed ones.

The Russian letters fall into three distinct classes: (a) those that have the same form and, very roughly, the same approximate value as their Roman counterparts (A, E, K, M, O, T); to these may be added one that comes quite close, the Cyrillic Z, which looks like the numeral 3; (b) Those that look deceptively like Roman letters, but have different values (B, H, P, C, Y, X; their value is, respectively, *v, n, r, s, oo, kh*); (c) The largest group consists of letters whose shapes are unfamiliar, or only vaguely familiar; here come the Cyrillic symbols for *b, d, g, s* of *pleasure,* two varieties of *i, l, p, f, ts, ch, sh, shch,* open *e, yoo, ya, y* used as in *boy,* and two characters that are no longer pronounced, but of which one indicates palatalization, the other nonpalatalization of the preceding consonant.

Some schools of thought advocate postponing the learning of the Cyrillic alphabet until some degree of spoken-language mastery has been achieved. It was proved, at least to my satisfaction, during the war that this presents no real advantage, and may confuse the learner. Teachers of Russian in the Army courses complained that once their students had grown accustomed to spoken Russian with English or phonemic transcriptions, they tended to fall apart six weeks later when they were introduced to the "real" spelling. Psychologically, they resented and hated it. They were now forced to adapt their acquired sound scheme to a system of writing which, while not as unphonetic as that of English, is still far from phonetic. They failed to recognize in the new written form even some of the simplest and shortest words with which they had become thoroughly familiar; and the adjustment was generally more difficult and longer than it would have been at the outset. This again seems to show that you cannot quite treat the adult as you do the child. The adult is capable of absorbing by a semi-intellective process what the child learns, over a much longer period, by trial and error; conversely, the adult does not have the time at his disposal, even if he had the inclination to do things the child's way.

Another interesting, but not too pedagogically sound suggestion for training yourself in Cyrillic was advanced by M. Swadesh, one of the Army's linguists, in a little manual he published: train yourself to use Cyrillic by transcribing into it English words: *dog* with Cyrillic *d* and *g* (the *o* is the same as ours); *cat* spelled KAT; etc. The reason why this is unsound is that it tends to confirm you in wrong values for Cyrillic letters; *dog* and *cat* transliterated into Cyrillic by this system would be pronounced by a Russian not as we do, but DAWK and KAHT.

My own preference for the learning of Cyrillic, as for all other forms of writing that are alphabetic or syllabic, and not pictographic-ideographic, like Chinese, is to take it at the very outset, learning to shape the letters, writing short words over and over again, pronouncing them at the same time with the correct pronunciation, and continuing this practice until thorough assimilation has been attained (Nikanov's *Russian Alphabet Chart* and its accompanying Folkways recordings are strongly recommended in this connection). In this fashion, the language you learn will always be thoroughly authentic, as to both speech and writing.

For what concerns the sounds of spoken Russian, by far the best advice, as usual, is to imitate and repeat after a native speaker or a good recording. Without going too deeply into a topic that would take many pages, these points may be worth while:

(a) Russian vowels are clear and even slightly drawled when stressed; they are slurred and somewhat indistinct when unstressed; but even the indistinct features fall into a fairly regular and predictable pattern. In addition, from the written-language standpoint, they fall into two distinct classes, one of which indicates palatalization, the other nonpalatalization of the preceding consonant (in transcription, *ya, ye, i* (often *yi*), *yo, yu,* (or soft sign), vs. *a, e,* velar *y, o, u,* (hard sign). The palatalization, or *y*-quality, however, is in the preceding consonant, not in the vowel, unless the vowel is initial in the word, in which case a full-fledged *y*-glide precedes it (*yazyk,* as against *uchit'sa, pol'e,* which are more accurate transliterations than *uchitsya, polye*).

(b) In connection with what has been said under (a), Russian consonants either carry in themselves an inherent palatalization, or they do not. An English approximation would be "he hit you" and "did you?" in fast speech vs. "he hit me" and "I did not." Listen to a Russian saying *manyi* for *many* when he speaks English to see what this palatalization does to a consonant. Nonpalatal consonants, on the other hand, are pronounced farther back in the mouth than their English counterparts. A word like *slushayu,* "I'm listening," commonly used for "hello!" on the phone, has the same sort of *l*-sound that we get in *milk.*

(c) Three of the Russian palatal consonants (transliterated as *zh,* or the *s* of *pleasure, sh,* and *shch,* are retroflex, and call for a curling of the tongue up toward the front of the hard palate.

(d) Final written voiced consonants (*-d, -b, -g, -v, -z, -zh*) are unvoiced in normal speech, and sound like *-t, -p, -k, -f, -s, -sh,* respectively. This is one reason why Russian family names often appear in double form (*Romanov, Romanoff*); *-ov* represents a transliteration of the spelling; *-off* represents the pronunciation.

(e) Russian stress is, unfortunately, unpredictable, and not indicated in writing. (In other Slavic languages the accent is fixed; always initial in Czech, always on the penult in Polish, which is a distinct break for the learner.) This means endless possibilities of error, and uncertainty occasionally hits even the Russians themselves. To make matters worse, several classes of words shift the stress from one syllable to another in the course of their declension or conjugation. Most neuter nouns, along with some feminines, shift regularly from the singular to the plural (*water* is vuh-DAH, but *waters* is VAW-dy). Nothing but practice will help here. Beginners' books and dictionaries regularly show how a word and its variant forms are to be accented, but a normal Russian book or newspaper does not.

(f) Russian, even more than German, shows certain consonant clusters which at first strike the English-speaking learner as impossible to pronounce. They are anything but impossible, as witnessed by the fact that over 200 million Soviet speakers pronounce them. Practice the initial *zdr-* of ZDRAHF-stvuy-t'eh ("hello," "good day"), the combination f SHEST' chuh-SAWF ("at six o'clock"), until they come out right. Most "impossible" Russian combinations occur in English, but in different positions. For *mchat'sa,* "to gallop away," try "I'm chary," then leave out *I;* for f SHEST', try "of show business," then leave out the *o* of *of;* for *mn'e,* "to me," try "I'm new," then leave out *I.* Difficulties are to be circumvented, not yielded to. The "impossible" is what takes a little longer. Again, remember that for the spoken language there is no substitute for the imitation and repetition of a native speaker or recording. Listen, learn, and, above all, puhf-tuh-R'EE-t'eh puh-ZHAHL-stuh, which means "Repeat, please."

When we come to grammatical structure, we are faced, in a modern, currently spoken language, with the setup that we have learned to associate with the Classical tongues, Latin and Greek. Russian nouns, adjectives, pronouns, are fully declined in six, occasionally seven, cases. For nouns, there are numerous declensional schemes. For adjectives, there are fewer, but there are extra forms to be learned if the adjective is used as a predicate adjective. For verbs, the forms would be relatively simple (present, past, and future) were it not for the Slavic dichotomy of aspect, which means that the verbs usually come in pairs, one imperfective, denoting that the action is incomplete, the other perfective, denoting that it is completed.

One modest break the learner gets is the absence of articles, definite or indefinite, exactly as in Latin. The gender system works out as in German, with males usually masculine, females usually feminine, but inanimate objects of any gender. Russian, however, is kinder than German in offering typical gender endings: nouns ending in consonants in the nominative singular are regularly masculine; those ending in -*a* or -*ya* are feminine (except those ending in -*mya*, or, better, -*m'a*, which are neuter). Those ending in -*o* or -*e* are neuter. The only ending that leaves you in doubt is palatalized consonant (such as -*t'*, -*d'*); this may be masculine or feminine.

The cases are almost, but not quite, as in Latin: nominative (subject, predicate nominative); genitive (possession); dative (indirect object); accusative (direct object); instrumental ("by means of," "with"); locative (most commonly, place where; this case is also called "prepositional," because it can be used only after a preposition). A few nouns have separate vocative forms (direct address: "O God!" "O Lord!"), but for the most part the nominative is used in this connection.

In Latin, only two cases, accusative and ablative, could be used with prepositions. In Greek, which had no ablative, it was genitive, dative, or accusative. In Sanskrit, which had eight cases, there were no prepositions. Russian rather surprisingly combines prepositions with any of its cases except the nominative. This means doubt as to which preposition to use, which case to use after a given preposition, and whether to use a preposition at all. Our common preposition "to" is translated by the dative case alone if it denotes an indirect object; by *v* plus accusative if it involves motion to; but by *k* with dative if the idea is rather that of motion toward; *na* with the accusative if the idea is that of "on to," or coming from above; *do* with the genitive if it means "as far as."

Only feminine nouns have a separate accusative case form, and that only in the singular. For masculines, neuters, and feminine plurals, the accusative takes the same form as the genitive if the noun is animate, as the nominative if inanimate.

It is perhaps worth mentioning as a memory device that the ending -*am*, -'*am* for dative plural, -*ami*, -'*ami* for instrumental plural, -*akh*, -'*akh* for locative plural are universal in nouns, and that adjectives use the same endings, but with *y* or *i* substituted for *a* or '*a*.

Adjectives agree with their nouns, but come in declensional schemes that diverge from those of the nouns. Predicate adjectives have short nominative forms (masculine, feminine, and neuter in the singular, a single merged form in the plural), but here one has to watch for shifts of stress from one form to another ("difficult" as a predicate adjective, for instance, is TROO-d'en, trood-NAH, TROOD-nuh, trood-NY). Comparative and superlative forms are in the nature of peace offerings to the learner. The former replaces the adjective ending with -'*eye*, and is, miraculously, invariable. The latter merely prefixes *samy* to the positive. The adverb is simply the neuter form of the predicate adjective (OOM-ny, "intelligent," oom-NAW, "intelligently").

Numerals present tough features. "One" is declined like an adjective, and agrees with its noun. All subsequent numerals (save compounds of "one," like 21, 31) are *nouns,* and require the following noun and its modifiers to be in the genitive singular after 2, 3, 4, and their compounds, the genitive plural from 5 on. So it's "one book," but "two, three, four of book," "five, six, seven of books." Fortunately, this rule holds only when the noun is in the nominative.

Personal pronouns are fully declined, and the nominative forms are generally used with verbs, in spite of individual verb endings. Possessive, demonstrative, interrogative, and relative pronouns show full declensional schemes, along with obvious descent from the same sources as English, German, Latin, and Romance (consider, for example, English *my, mine,* German *mein,* Latin *meus,* French *mon,* Italian *mio,* Russian *moy;* or Latin *suus,* German *sein,* Russian *svoy,* which English has replaced with *his,* obviously the genitive form of the personal pronoun *he;* or Russian *chto,* which less visibly, but just as surely, goes back to the same original form as Latin *quid,* English *what* [earlier *hwat*], German *was;* here an original Indo-European *kw, represented by Latin *qu,* turns the *k* into *h* in Germanic, but palatalizes it into *ch* in Eastern members of the family, such as Slavic and Sanskrit).

In the matter of verbs, the Russian aspectual dichotomy calls generally for two verbs where we have one. "To write" is basically *pisat';* but this means "to be writing" without any fixed point of time or indication as to whether the writing came to an end. "To write" once, and then be finished writing, is *napisat'*. *D'elat'* is "to do" in general; but "to do" something and then be through is *sd'elat'*. It will be noticed that the perfective verb, which shows the action carried through, is often formed by putting a prefix on the base, represented by the imperfective verb. Some inkling of the concept of aspect appears in Romance tenses such as the simple past vs. the imperfect (Spanish *escribía*, "he was writing, used to write," vs. *escribió*, "he wrote"). One might even bring in such English verbs as "to speak," which more often refers to a general, indefinite action ("he speaks English") vs. "to say" or "to tell," which are usually specific in time and mode of action ("he said to me in English," "he told me in English"). The very indefiniteness of the two concepts and the border between them, however, makes the full assimilation of the proper use of Russian perfective and imperfective forms a difficult and slow task. One Slavic expert suggests some striking examples: *"Chto d'elal?"* *"Vs'o."* ("What was he doing, trying to do?" "Everything."); *"Chto sd'elal?"* *"N'ichevo."* "What did he do, accomplish?" "Nothing." *"Kogda otkryval"* ("at the time when he was discovering"); *"Kogda otkryl"* ("when he discovered").

The imperfective verb has a present, a past, and a future ("I do" normally or usually; "I am doing"; "I was doing or used to do"; "I shall be doing"). The perfective verb has a present form which carries a future meaning ("I shall do," and be through), and a past ("I did, have done"). The two presents are fully conjugated, and have separate personal endings, in spite of which they are generally used with subject pronouns. The past is a mere participle, with auxiliary understood, and behaves like a predicate adjective, with masculine, feminine, and neuter singular forms, and a single plural form for all three genders. It naturally requires the subject pronoun, and has the same variations of stress that affect predicate adjectives generally. The imperfective future is simply the future of "to be" (*budu*) with the infinitive following it. Conditional and subjunctive concepts are taken care of by the past indicative with appropriate particles or conjunctions. The imperative is simple, and reminds you of the imperative of Latin. The reflexive is abundantly used (it merely calls for the addition of an almost invariable reflexive pronoun to the plain verb), and does service for the passive as well (*uchit'sa,* "to teach oneself," "to be taught," "to learn"). Russian, like Latin and particularly Greek, has an abundance of participial and gerundial forms, which often replace what in the Western languages would have to be subordinate clauses.

The question now comes up: How do you learn this sort of language? By mere repetition of pattern phrases and sentences, with appropriate substitutions, as called for by the audio-lingual method? Or by plodding memorization of paradigms and declensional schemes, as used to be done, and is still done, for Latin and Greek? Or by a combination of both methods, plus the working in of a number of cliché expressions of the ultra-frequent colloquial type?

Before we attempt an answer, let us recall that Bloomfield, speaking of morphemes, which are basic, indivisible units of meaning, subdivides them into what he calls free and bound. The free morpheme is one that can be used in isolation, like *wall, tell, good.* The bound morpheme is one that can be used only in connection with another morpheme, and never appears by itself, like the *-s* that gives *walls* its plural connotation, or the *-s* that marks *tells* as third person singular, or the written *-ed,* (spoken *-d*) that you add on to *love* to get the past *loved,* or the *re-* that you prefix to *tell* to give it the meaning of "tell again." This classification is quite useful in a language like English, which uses nouns, adjectives, and verbs in root forms. In languages like Russian, Sanskrit, Greek, or Latin, practically every morpheme is bound, except for the limited number of prepositions, conjunctions, interjections, and adverbs that don't come from adjectives. In English you can use *wall* in isolation, but in Latin you cannot use *mur-* without a case ending; in Russian, only one case form (nominative singular, for the most part, in masculine nouns, genitive plural, usually, for feminines and neuters) happens to coincide with the bare stem.

The use of pattern sentences and the substitution method work out very well in Chinese; moderately well in languages like Spanish and French, where all you have to worry about is a singular or a plural noun form; not very well in languages like Latin or Russian, where the multiplicity of case forms and declensional types leads to confusion. After "I see," the student wonders why the word for "officer" has an *a*-ending, the word for "village" an *o*-ending, the word for "book" a *u*-ending, the word for "house" a consonant ending. Then, in another pattern, he finds "officer" with consonant ending, *u*-ending, *om*-ending, *e*-ending; "book" with *a*-ending, *y*-ending, *e*-ending, *oy*-ending. He starts asking questions: "Why does one noun used in this pattern have an *a*-ending, another a *u*-ending, another an *o*-ending?" If he is told not to worry about it, but just memorize the phrase, he is baffled and perturbed. If you undertake to explain the reason why, you are going into the traditional paradigm method. Under the circumstances, it seems to me best, in languages of the heavily inflected type, to start with a grammatical explanation before you attempt too much in the way of pattern phrases, so as to set the learner's mind at rest and make him feel that there is rhyme and reason to the language he is learning. Also, the learner should be allowed, and even encouraged, to indulge in a considerable amount of memorization of paradigms, declensional and conjugational schemes, so that his inductive process of learning from direct examples and practice may be supplemented by a certain amount of deductive methodology enabling him to go through this logical mental process: "Feminine nouns have -*a* in the nominative singular, -*u* in the accusative, as I learned from my paradigm *kniga; minuta* is a feminine noun, obviously of the same type as *kniga;* therefore, if I want to use it in the accusative, I must give it a *u*-ending." This conscious intellective process does not hurt or interfere with the pattern learning, but rather serves to clarify and explain it, and make it satisfactory and acceptable to the learner. The inductive process works to best advantage where the language has a majority of free morphemes. The deductive process can be called in to help where there is a majority of bound morphemes. In Monterey, I never heard any complaint about the prevailing audiolingual methodology from students of Chinese. I heard plenty from students and instructors of Russian. Be elastic and eclectic, and modify your language-learning method to fit existing language conditions. Above all, do not scorn the power of rote memorization, not only for what concerns pattern phrases, but also for what concerns paradigms, where they exist.

The study of Russian offers many distinct advantages to the learner. On the practical, utilitarian side, it gives access to a nation that covers one sixth of the earth's land surface, and has a growing population that outnumbers our own. Russian is expanding, particularly in European Communist countries. It is a language whose political-military importance, at the present time, is second only to our own; whose scientific achievements have been, in a sense, earth-shaking; whose literary and cultural merits are indeed vast, and far transcend any political implication; and whose possibilities of economic and business use may, if things go well, be far greater in ten years than they are today.

In addition, on the purely linguistic front, Russian offers a rather easy transition to other Slavic languages, some of which (Polish, Czech and Slovak, Serbo-Croatian) are quite important in their own right, even if they are not of first rank for what concerns number of speakers. It also affords a clear and valuable insight into the original structure of the Indo-European languages, of which English, German, and Romance form a part, along with most of the tongues of India. It is particularly valuable in giving us a present-day insight into the spoken nature of the two great languages of antiquity, Greek and Latin, in the living reality of which in their heyday some people, including linguists, still refuse to believe, at least by implication. In my own case, I put my previously acquired Latin and Greek to work in learning Russian. But there is nothing to prevent the process from being operated in reverse; one who has acquired living, spoken Russian will find that it greatly smooths his path as he endeavors to gain a knowledge of the Classical tongues.

All in all, Russian is a language well worth learning, even if it does call for a greater effort than the traditional languages of the American curriculum.

24

How Do You Learn a Classical Language?

For Reading Purposes Only?—The Tongues of Literature and Philosophy—The Historical Sense—The Triple Function of Greek and Latin—Problems of Learning Latin and/or Greek—The Special Problem of Hebrew

IN the days that preceded the First World War, Latin and Greek together accounted for a greater percentage of foreign language enrollments in our high schools and colleges than all modern languages put together. The immediacy of modern life and its problems has reversed that situation. The major of the "leisure" languages, Latin, has now fewer followers than either French or Spanish, while students of Greek have dwindled to a mere trickle.

Nevertheless, the pursuit of the Classics goes on apace, even though a good deal of it is done in translation, in Humanities and Great Books courses. But one of the two great languages of the past, Latin, still has a large number of devoted followers. Well over one million high school students selected Latin in 1963.

Latin for speaking purposes? Or Latin for reading purposes only? The fact of the matter is that while there is still an opportunity to use Latin as a spoken tongue if you are a member of the Catholic clergy, and that it can sometimes be used as a final resort in attempts at international communications (particularly in the Vatican State, where Latin is co-official with Italian), the true usefulness of the Classical languages lies elsewhere than in speech.

It used to be claimed that there was in the study of the Classical languages a transfer discipline value, that they taught you how to think logically and follow through to a correct conclusion. Modern psychologists are in doubt concerning transfer discipline values, though it is undeniable that if you are not given instruction in logical thinking somewhere in your course of studies, there will always be snarls along your line of thought. If this is so, then Latin and Greek supply good training, for in getting at the meaning of a passage in either language one usually has to exercise his mind and ingenuity, and string together the linguistic clues that ultimately solve the puzzle. It is obvious, however, that this intellective process would have to be exercised on the written rather than the spoken form of the language.

Again, both Latin and Greek are of tremendous value in unlocking the treasure houses of Indo-European roots and etymological meanings. It is no accident that all books and articles dealing with word power and control over English vocabulary invariably present the etymological derivations of the words they describe. In a great many cases, the etymological derivation serves to concretize the meaning of the modern word. "Perfect" is something that is "done through." "Supernumerary" is "above the number" required. All this can be of immediate and even practical value. But again, etymology is a time-consuming process, and has to be done at leisure, preferably in the privacy of one's study, rather than in the midst of a heated conversation.

We have already seen that some modern languages of the Indo-European family, notably Russian, have a great deal of grammatical structure in common with the ancient languages of the group. This means that we can transfer with relative ease from our acquired Classical Latin or Greek a large bundle of grammatical concepts, features, and processes to a Slavic tongue. We have also seen that not only the English but to an even greater degree the Romance vocabularies are largely based on both Latin and Greek, and this means that a knowledge of Latin will certainly aid us when we undertake the study of French or Italian. But in establishing both the structural and the lexical links, the process will be largely intellective, and in slow motion.

Lastly, once you come to the upper, literary reaches of both Latin and Greek, there begin to appear not only linguistic, literary, and cultural connections, but profound historical lessons that modern man perhaps needs. As we read the Classical authors, we begin to see that many of the problems that beset us have appeared before—democracy, tyranny, political maneuvers, international diplomacy, war and aggression, conquest and colonialism, slavery and class distinctions, poverty and its relief, propaganda of all types, even foreign aid. The city-states of Greece, Republican and Imperial Rome, went through all these phases. How the problems were solved, how they failed to be solved, what the failure to solve them led to, can be of intense interest, and teach us enduring lessons. It is true that to reach the stage where one can handle these ancient examples in the original one must be rather far advanced. It is also true that they can be read in translation. But the effect is not quite the same. What sounds natural in Cicero's own words sounds stilted in the words of his English translator; also, there is not the same incentive to read him if one has not been introduced to him in high school.

Once more, it will be seen that this last-named value for the Classical languages involves an intellective rather than a spontaneous reflex process. From the standpoint of philology as well as of philosophy, of history as well as of literature, the omens point overwhelmingly to a written-language rather than a spoken-language use and value for the Classical languages. It may therefore be just as well if in connection with them we disturb the traditional method of learning as little as possible, and do not attempt too many experiments in the way of teaching Latin and Greek as spoken tongues.

Nevertheless, there is no really good reason why on the not too infrequent occasions when we attempt to pronounce Latin and Greek words and expressions we should not strive for some measure of authenticity. Painstaking research has long since established at least a reasonable approximation to the sound schemes of both languages in their respective Classical periods. We may aim for this, or, if we prefer, we may take both in the spoken forms in which they survive to the present day. Greek is still a spoken popular tongue, and has enjoyed unbroken use since the days of Homer and Plato. It has gone through somewhat drastic sound transformations in the course of three thousand years, but the Greek classics are still read and expounded today in the high schools and universities of Greece in the modern Greek pronunciation. As for Latin, the so-called "Church" or "Italian" pronunciation seems to be the closest descendant of the tongue of Caesar in its fifth-century version, and this, too, is used, both in the universal Roman Catholic Church and in the high schools and universities of Italy. It might be suggested that if our institutions of learning do not care to reconstruct the Classical pronunciation of either tongue, they might do well to fasten on these modern versions, which at least have the merit of authenticity. It always makes me shudder to hear the British public school pronunciation of *pater* as PAY-tuhr, or the American version of *bona fide* and *alibi*. I once heard an American politician pronounce *sine die* so that the first word sounded like the trigonometric function and the second like the synonym of "expire," and I found it difficult to fall asleep that night.

Approaching both languages firmly on a traditional basis, from the written-language angle, we are at once confronted, in the case of Greek, with that great bugaboo of American language learners, a strange alphabet. It matters little that this alphabet gave rise to our own, that it is copiously used in our mathematical and scientific sets of symbols (*pi, sigma, epsilon*), and that it enters all our Greek-letter fraternities and sororities (Phi Beta Kappa, Alpha Phi Delta, etc.). It still frightens the learner.

It needn't and shouldn't, though the learner should be cautioned that he will never achieve in it, or any other strange alphabet, the reading and writing fluency he has in his own. Strange alphabets are to be taken in one's stride, deliberately, slowly if need be. My own recollection is that our first semester of Greek in high school was devoted largely to assimilating the alphabet, learning to read it, at first in short words, then in longer words and passages, which we pronounced as we learned to read them, writing the alphabet over and over, then writing words and phrases, until it had become a second (but not a first) nature.

The use of every alphabetic form is in the nature of a habit, just as is the use of a spoken language. Habits are not formed overnight, but they can be formed—good ones, fortunately, as well as bad ones. The Greek alphabet, like the Cyrillic, is one of the easier alphabetic forms for one who starts from Roman. It is much more difficult to memorize the Hebrew, or the Arabic, or the Armenian, or the De-vanagari. Yet, with time and interest, they can all be memorized. I have memorized all of them, and several others besides, at various times, and temporarily forgotten half of them by reason of lack of practice; but I have no doubt that with a little practice they would all come back with relative ease, as do spoken languages.

In the matter of grammatical structure, enough has been said in the preceding chapters to make excessive repetition unnecessary. The following points are worth summarizing:

(a) Latin uses no articles, definite or indefinite. Greek has a fully declined definite article, which it uses approximately as we use ours. This means that in Latin *vir* (or *homo*) may mean "man," "a man," "the man." In Greek *anthropos* is "man" or "a man," but "the man" is *ho anthropos*.

(b) Both languages have the same semilogical gender categories. Males are usually masculine, females feminine, but inanimate nouns may be anything. Greek has, in addition to singular and plural, a scantily used dual number, which it uses for "two," reserving the plural for more than two. The same dual appears in other ancient Indo-European languages, notably Sanskrit, as well as in the Semitic tongues (Hebrew, Arabic, etc.).

(c) Latin has five cases (six if you count the vocative, or case of direct address, which appears only in a limited category of nouns as separate in form from the nominative): nominative, genitive, dative, accusative, ablative. Greek lacks the ablative, and its functions are distributed among the other cases (Sanskrit, oldest of the Indo-European languages on record, had eight cases, including both Latin's ablative and Russian's instrumental and locative). Both languages have copious declensional schemes, which to some extent give indication of gender, but almost as often do not.

(d) Adjectives agree in gender, number, and case, both in the attributive and in the predicate position. They fall into declensional classes similar to those of nouns, but there is no guarantee of identical endings, since the adjective may belong to a different declensional class from the noun it modifies. Comparative and superlative are formed by means of appropriate suffixes, to which declensional endings are added. Adverbs are usually formed on the stems of adjectives by means of special suffixes; they, too, are compared, but not declined.

(e) Prepositions may be used in Latin only with the accusative and ablative; in Greek with the genitive, accusative, or dative. In many instances, the mere case ending suffices where a modern Western language would require a preposition.

(f) Verbs show complex systems of conjugations, with personal endings; plenty of clearly defined tenses; moods which in Latin include indicative, subjunctive, infinitive, imperative, to which Greek adds optative; and voices, which in Latin are active and passive; but in Greek there is also a middle voice, which functions somewhat like a reflexive. Greek, even more than Latin, has abundant participial and gerundial forms, and these are often used, as in Russian, where modern Western languages would prefer subordinate clauses.

(g) Among the indicative tenses, Latin has present, imperfect, future, perfect, pluperfect, future perfect. Greek has in addition an aorist, which takes one of the two functions of the Latin perfect ("I saw"), so that the Greek perfect is restricted to the function "I have seen." The functions of the conditionals of modern Western languages are for the most part fulfilled by the subjunctive.

(h) Syntactically, both languages offer far greater freedom of position and elasticity than most modern languages, by reason of the morphological endings of the main parts of speech (nouns, adjectives, pronouns, verbs), which clarify the meaning and function of the word in the sentence. This freedom of word order is what causes most of the translation difficulties, as the learner has to reassemble his words in the order which is compulsory in English. The learner must watch for morphological clues, and learn to put together what the endings indicate should go together. In Virgil's *litora curvae praetexunt puppes* ("the curved sterns occupy the beaches"), the line of reasoning runs something like this: *litora,* which is neuter plural, could be nominative or accusative; so could *puppes,* which is feminine plural; but *curvae,* the adjective, clearly indicates nominative plural feminine; so it can only go with *puppes,* which must be nominative; therefore, *curvae puppes* must be the subject of the verb *praetexunt,* and *litora* its object.

It is not only possible but altogether likely that both Latin and Greek could be learned and used, even today, as spoken languages, as, in a sense, they are. In the Middle Ages and through most of the Renaissance, Latin was not only the language of scholarship in the West (just as Byzantine Greek was in the East until the fall of Constantinople to the Turks in the middle of the fifteenth century); it was also the spoken language among scholars, students, and clerics of different nationalities. There is no indication that modern imitation-repetition or audio-lingual methods of pattern phrases and substitution frames were used in the instruction that future scholars received. They learned by rote, by memorization and recitation of paradigms, by constant reading, by written and oral composition. All this lore was then transferred to the speaking and understanding process, with seemingly little difficulty. There is little doubt that this could be done today if the occasion arose, as it frequently does in the training of the Catholic clergy. Without going overboard for the traditional method, it might be well if it were accorded the recognition to which it is entitled on the basis of its past achievements.

Some special problems arise in connection with the learning of Hebrew, which is also, in a sense, a Classical language, probably more ancient than Greek and definitely more ancient than Latin, and a fundamental part of our Western tradition. The problems are occasioned by the fact that in recent times Hebrew, long a liturgical language among the Jewish communities all over the world, and learned by rote in a highly traditional method, has become also a modern, national, official, spoken language in the state of Israel. This has involved a thoroughgoing transformation of the old Biblical language, at least for what concerns vocabulary, with the introduction of thousands of new terms, some directly borrowed from the Western languages, others ingeniously coined on Semitic roots by the loan-translation process.

For what concerns the sound scheme of the new popular tongue, a choice or compromise had to be made between the two liturgical systems of pronunciation that had become current in the Jewish communities, the Ashkenazic, favored by Northern European Jews, and the Sephardic, used by Jewish groups living in the Mediterranean basin. The latter, more indigenous to the original Palestinian Jews, generally prevailed; but since the differences between the two are not startling, the transition was not difficult for Northern European Jews. A greater problem, perhaps, was their tendency to use Yiddish, which is basically a medieval German dialect. This, too, seems to be under control.

The American learner of Hebrew, however, is faced with a definite choice. He can restrict his efforts to the old liturgical language of the Talmud and Torah, and approach it in the traditional, written-language fashion; or he can go in for the full-blown new spoken tongue of Israel, in which case he will attack the language as he would any spoken tongue for everyday use. The latter is for the most part the approach used both in the high schools and in colleges where Hebrew is taught, and among private learners, as evidenced by the abundant sales of spoken Israeli Hebrew recordings.

Viewed from this angle, Hebrew belongs among the modern spoken languages, and will be referred to in the next chapter.

25

What Other Languages Are Important?

Present Position of Chinese, Japanese, Arabic, Hindustani, and Indonesian—How to Learn One of Them if Necessary—The World's Lesser Languages—The Effects of Linguistic Colonialism —The Gamble on an International Language

ONCE we step beyond the range of Latin and the Inner Six among the modern languages (English, French, Spanish, German, Italian, Russian) we find ourselves lost in the great language forest, with its three thousand and more trees. Here it is every man for himself. You cut down the tree you happen to need.

Yet the trees are not all of the same size or quality, and the purpose for which you want one of them becomes important. Consider, first of all, the Outer Seven, which include some of the biggest languages in the world, not only for what concerns population but in other significant respects, such as ancient culture, present commercial possibilities, however specialized, and what the stockbrokers call "growth potentialities."

Portuguese, the language whose existence most Americans refuse to recognize, has already been described. Chinese is the living tongue of one out of four people in the world, and China has of late been making the headlines. However things may go in days to come, Chinese is bound to become a language of great practical significance to us. In addition, it is the vehicle of a great and noble civilization. However much we may disagree with China's present rulers, the great reality of China and the Chinese race remains. In the mighty tapestry of history, Communism in both China and Russia is a temporary, insignificant episode.

Japanese, the language of one hundred million, represents one of the most progressive forces in the world, as proved by Japan's astounding recovery in the past twenty years. The language is worthy of very serious consideration. Arabic is another tongue with a large and growing population, a huge area, widespread influence beyond its own speaking borders, and a noble tradition of civilization in the scientific field (mathematics, astronomy, and chemistry, as modern sciences, may be said to have been initiated by the Arabs). There is nothing to prevent the scientific flair of the Arabic speakers from suddenly bursting into flame again. Hindi-Urdu and Indonesian are two developing languages, each of which is making a bid to become predominant in a vast area. Both, along with Bengali, have cultural traditions, with their roots deep in the past, and the two leading languages of the Indian subcontinent go back to Sanskrit, the language that best illustrates the original unfolding of Indo-European civilization.

The study of each and any of these languages is highly legitimate, even though they do not form part of America's educational inner circle, and have to be taken up either at institutions of higher learning or privately.

In the latter eventuality, it may be well to keep in mind that Chinese is a language that lends itself superbly to the modern methodology of listen-and-repeat, accompanied by pattern phrases and substitution frames. Chinese is a language of significant tones, monosyllabic root words that tolerate no endings or prefixes, a grammatical structure that depends altogether on word order, and not at all on morphology, and a vocabulary that has no links whatsoever to our own, save for a few barely recognizable loan words. This means that the imitation and repetition of native speakers, whether live or recorded, is imperative. In connection with Chinese (and Japanese as well) there is the possibility (in fact, the desirability) of isolating the spoken from the written language, concentrating first on the former, using as a written aid one of the many systems of transcription that have been devised for the purpose, and taking up the writing, if at all, at a considerable distance of time. The reason for this is that both languages use a pictographic-ideographic system of writing, in which there is practically no connection between the spoken sounds and the written symbols. The latter are thoroughly arbitrary, and far too numerous to be readily learned (the knowledge of 4,000 characters is the minimum that will enable you to read a newspaper; if you wish to be a Chinese scholar, you can go up as far as 40,000 characters). Japanese has, in addition, devised two sets of syllabic characters which could be, but usually are not, used to represent the language phonetically, and whose main function is to represent the flectional endings which Japanese, unlike Chinese, possesses in great abundance.

Japanese has plenty of morphology, as well as syntax, and no tones. It also has a fairly simple sound structure, and a system of Roman-alphabet transcription which many Japanese advocate as a replacement for their Chinese ideographs and native syllabaries. This means that Japanese, far more than Chinese, lends itself to study out of books rather than by the imitation-repetition method. The latter, however, will be of considerable help in fixing spoken-language forms in the learner's mind.

Arabic is a tongue of strange and unfamiliar sounds, calling for special training of the muscles of the throat. Imitation of a native speaker or recording is strongly recommended for this language. Its grammatical structure and vocabulary are Semitic, which means that anyone already acquainted with Hebrew will not have too much trouble with them. The learner may be cautioned that present-day spoken Arabic comes in several widely divergent dialectal forms, so that the Arabic speaker from Morocco will have considerable difficulty in understanding his fellow speaker from Iraq or Sa'udi Arabia. The compromise language that is common to all Arabic speakers, and that generally appears in written form, is squarely based on the Classical Arabic of the Koran; but this has the drawback of being the spoken language of practically nobody outside of a few scholars. The Arabic variety spoken in Egypt presents the double advantage of having the greatest number of speakers and being most central with respect to the North African and Middle Eastern varieties, and is the form most often presented on the colloquial level. The written form employs the Arabic alphabet, which is somewhat complicated (each letter has four possible forms, according as it comes in the initial, medial, or final position in the word, or stands alone), runs, like the Hebrew, from right to left, and indicates vowel values, if at all, by small suprascript or subscript characters. It presents no insurmountable difficulties, and should be learned at or near the outset of your studies.

Hindi-Urdu and Bengali are both direct descendants of Sanskrit, the earliest recorded Indo-European tongue. But while both have kept virtually intact the sound structure of their ancestor, they have made grammatical innovations of a "simplifying" nature that make them rather easy to assimilate. In written form, Hindi and Bengali continue to use the old Devanagari alphabet of Sanskrit, while Urdu, official in Moslem Pakistan, uses a variant of the Arabic alphabet. Urdu, in addition, shows a preference for Arabic and Persian words which the Hindi speaker may understand, but will not normally use, replacing them with Sanskrit-derived words. Yet Hindi and Urdu are close enough to be rated by most linguists as variant or dialectal forms of the same language, Hindustani. The sound scheme, while smooth enough and rather pleasant to the ear, involves certain sound distinctions which run counter to our habits (*bh* vs. *b,* for instance, represented by two different characters in the Devanagari alphabet, and making for a difference of meaning in two words where everything else is the same). The imitation of native speakers or recordings is therefore recommended, along with the study of the language out of books.

Indonesian, or its older and more widespread, but less official, variant, Malay, is a language of smooth and easy sounds, and has the added advantage of appearing in a highly phonetic Roman alphabet. This gives easy initial access to it, and obviates the need for too much imitation-repetition. Its grammatical structure, while unfamiliar, is not too difficult, and its main problems reside in the strangeness of its vocabulary, which belongs to the same family as Hawaiian and most of the Philippines languages.

Among these "Outer Seven" languages, four are rather widely taught at colleges and universities. They are Portuguese, Chinese, Japanese, and Arabic. Courses in Hindi, Urdu, Bengali, and Indonesian are few and far between. On the other hand, a good many private language schools have them on their list, and the larger producers of language recordings have most of them among their offerings. For grammars and dictionaries of "unusual" languages, there is one American bookseller, Stechert-Hafner, 31 East 10 Street, New York 10003, that has a very extensive offering, and will mail you its catalogue of language books on request. It will even import what you want from Europe or elsewhere.

Hebrew, which was listed in the previous chapter among the Classical languages, rates, as a spoken tongue, with the major four of the Outer Seven, outstripping some of them both as an institutional language and in sales of recordings.

It will be recalled that for what concerns our high schools, as compared with about four million students of Latin, French, Spanish, German, Italian, and Russian, total enrollments in all other languages barely reached 10,000, and that in all our institutions of higher learning, as against over one million learners of the same six big languages, enrollments in all other tongues (nearly seventy in number) did not quite reach 20,000. There seems to be a somewhat better balance in both private language schools and private study, as evidenced by sales of recordings, where the "exceptional" languages come up to perhaps 20 per cent of the total.

It is nevertheless a fact that such languages are normally studied for specific rather than for general reasons. The specific reasons may include family, national, or religious ties (this factor is undoubtedly strongly operative in the case of Polish and other Slavic languages outside of Russian, Scandinavian tongues like Swedish and Norwegian, Hebrew, modern Greek); they may include business or professional reasons (Portuguese, Scandinavian tongues, Dutch, Arabic, Indonesian, easily fall within this category). Then there are military reasons (Korean, Vietnamese, Pidgin English). The reasons may involve missionary or welfare work of the Peace Corps variety (here we may find almost anything, down to the most obscure tongues of Africa, Asia, South America, and New Guinea); they may involve linguistic interests of the scientific variety (American Indian, African, Asian, Pacific languages); they may involve sheer tourist curiosity, or curiosity without further qualification (I have been asked on one or two occasions how one may go about learning Hawaiian or Papiamento).

For some of these languages, courses and materials are as plentiful and readily accessible as for the Outer Seven. No serious difficulty will be encountered, for instance, if one wants to study Polish, or Czech, or Dutch, or Danish. If regular institutional courses are not available in your area, you will be able to cover the language by yourself, if you are really so minded, by a judicious investment in grammars, dictionaries, readers, and recordings. Things become a little tougher if your specialized interests lie in Swahili, Hausa, Tamil, or Aranta. But even here there are few difficulties that cannot be solved for you by a combination of inquiries directed at the Library of Congress, a specialized bookstore like Stechert-Hafner, a specialized school of languages like Berlitz, specialized recording houses like Linguaphone and Holt. Remember also that the British, by reason of their long colonial experience, have gone in for unusual languages to a far greater extent than we have, and that much of their production is available to us through the proper channels.

As for the method of learning a "minor" language, that is up to you. If you register for a duly constituted course, in a regular university or a private language school, the methodology will be laid out for you. If you are forced to or prefer to study by yourself, everything we said in the earlier chapters of this book becomes operative. For the spoken language, get a native speaker and converse with him if you can; if you can't, get a good set of records, and follow the directions for imitation and repetition. For the grammatical structure, get and use a good, up-to-date grammar. Follow this up with a good reader, and have a good, modern dictionary by your side. Don't hesitate to read out loud; memorize and declaim poetry. By all means attempt writing, even if you have no one to correct it for you. Writing practice enlists kinesthetic memory in your service, to supplement auditory and visual memory.

Without wishing in any way to disparage the languages of small and occasionally still backward groups, you may be reminded that colonialism, however you may feel about it politically, survives and will survive for some time to come in its linguistic effects. As an all-purpose language in either Congo, French is more likely to serve you than any one of the native languages. You may also do better with it in Algeria, Tunisia, and Morocco than with your own attempt at Arabic, which you may be learning in its Egyptian or Classical variety. Spanish will in one fashion or another carry you through even the Quechua, Aymará, and Tupi-Guaraní areas of Peru, Bolivia, and Paraguay. German may easily serve your purpose in the cities of Hungary, Czechoslovakia, and northern Yugoslavia, and Italian may perform the same service in Dalmatia. English will probably carry you quite well through India, Pakistan, Burma, and various new African countries. Russian will almost surely work out in the non-Russian sections of the Soviet Union, and you may find enough Italian speakers in Buenos Aires and São Paulo to fill your needs if you happen to have studied Italian instead of Spanish and Portuguese.

Is there any possibility of using one of the thousand or so constructed, artificial languages that roam the earth? Is any one of them worth spending time and effort on? How do you go about learning it?

Interlinguistics (the study of international languages and the possibility of their application) is a semiscientific pursuit in its own right, though somewhat of the hobby variety, like stamp collecting. If it interests you, the best thing you can do is to subscribe to *International Language Review,* Box 393, Denver 1, Colorado, which presents and discusses the various plans of the past, present, and future.

On the practical side, the most extensively used constructed language is Esperanto, which is in all senses of the word a spoken and written language, with an undetermined number of speakers scattered throughout the world which has been estimated as high as eight million, is used in spoken form at congresses and whenever two or more Esperantists of different language backgrounds meet, and has a large number of books, both original and in translation, and of regularly published periodicals. It also enjoys some measure of official recognition, which varies from country to country. Some nations even put regular Esperanto programs on their national radio.

It is perhaps more widely studied abroad than in America, but even here it has made its appearance in several public high schools and colleges. It is, of course, taught in special private schools, and plenty of grammars, dictionaries, readers, and even recordings are available.

Its sound scheme is simple, its system of writing has absolute sound-for-symbol correspondence, its grammatical structure is deliberately simplified, to the point where it can be easily learned in one hour. There is, of course, a vocabulary, which has to be acquired in the usual hard way, by memorization, reading, and writing.

Esperanto is recommended to anyone who wishes to see what can be done in the matter of making language learning as easy as possible to one who is not born to it. It can be practically useful to the extent that if you know it, you may meet in the course of your wanderings another person who wears the symbol of the little green star in his buttonhole, and you may address him without fear.

If the nations of the world ever decide to institute a single language, valid for international use, which they may be forced to do by reason of increased travel and communications before the end of this century, and if their spirit of nationalism prevents them from selecting one of the national tongues, they may have to fall back on a constructed, "neutral" language, and if this comes to pass, Esperanto is the most likely candidate, by reason of the progress it has already made.

26

The Problems of Learning English

How "Easy" Is Our Language?—Spelling, Pronunciation, and Standardization—The Deceptive Ease of the Grammatical Structure—The International Vocabulary—The World's Favorite Language

DURING the Second World War, I was requested by Governor Nelson Rockefeller, then Coordinator of Inter-American Affairs, to prepare scripts for an extensive series of English lessons for Spanish speakers, to be broadcast every week over local radio stations in Latin America. The series, I was informed much later, was highly successful, and the lessons were also adapted by OWI for extensive use in Europe, Africa, and Asia.

This was my first attempt at teaching English to foreigners. Considering that I had myself acquired English by the process of osmosis at an early age, I had never given the structure of the language, or its difficulties, any serious thought. All my conscious efforts had been directed at languages I had had to study the hard way. If anything, I had supinely subscribed to the widely held theory that English is a very "easy" language, by reason of its dearth of inflectional endings, its "logical" syntax, and its international vocabulary. It was not until I found myself squarely up against the necessity of explaining that "simple," "analytical" structure to people whose linguistic habits were different that I began to realize what difficulties English presents to those who face it at the adult stage, if one wishes to handle it in anything like correct native-speaker form (English is a language that lends itself superbly to pidginization, so that it can be spoken in forms that make your hair stand on end, but can still be understood).

A few words about the difficulties I encountered and attempted to solve in my radio series may be of some value to two categories of readers: foreigners who are studying English, and teachers of English to foreigners. The latter, as specialists in the field, are probably aware of everything I am going to say; nevertheless, they may at times, by reason of the fact that they are themselves native speakers, and that they may not know too much about their students' native languages, be tempted to minimize some of the troubles that beset their students, and not view them in proper perspective.

The spelling-pronunciation hurdle, one of the most serious in the world, is something that the foreign adult learner shares with the native child speaker. Both must learn in the hardest possible way how to spell words they may chance to hear first in spoken form, and how to pronounce words they may first see in written form. For this there is no help, save what would be vouchsafed by a wholesale reform of either English spelling or English pronunciation. Since the latter is practically unthinkable, and the former seems too remote a possibility to contemplate seriously, the only advice that can be given is to exercise patience and submit to hard work. The English speaker goes through the painful process of learning to spell from the time his schooling begins until he emerges from college or graduate school. People with Ph.D. degrees and linguistic specialization, like myself, occasionally have to pause and look in our English dictionaries to find out how a word is spelled or pronounced. The system of phonics used in some of our schools, whereby generalized rules of spelling-pronunciation are attempted, is of some value. But the number of exceptions is still too great for comfort.

For what concerns the pronunciation itself, divorced from the spelling, trouble is occasioned by the fact that there is no real English standard. The King's (or Queen's) English of Britain is only a pale reflection of standard Parisian French, standard Tuscan Italian, standard Castilian Spanish, standard *Bühnenaussprache* German. The British, as attested by Shaw, refuse to speak it, and lapse all too frequently into their own local or class dialects. As for American English, which diverges to a rather startling degree from any British variety, it is, if anything, even less standardized, with its three main varieties (Eastern, Southern, Midwestern) and its 25 or more lesser variants. While this permits the foreign learner some leeway in his own attempts at English pronunciation, it also occasions far greater confusion than occurs in the learning of more standardized Western tongues.

Among the features of English pronunciation that may generally be expected to cause trouble to a foreign learner are:

(a) The drawled stressed vowels, which more often than not turn into diphthongs by reason of added off-glides, and which in any case diverge considerably from the scheme of predominant cardinal vowels that prevails in most other Western languages. It is the tendency of the foreign learner to pronounce pure vowels where English has a single vowel symbol in spelling, but a diphthong in pronunciation (*a* of *late, o* of *note*). Additional difficulty is encountered in the case of those diphthongs which present a standard phonetic difference in British and American English, or among the various dialects of American (*o* of *note, ou* of *house*).

(b) The slurred, somewhat indistinct unstressed vowels, as illustrated by the unaccented vowels of *general* and *singing*. Again, regular phonetic differences between British and American (*o* of *hot*) add to the confusion. Most Romance speakers will have trouble with vowel sounds that do not appear in their sound schemes, even by approximation (*bat, bit,* unstressed *the, but, girl*). They will also find it difficult to establish the proper phonemic distinction between *hall* and *hull, leave* and *live, food* and *good*. For this there is no remedy save long, painstaking imitation and repetition, either of native speakers or of recordings, with particular stress on those phonemically distinct vowel sounds which do not constitute a phonemic distinction in the learner's own language.

(c) Among English consonant sounds, most troublesome are our alveolar *t, d, s, z, n, l,* which correspond in many foreign languages to postdentals, with a lower point of articulation; our two dental or interdental spirant *th* sounds (*thing, this*), which have no counterpart in most foreign languages, and for which various substitutions tend to be made by the foreign learner (*dees, zees,* etc. for *this*); our *h,* nonexistent in many languages, which Italians tend to ignore and Spanish speakers to overrate (they use the *j* of *jarra* instead); our *w,* which tends to be replaced by *v* in the pronunciation of German and Russian speakers, but with plenty of overcorrection, whereby *veal* comes out as *weal;* our *r,* far from standardized in the English-speaking world itself, which tends to be replaced by a uvular *r* in the mouths of French and German speakers, by a trill in the mouths of Slavic and other Romance speakers; our *ng* in final position, for which *-nk* is a common substitution. Russian speakers must be cautioned not to palatalize their consonants before *i* (*manyi, onlyi*).

Again, the only cure is the imitation and repetition of native speakers or recordings.

(d) English offers some bad initial and final consonant clusters (*shriek, desks, pests, ends, ribs*). Spanish speakers, in addition, will find difficult any initial group of *s* plus consonant (*speak, star, strive*), will tend to prefix an *e*-sound, and must be drilled out of it.

(e) English word stress, intonation, juncture, and syllabic division must be learned from experience, imitation, and repetition. Generalizations are of limited help (one may say, for instance, that in native Germanic words English usually stresses the initial syllable; but since more than half of all English words are borrowed from other sources, this hint is of limited value to a learner who is not an etymologist; we may also inform the learner that English favors the syllabic pattern consonant-vowel-consonant, or vowel-consonant, as illustrated by *gen-er-al;* but the exceptions are quite numerous; we may offer for imitation and repetition such examples as *blackbird* and *black bird,* illustrating various types of word stress and juncture, and such phrases as "What are we having for dinner, Mother?" and "What are we having for dinner, liver?" to illustrate English sentence stress; but again we run into strong individual and local divergences).

In the matter of grammatical structure, English looks deceptively simple. Our definite article is invariable, at least in written form (in speech, *the man* is opposed to *the egg*). Our indefinite article has two forms, but they are used in accordance with the sound that follows. Our gender and number system is quite logical (let us not worry too much about such exceptional forms as "she" for "ship," "it" for "baby," "five-foot pole," "two dozen eggs"). Our adjective is quite uninflected and invariable, save where it is substantivized ("young marrieds," "the screen greats"); its system of comparison (*-er, -est,* or *more, most*) is simple, and only occasionally leaves you in doubt ("coffier coffee"; or is it "coffeyer"?). Our noun has a very simple declensional scheme, with only a separate genitive form (*boy, boy's, boys, boys'*).

But here some of our troubles begin. Outside of our few irregular plurals (like *feet, mice, oxen, men, children*), our general plural suffix *-s* may assume in writing the form *-es,* often with a change of what precedes (*lady, ladies; knife, knives*). In speech, it may take three forms: /s/ if it follows an unvoiced consonant (desks); /z/ if it follows a voiced consonant or a vowel (*boys, limbs*); /iz/ if it follows an *s*- or *z*-sound (*glasses, sizes*). All this has to be carefully explained and illustrated to your foreign learner, under penalty of painful mispronunciations and misspellings. What has been said for the apparently simple -*s* plural of nouns applies equally to the equally seemingly simple -*s* that marks the third singular of verbs (*walks; loves, tidies; pierces, fizzes*).

The English verb is, in theory, a very simple thing. Basically, we are afflicted with only two types of verbs, the weak (*love, loves, loved*) and the strong (*see, sees, saw, seen*). The three morphological forms (plus the universally regular present participle in -*ing*) of the weak verb, and the four of the strong verb, are all one need memorize. A very considerable number of auxiliaries that have to be properly used removes some of this advantage (*have, be, may, might, can, could, shall, should, will, would, must,* etc., with all their compound forms). Our universal use of subject pronouns and our reduction of all forms of address to a single *you* (*youse, you-all, you'uns* are recognized as dialectal and substandard even by the apostles of usage), help out.

One initial difficulty that presents itself in connection with English verbs is the multiplicity of negative and interrogative formations. The use of *do* as an auxiliary for questions and negations presents some thorny aspects to speakers of other languages that merely invert or use one or more negative particles. Consider, for example, "he goes," but "he does not go," "does he go?"; "has he?", "does he have?" (Americans use these two forms more or less interchangeably, but the British use them only in given situations); "is he?", but not "does he be?" The use or non-use of *do* may come natural to an English speaker, but it is anything but natural to a foreign learner, and calls for heavy practice.

The real trouble with the English verb is the way it combines with an almost endless list of prepositions and adverbs to supply new and highly idiomatic meanings. Merely learning *look* and *out* will not give the learner the idiomatic meaning of the combination *look out* ("be careful"); "see through something" and "see something through," "go fast" and "stand fast," "run down," "run up," "run through," "make up," "make out," "give up," "give in," "give out," "play up," "play down," "call for," "call up," "call down," are all combinations that have to be learned as expressions altogether different in meaning from their component parts. English is a language in which the by-verb (to give this combination its technical name) is basic; in fact, it is so basic that it forms the backbone of that semi-artificial linguistic system which other languages have in vain tried to duplicate, Basic English. Here, fewer than twenty verbs are allowed; they are merely combined with various prepositions and adverbs to give you thousands of verb meanings that other languages would be forced to convey by means of separate, individual verbs. But to think that these idiomatic combinations are easy to anyone not born to them or brought up with them is one of the worst snares and delusions ever concocted by the human mind. They must be learned, and learned the hard way, if English is to make any sense at all to a foreign learner. The worst feature about them is that their existence and paramount importance in the process of learning English is not even generally recognized. Repeated suggestions to American publishers that they bring out word lists and dictionaries of English by-verbs, with their foreign-language equivalents, for the instruction of foreign learners, have met with stubborn refusals.

It is hard to tell whether the English by-verb pertains to the domain of morphology, to that of syntax, or to that of vocabulary. Outside of them, English syntax does not present any overwhelming difficulties. The word order is fairly well fixed, with a general arrangement of subject-verb-object, and a strong tendency to place the modifier before the modified word (articles and adjectives before nouns, adverbs before adjectives and participles).

It is often difficult in English to tell apart the parts of speech, by reason of an almost deliberately planned scarcity of flectional endings or other distinctive terminations, and of the freedom of functional change (a noun turns into a verb with no ceremony of ending change, as with *contact, screen, poll, mail;* in like manner a verb may turn into a noun, as with *show, hit, shave, find;* and, of course, nouns may be used as adjectives (*a class distinction*) and many adjectives as nouns (*soup greens*). This feature, which gives English a faint resemblance to Chinese, can be quite bewildering to the foreign learner, and even to the native, when it appears in newspaper headlines

("Police police police poll," meaning that the police policed a poll dealing with the police themselves).

The English vocabulary is the richest in the world, by reason of the numerous sources from which the language has abundantly and freely borrowed, its free and easy tendency to coin words, and its leading position as the vehicle of many branches of science and technology, each of which has its own specialized vocabulary, or jargon.

While this constitutes an advantage, by reason of plentiful synonyms, it also lends itself to the creation of an extraordinarily large number of confusing homonyms, homophones, and other picturesque but disagreeable features, involving sound, form, spelling, and meaning (*him, hymn; time, thyme; pole, Pole; fare, fair; post,* in its various meanings and derivations). All these things must be acquired and assimilated for proper use of the language in anything but pidgin form.

In connection with the learning of English, the use of native speakers or recordings should go hand in hand with intensive grammatical practice of the pattern and frame variety, and extensive reading of all types of material. But even before the learner starts, he should make up his mind on one important point, namely, which main variant of English he wants, the British or the American. Continental Europeans who have learned British English in their schools are often confused on coming to America because American English presents too many unfamiliar features, not only of pronunciation and intonation but also of grammar and spelling and, above all, of vocabulary and idioms. It would be highly desirable if European schools and colleges were to institute parallel courses in the two main branches of the English language. At the very least, they might add some of the most important American variants to their British English, considering that not only foreign learners but even native Americans and Britons are occasionally confused and stumped by each other's language; and considering also that American speakers now constitute an absolute majority of all native speakers of English.

All the language-learning processes that have been mentioned in connection with other tongues are fully operative in the learning of English, with one or two added features. The learner should no doubt go through the listening and imitating procedure, the pattern and word substitution drills. But he should certainly supplement them with abundant reading practice, for the proper acquisition of idioms and by-verbs, taking them not only in a fleeting spoken context but also in a written context where they can be considered, studied, and assimilated at leisure. Since he is spared the chore of memorizing endless paradigms of declensions and conjugations, which face him elsewhere, he should not mind devoting some of the time saved to that peculiarly English chore which consists in linking the spoken with the written form—in other words, spelling and pronunciation drills. English lends itself to pidginization and use by functional illiterates. But English is also a language of mighty literary and philosophical content, and, above all, the language of business, science, and technology par excellence. Hence it should be acquired contemporaneously in both forms, the spoken and the written.

As the language having the second highest number of native speakers in the world (over 300 million, or slightly better than one person out of every ten on earth), plus at least another 100 million who use it in acquired or pidgin form; as the language most widely distributed and most widely studied in the world; as the language which possesses the largest quantitative amount of books, magazines, newspapers, radio and TV programs (the quality is occasionally something else again); as the language most widely favored in all polls taken so far for the post of international tongue, English is well worth a sincere and determined effort.

As a further inducement, it may be added that English is fully and solely official in the following countries to which it is not native: Kenya, Liberia, Nigeria, Sierra Leone, Rhodesia, Uganda, Zambia, Gambia. It is co-official with one or more other languages, native or colonial, in the following countries: Cameroon, Ghana, Mali, Somalia, Malawi, South Africa, Sudan, Tanzania, Burma, Ceylon, India, Israel, Jordan, Kuwait, Malaysia, Singapore, Nepal, Pakistan, the Philippines, Thailand, Tonga, Samoa, Ireland, and the Isle of Jersey.

Appendix I. Alphabets and Language Sounds

The purpose of this Appendix is to describe what the letters of the Roman, Greek, and Cyrillic alphabets mean, in terms of sounds, to the speakers of languages using those three closely related writing systems. This puts into reverse the more modern trend to describe languages in terms of sounds, then proceed to describe how those sounds are alphabetically represented. However, from the standpoint of the layman, who is faced with foreign words and names in written form, and wonders how the words or names may be pronounced, the approach we are using is intensely practical. It is also of general interest to the language learner, supplying him with a ready table of reference to information that would otherwise have to be sought in many different manuals.

The languages wholly or partly covered in this Appendix are:

(Germanic): German, Dutch, Swedish, Norwegian, Danish, Icelandic.

(Latin-Romance): Classical Latin, French, Spanish, Portuguese, Italian, Rumanian.

(Slavic): Russian, Ukrainian, Polish, Czech, Serbo-Croatian (with Croatian in Roman alphabet, Serbian in Cyrillic), Bulgarian.

(Baltic): Lithuanian, Lettish (or Latvian).

(Greek): Classical Greek, modern Greek.

(Celtic): Irish, Welsh.

(Ural-Altaic): Finnish, Hungarian, Turkish.

(Otherwise classified): Albanian, Malay-Indonesian, Esperanto.

To these have been added languages that most frequently appear in standardized Roman alphabet transliteration or transcription (Sanskrit, Hindi, Japanese); also, in part, Arabic and Hebrew. Omitted are Chinese, because of lack of standardization in transcription, particularly with regard to tones; Vietnamese, which uses the Roman alphabet, but has an extremely complicated system of written diacritics and tones; Basque, which uses the Roman alphabet but has no standardized written form (though one or two occasional letter-groups on which there is agreement are mentioned). Mention also appears, where relevant, of Catalan and Old Provençal, as well as of Anglo-Saxon and Breton. Omitted are also a few languages which are close variants of others that appear (Slovenian, Slovak, Macedonian, for instance).

Within the same language, multiple pronunciations for the same symbol or group of symbols are by no means an exclusive prerogative of English. In most languages, however, there is a possibility of classifying variant pronunciations, according to position in the word or other consistent rules. Irish seems to be the only language that outstrips English in erratic features of pronunciation in relation to spelling.

In this study, each letter of the Roman alphabet is first presented uncombined and unmodified by diacritic signs, with full explanation and exemplification for the more commonly studied languages (German, Classical Latin, French, Spanish, Portuguese, Italian), and occasionally for others; next, the letter appears with modifying diacritic signs; lastly, the letter is given when it is the first element of a group of letters used with a special phonetic value.

The Greek and Cyrillic alphabets are treated in the same fashion. For Greek, the two pronunciations selected are the Classical Attic of the fifth–fourth centuries B.C., as reconstructed by the Erasmian scholars of the Renaissance; and the current official modern pronunciation. For Cyrillic, the languages selected are modern Russian, Ukrainian, Serbian, and Bulgarian, with occasional reference to Byelorussian.

Of particular importance in the relationship between spelling and pronunciation are the factors of stress (the place where the accent falls in a given word); vowel quantity (significant length or shortness of a vowel sound); length of spoken consonant sounds (usually indicated in writing by gemination, or writing the consonant double); and diacritic marks (symbols placed above, beneath, or to the side of given letters to indicate a modified pronunciation). These factors are separately and briefly described below.

STRESS

The stress normally falls on the initial syllable of the word (save for foreign loan-words and native words beginning with certain prefixes) in the Germanic languages (English, German, Dutch, Swedish, Norwegian, Danish, Icelandic). However, all these languages, English more than the others, have borrowed a large portion of their vocabulary from other, non-Germanic tongues, especially from Latin, Greek, and Romance sources; in such borrowed words the rule of initial stress does not hold. Also, there are some native Germanic prefixes that refuse to take the stress, which then falls on the second, or root, syllable. Some of the more common of these are represented in English by *be-* of *behold, for-* of *forswear, mis-* of *mislead, to-* of *today, un-* of *unborn, with-* of *withdraw*. The list varies from one Germanic language to another; German, for example, stresses initial *zu-, un-, mit-,* which etymologically correspond to English *to-, un-, with-,* but adds *emp-, ent-, er-, ge-, ver-, zer-* to the stress-rejecting prefixes.

Other languages that regularly stress the initial syllable are Czech, Hungarian, Finnish. Japanese and Serbo-Croatian most often, but not invariably, have initial stress.

Languages that regularly stress the penult (next to the last) syllable are Polish and Esperanto. The penult is most often stressed in Spanish, Portuguese, Italian, Rumanian, Welsh, and Malay-Indonesian; but sometimes these languages stress the last syllable, or the third from the end. Spanish and Portuguese give indication of this "irregular" stress by marking the vowel with an acute accent. Italian indicates a final stressed vowel by a grave accent, but offers no written indication of penultimate or other accent. In Classical Latin the stress falls on the penult or third from the end, but without written indication.

Final stress appears with some regularity in Turkish and French; in French, however, if the final syllable has a so-called mute *e* that is pronounced (*notre, livre*), the stress is on the penult.

Generally unpredictable is the position of the stress in Lithuanian, Lettish, Irish, Albanian, Sanskrit, Hindi, Greek, Russian, Ukrainian, Bulgarian.

VOWEL QUANTITY
(LONG AND SHORT VOWEL SOUNDS)

Distinctions that are phonemic (i.e., significant in distinguishing meanings between two words that are otherwise alike) between long and short vowel sounds appear in English, German, Dutch, Swedish, Norwegian, Danish, Icelandic, Classical Latin, Czech, Serbo-Croatian, Finnish, Hungarian, Lithuanian, Lettish, Irish, Welsh, Arabic, Hebrew, Sanskrit, Hindi, Japanese, Classical Greek. These distinctions may be indicated in writing by a double vowel (as in Finnish); by the use of an accent mark or other diacritic sign (as in Czech, Hungarian, Lettish); by the use of an *h* after the vowel (as in German); or by the position of the vowel in relation to other letters in the word (German *loben* vs. *voll*). In some languages there is often no distinction in writing (English *boot* vs. *foot*).

Distinction between long and short vowel sounds appears occasionally in French (*notre* vs. *nôtre*) and Portuguese (*a* vs. *à*); but the distinction in length is usually accompanied by a modification of sound as well as of semantic value.

Languages in which there is little if any distinction between long and short vowel sounds, save to the extent that the stressed vowel of the word may be non-phonemically lengthened by some speakers or under special circumstances of emphasis, excitement, etc., are Spanish, Italian, Rumanian, Polish, Turkish, Albanian, Malay-Indonesian, modern Greek, Russian, Ukrainian, Bulgarian.

GEMINATION (DOUBLING) OF CONSONANTS

Written double consonants are particularly significant for distinction of meaning (phonemic) in Classical Latin, Italian, Finnish, Hungarian, Arabic, Hebrew, Sanskrit, Hindi, Japanese, Classical and modern Greek. They are not generally significant to pronunciation in English, French, Portuguese, Polish, Czech, Lithuanian, Lettish, Irish, Malay-Indonesian, Esperanto, Russian. In some of these languages (English, French) the use of the written double consonant is etymological and traditional. In others (Spanish, Portuguese, the Slavic languages) written double consonants seldom appear. Occasionally the written double consonant indicates a different spoken value rather than a lengthening for the consonant sound; this is true of Spanish *ll*, French and Portuguese *ss* between vowels, Welsh *ff* and *ll*, Icelandic double consonants which indicate an *h*-sound before the consonant doubled. Some doubt attaches to the value of written double consonants in German, Swedish, Norwegian, Danish, Russian, where the speaker, influenced perhaps by the spelling, often tends to lengthen the consonant sound. In some languages that normally do not distinguish in speech between a single and a double written consonant, there is an occasional lengthening, or even repetition of the consonant sound when the word is felt to be a compound (English *innate, unknown,* vs. *inane, unable;* Spanish *ennoblecer*).

The phonetic process of pronouncing a "double" consonant consists of lengthening the period of production of the sound, save in the case of plosives (*p, b, k, g, t, d*), where the production of the sound consists of gathering the breath behind a complete obstruction somewhere in the vocal passage, then suddenly releasing the obstruction. For plosives, the doubling process consists phonetically of prolonging the period of retention before the release, which is by its nature invariable.

DIACRITIC SIGNS

´ (acute accent)—indicates length of vowel (not necessarily place of stress) in Czech, Hungarian, Icelandic, Irish; it generally indicates the place of the stress in Spanish, Portuguese, Albanian; a modification of the vowel sound in French, Polish; a palatalization of the consonant sound in Polish, Croatian. In the Yale transcription of Chinese, it indicates a rising tone.

` (grave accent)—indicates final-vowel stress in Italian; the place of the original stress in compound words in Portuguese; distinction between short words having identical spelling and pronunciation in French (*la, là; ou, où*); but also a modification in pronunciation of *e* (*père*). In Yale transcription of Chinese, it indicates a falling tone.

^ or ˆ (circumflex accent; the second symbol seldom appears save in Greek)—indicates place of stress, modification of vowel sound, and some measure of length in French and Portuguese; modification of vowel sound in Rumanian; modification of consonant sound in Esperanto. Appears occasionally in other languages to indicate contraction of two vowels into one.

¯ (macron)—indicates length of vowel sound in Latin (but is not always used); Sanskrit and Hindi transliterations (where it may also indicate a modified value for consonants); Lettish; Japanese (in Japanese transcriptions, *ii* often replaces *ī*). In Chinese transcriptions, indicates level tone.

˘ (breve)—indicates modification of vowel sound in Rumanian, Malay-Indonesian; modification of consonant sound in Turkish; shortness of vowel sound in Latin, but is seldom indicated. In Chinese Yale transcription, indicates falling-rising tone.

¨ (umlaut or diaeresis)—as an umlaut sign, indicates modification of vowel sound in German, Swedish, Norwegian, Danish, Icelandic, Albanian, Finnish, Hungarian, Turkish. As a diaeresis sign over the second of two contiguous vowels, it indicates in French, occasionally in English, that the two vowels are to be pronounced separately instead of combining in pronunciation (*Noël, coöperate*). In Spanish and Portuguese, over the first of two contiguous vowels, it indicates that a *u* following *g* or *q* and preceding a vowel is to be pronounced where it would otherwise be silent (*vergüenza, conseqüéncia*).

˝ (umlaut)—this modified version of the preceding sign may be used interchangeably with it save in Hungarian, where it indicates length for the middle rounded vowel over which it appears, while the double dot indicates short quantity.

° —indicates modified value for the vowel over which it appears in Swedish, Norwegian, Czech.

˛ —indicates nasalization of vowel under which it appears in Polish, Lithuanian (but in Lithuanian the nasalization has disappeared in modern pronunciation). It is occasionally used in historical linguistics to indicate an open quality for vowels, particularly *e* and *o*.

˛ (cedilla)—indicates modification of consonant sound in French, Portuguese, Rumanian, Lithuanian, Lettish, Turkish.

˜ (til or tilde)—indicates palatalization of *n* in Spanish, Sanskrit, Hindi; nasalization of vowel in Portuguese.

ˇ —indicates palatalization of consonant in Polish, Czech, Croatian, Lithuanian, Lettish; modification of vowel sound in Czech.

. —under consonant, indicates modification of consonant sound in Lithuanian, Sanskrit, Hindi, Arabic. Occasionally used in historical linguistics to indicate closed quality for vowels, particularly *e* and *o*.

˙ —over consonant in Polish, over vowel in Lithuanian, indicates modified value. The *absence* of the dot over *i* in Turkish indicates modified value.

/ or ⁄ bar across *l* indicates modified value in Polish; across *o* indicates modified value in Norwegian, Danish.

' —(smooth breathing)—in Greek, indicates lack of *h*-sound before initial vowel; in Arabic, Hebrew transliterations, indicates a glottal stop, similar to English *co-operate*, German *die Eier*.

' (rough breathing)—in Classical, but not in modern Greek, indicates *h*-sound before initial vowel or *r;* in Arabic, Hebrew transliterations, indicates constriction of pharynx; but while this is still alive in Arabic, it has practically disappeared from modern Hebrew.

⌢ —occasionally used in linguistics under the vowels *i* and *u* to indicate a semivowel value (*y* of *yet* or *boy; w* of *wow*).

NOTE ON THE TRANSCRIPTION OF CHINESE TONES

In the older Wade transcription, the tones are indicated by numerical exponents, as follows: (level tone) Yale *mā*, Wade *ma*[1]; (rising tone) Yale *má*, Wade *ma*[2]; (falling-rising tone) Yale *mă*, Wade *ma*[3]; (falling tone) Yale *mà*, Wade *ma*[4]. Another system of transcription uses the symbols ⁻, / , ∨, \ before the word instead of over the vowel.

THE ROMAN ALPHABET

A

Generally represents a sound ranging between the *o* of American *not* and the *a* of *father,* more usually the latter. In some languages and transliterations, it indicates a sound close to the *u* of *but.*

German—distinguishes between long *a* (V*a*ter = f*a*ther, somewhat prolonged), and short *a* (W*a*sser = *a*ha). The same distinction occurs in Classical Latin (lātus vs. lătus), Swedish, Norwegian, Danish.

French—usually = h*a*t, but slightly more open (m*a* mère); occasionally = f*a*ther (p*a*s). The same distinction holds in Dutch (k*a*t vs. r*a*men).

Spanish—regularly = f*a*ther (*a*gua).

Portuguese—stressed, = f*a*ther; unstressed, = b*u*t (*á*gua).

Italian—regularly = f*a*ther (*a*cqu*a*).

Icelandic, Rumanian, Polish, Czech, Croatian, Lithuanian, Lettish, Welsh, Albanian, Finnish, Turkish, Malay-Indonesian, Esperanto, transliterations of Hebrew, Japanese— = f*a*ther (more or less prolonged).

Irish—variations include h*a*t, n*o*t, m*e*t, b*u*t.

Hungarian— = n*o*t in British pronunciation.

Sanskrit, Hindi transliterations— = b*u*t (note translit. of *Panjab* as *Punjab*).

Arabic— = m*a*n.

With Diacritic Signs

á—Spanish, Portuguese: indicates place of stress (hablar*á,* *á*gua); Czech, Hungarian: = f*a*ther, somewhat prolonged; Icelandic: = f*a*ther or c*o*w; Irish: = l*a*w.

à—French: = h*a*t, slightly more open; Italian (occasionally also Rumanian): indicates stress on final vowel (citt*à*); Portuguese: in compound words, indicates place of original stress, but is seldom used (m*à*zinha).

â—French: = f*a*ther (*â*ge); Portuguese: = see *â*m, *â*n, below; Rumanian: in older spelling = rhythm (c*â*nt*à*).

ā—Classical Latin: = f*a*ther prolonged, but is not always used; Lettish: = f*a*ther prolonged. Used in transliteration of both ancient and modern languages (Indo-European, Sanskrit, Hindi, Greek, Hebrew, Japanese): = f*a*ther prolonged. Arabic: = m*a*n prolonged.

ă—Rumanian: = bac*o*n (ap*ă*); used occasionally to indicate sound of short American n*o*t in ancient languages (Latin lătus vs. lātus).

ä—German: long = th*e*re (wählen); short = m*e*t (Männer); Swedish, Norwegian, Danish: = m*e*t (before *r*, = m*a*n); Finnish: = m*a*n.

ã—Portuguese: = f*a*ther with nasal passage closed off (irm*ã*).

ą —Polish: = f*o*r with nasal passage closed off.

å—Swedish, Norwegian: long = s*aw;* short = British n*o*t.

In Combination

aa—German, Dutch, Finnish: = f*a*ther prolonged (P*aa*r, r*aa*d, s*aa*); Danish: = s*aw*.

ää—Finnish: = h*a*d prolonged.

aai—Dutch: = s*i*gh.

ae (or æ)—Classical Latin, Icelandic: = tr*y;* Norwegian, Danish: = b*a*d or b*e*d; Anglo-Saxon: = h*a*t (æ = b*a*d prolonged).

ãe—Portuguese: = l*ie* with nasal passage closed off (*cães*).

ah—German: = f*a*ther prolonged (f*a*hren).

ai—French: at end of verb-form = f*a*te without final glide (j'aur*ai*); elsewhere = b*e*t (f*ai*re); Irish: = m*e*t; in other languages, generally = s*i*gh.

ái—Irish: = l*aw*.

aim, ain—French: final or before consonant = m*e*n with nasal passage closed (f*aim*, m*ain*, m*ain*tenant).

aj—Swedish, Norwegian, Danish, Dutch, Czech: = s*i*gh.

am, an—French: final or before consonant = f*a*ther with nasal passage closed (fl*am*bé, *an*).

an—Portuguese: before consonant = f*u*n with nasal passage closed (dist*ân*cia).

ão—Portuguese: = c*ow* with nasal passage closed (c*ão*).

aoi—Irish: = s*ee*.

au—German, Dutch, Swedish, Norwegian, Danish, Spanish, Portuguese, Italian: = h*ow* (Ger. *au*s; Sp. f*au*sto; Pt., It. *au*mento); French: = g*o* without final glide (*au*rai).

äu—German: = b*oy* (Br*äu*haus).

auw—Dutch: = h*ow* (g*auw*).

B

Generally pronounced as in English.

German—final = la*p* (a*b*); also Dutch, Catalan.

Spanish—between vowels, even in two separate but closely linked words,

= li*v*e pronounced bilabially (both lips, not lower lip and upper teeth) (Ha*b*ana, la *b*arraca). Elsewhere, as in English.
Finnish—not used, save in foreign names and loan-words.

In Combination

bb—prolong period before release in Italian (a*bb*iamo), Hungarian, transliterations of Sanskrit, Hindi, Arabic, Hebrew, Japanese.
bh—Irish: = *v*at or *w*et; Sanskrit, Hindi transliterations: = Kno*bh*ill (*Bh*ārāt, Hindi name for India).

C

Seldom used save in foreign names and loan-words in German, Dutch, Swedish, Norwegian, Danish, Icelandic, Finnish, Malay-Indonesian; in native words in the Germanic languages, it is generally combined with *h* or *k* (see below).

German—before *e, i, ä, ö, ü* = i*ts* (*C*äsar); before *a, o, u,* consonant = *c*at (*C*afe).
French—before *e, i* = *s*o (*c*ici); before a, o, u, consonant = *c*offee (*c*afé, *c*rème).
Spanish—before *a, o, u,* consonant = *c*at (*c*asa); before *e, i* = *s*o (generally in southern Spain, Spanish America) or = *th*ing (northern Spain; *c*ielo).
Portuguese—before *a, o, u,* consonant—*c*at (*c*asa); before *e, i* = *s*o (*c*idade).
Italian—before *a, o, u,* consonant = *c*at (*c*asa); before *e, i* = *ch*urch (*c*era). Likewise in Rumanian.
Swedish—before *e, i, y* = *s*o; Norwegian, Danish—before *ä, ae, e, i* = *s*o; elsewhere = *c*ome.
Polish, Czech, Croatian, Lithuanian, Lettish, Albanian, Hungarian, Esperanto—regularly = i*ts*.
Classical Latin, Irish, Welsh—regularly = *c*at (Lat. *c*auda, *C*icero).
Turkish— = *j*et.
In transliteration of Sanskrit, Hindi— = *ch*urch.

With Diacritic Signs

ç—French, Portuguese, Catalan: = *s*o (Fr. fa*ç*ade, Pt. ca*ç*ador); Turkish, Albanian: = *ch*urch; Sanskrit, Hindi transliterations: a*sh* (*Ç*iva).
č—Czech, Lithuanian, Lettish: = *ch*urch.

c—Esperanto: = *ch*urch.

ć—Polish, Croatian: = hi*t* *y*ou or *ch*urch.

In Combination

cc—Latin, Italian, Sanskrit and Hindi transliterations: prolong period before release of *c,* with whatever value *c* has in that position in that language (Lat. fla*cc*us, It. Ba*cc*o, la*cc*i).

cch—Italian, Sanskrit and Hindi transliterations: prolong period before release of *ch,* with whatever value *ch* has in that position in that language (It. fa*cch*ino).

ch—French, Portuguese, Breton: = *sh*ore (Fr. *ch*er, Pt. *ch*amar); Spanish: = *ch*urch (le*ch*e); Italian, Rumanian: before *e, i* = *c*at (It. *ch*i, *ch*e); German: *after a, o, u* = Scottish lo*ch* (Ba*ch*); *after e, i, ä, ö, ü,* consonant = strongly articulated *h*uge (i*ch*); Swedish: *sh*ore (usually in loan words from French); Dutch, Polish, Czech, Croatian, Irish, Welsh, transliteration of Hebrew: = lo*ch;* Japanese transliteration: = sound intermediate between *ch*urch and hi*t* *y*ou; Catalan: in final position = sa*c*.

c'h—Breton: = Scottish lo*ch*.

ci—Italian: followed by vowel = *ch*ill (*ci*ascuno); Polish: = wha*t's* *y*our.

ck—German, Swedish: as in English; Polish, Czech, Croatian, Lithuanian, Lettish, Albanian, Hungarian, Esperanto: = i*t's* *k*illing; Dutch, Norwegian, Danish, French, Spanish, Portuguese, Italian, Rumanian: used only in foreign words.

cq—Italian: = *c*ool, with holding period prolonged before release (a*cq*ua).

cs—Hungarian: = *ch*urch (*cs*árdás).

cz—Hungarian: = i*ts;* Polish: = *ch*urch.

D

Save in the Germanic languages (English, German, Dutch, Swedish, Norwegian, Danish, Icelandic) it is rather dental than alveolar (tip of tongue against back of upper teeth rather than against ridge of upper gums). This is particularly true of the Romance languages.

German— = *d*ear (*d*er); in final position = le*t* (Ba*d*). Likewise in Dutch (raa*d*), Swedish.

French— = dental *d*ear or A*d*am (*d*ouce); final and linked to initial vowel sound of following word = le*t* (gran*d* homme).

Spanish— = dental *d*ear, ban*d*y (*d*uro, an*d*ar); between vowels, even in

two separate but closely linked words, = o*t*her (to*d*o, la *d*ueña); final
is often silent or = *th*ing (Uste*d*).

Portuguese— = dental *d*ear, A*d*am.

Norwegian, Danish—between vowels, often = fa*t*her; final, often silent
after *l, n, r,* or before final *s, t.*

Catalan—final = le*t.*

Finnish—not used save in foreign words and names.

With Diacritic Signs

dˇ—Czech: = di*d* you.

ḍ—in Arabic transliteration, indicates emphatically uttered *d* (blade of
tongue pressed against palate); in Sanskrit, Hindi transliteration indicates English alveolar *d* (as against the transliteration *d,* which indicates
the Romance dental *d*).

ᚦ —Icelandic: = *th*is; Anglo-Saxon: = *th*is or *th*ing.

In Combination

dd—Welsh: = *th*is; Latin, Italian, Hungarian, transliterations of Sanskrit,
Hindi, Arabic, Hebrew, Japanese: prolong period before release (Lat.
a*dd*ere, It. a*dd*etto).

dh—Irish: generally silent; Albanian: = *th*is; Sanskrit, Hindi transliterations: = ba*d h*ome.

dj—Swedish: = *y*et; Croatian: = di*d* you; Catalan, Malay-Indonesian: =
*j*oke.

ds—Hungarian: = *g*in.

dz—Polish: = a*dz*e.

dź—Polish: = di*d* you.

dż—Polish = *j*ump.

dž—Croatian, Lithuanian, Lettish: = *j*ump.

dzs—Hungarian: = *j*ump.

E

Generally ranges between m*e*t and th*e*re (or g*a*te without final glide).

German—if long, = th*e*re or g*a*te (l*e*ben); if short, = m*e*t (F*e*nster);
final, generally as in fath*e*r, though some tend to pronounce as in m*e*t
(Glock*e*). The same holds generally for Swedish, Norwegian, Danish.

French—followed by consonant in the same syllable, = m*e*t (l*e*ttre); in
-*er* and -*ez* verb endings, = g*a*te without final glide, and somewhat

shorter (ferm*er,* ferm*ez*); is silent in *-e* and *-es* endings of words of more than one syllable (port*e,* port*es*), and in 3rd person plural verb endings (port*ent*); elsewhere = th*e* man (l*e,* remettr*e*).

Spanish— = th*e*re, or g*a*te without final glide (*este*).

Portuguese—stressed and open, = m*e*t (t*e*rra); stressed and closed, = g*a*te without final glide (m*e*sa); unstressed, fluctuates between p*i*n and th*e* man (pr*e*sente); initial and followed by *s* plus consonant, is silent or = th*e* man (*e*scudo); final, or preceding final *s,* = th*e* man in Portugal and parts of Brazil, = p*i*n in other parts of Brazil, notably Rio de Janeiro (present*e*).

Italian—stressed and open, = m*e*t (b*e*ne); stressed and closed, = g*a*te without final glide (fr*e*ddo); unstressed, generally = g*a*te without final glide (b*e*ne, pr*e*sente).

Dutch—long, = g*a*te without final glide; short, = m*e*t; final, and in prefixes, suffixes, and articles, = th*e* man.

Rumanian—initial = y*e*t; elsewhere = m*e*t.

Polish, Czech, Croatian, Lithuanian, Lettish, Irish, Welsh, Albanian, Finnish, Turkish—generally = m*e*t.

Breton—sometimes = French *é,* sometimes = French *è;* never French *e* of l*e.*

Hungarian— = h*a*t.

Esperanto— = g*a*te without final glide.

Latin—quantity distinction between long (m*ē*) and short (b*ĕ*ne) at first did not affect open or closed quality, but at some point in historical development which is still uncertain long *ē* assumed the quality of g*a*te, short *e* that of m*e*t, while quantity distinctions became blurred. Quantity distinctions appear in transliterations of Sanskrit, Hindi, Arabic, Hebrew, Japanese, with degree of openness a matter largely of speaker's choice or dialectal variation.

With Diacritic Signs

é—French: = g*a*te, closed and short (port*é*); Spanish: indicates place of stress (habl*é*); Portuguese: = m*e*t (caf*é*); Hungarian: = g*a*te, closed and prolonged.

è—French: = m*e*t (m*è*re); Portuguese: in compound words, indicates place of stress in original form (caf*è*zinho); Italian: indicates stress on final vowel (which may be open or closed: caff*è,* ricev*è*).

ê—French: = m*e*t, sometimes prolonged (*ê*tre); Portuguese: = g*a*te, closed and short (*ê*ste).

ē—Latin: = g*a*te, long and without final glide, but not always used (m*ē*); Lettish: = g*a*te, prolonged and without final glide.

ĕ—Latin: = mɛt, but not always indicated (bĕne); Malay-Indonesian: = thɛ man or is silent (pĕlan).

ë—French: = mɛt, to be pronounced separate from preceding vowel (Noël); Albanian: = the man.

ę—Polish—mɛt with nasal passage closed: Lithuanian: = mɛt (former nasalization now lost); in historical linguistics sometimes used to indicate open quality of *e* (= mɛt).

ě—Czech: = yɛt.

ė—Lithuanian: = gɑte or ɑisle.

ẹ—in historical linguistics, sometimes used to indicate closed quality of *e* (gɑte).

In Combination

ea—Rumanian: = yɑrd, or mɛt + yɑrd, with stress on *a;* Irish: = tin or nɔt.

éa—Irish: = hɑd.

eau—French: = gɔ without final glide (bɛau).

ee—Dutch: = gɑte prolonged, without final glide; Finnish: = mɛt prolonged.

eeuw—Dutch: = mɛt + fool.

eg—Norwegian, Danish: = *eight.*

eh—German: = gɑte without final glide, prolonged (zɛhn).

ei—German: = mine (ein); Portuguese, Italian, Norwegian, Danish, Finnish, Japanese transliteration: = *eight* (Port. leite, It. bei); Irish: = mɛt; Dutch: = *eight* or bite.

éi—Irish: = hɑd.

ein—French: final, or before consonant, = mɑn with nasal passage closed (sein).

ej—Norwegian, Danish, Czech: = *eight.*

em—French: final, or before consonant, = fɑther with nasal passage closed (embêter); Portuguese: = gɑte, *with* final glide and nasal passage closed (homem, em).

en—French: before consonant, = fɑther with nasal passage closed (encore); in final position, especially preceded by *i,* often = mɑn with nasal passage closed (rien, italien).

eu—German: = bɔy (treu); French: = mɛt with rounded lips (a lesser degree of rounding (seul) and a greater degree, amounting to a pout, especially in final position (feu); Norwegian, Danish: = French *eu* + v (oeuvre); Dutch: = mɛt with rounded lips; Spanish, Italian, Portuguese, Latin: = stressed mɛt + fool (Europa).

F

Generally as in English, with air escaping gradually between lower lip and upper teeth.

Japanese transliteration (regularly followed by *u*)—air escapes between lower and upper lip, as when one blows out a match (*Fu*ji).

Welsh— = A*v*on.

Anglo-Saxon—between vowels = se*v*en.

Icelandic— = se*v*en, lo*v*e between vowels and in final position.

Not used save in foreign words and names in Finnish, Malay-Indonesian.

In Combination

ff—Welsh: = sa*f*e; Latin, Italian, Finnish, Hungarian, Arabic, Hebrew transliterations: = *f* prolonged (Lat. of*f*icium, It. uf*f*icio).

fh—Irish: generally silent.

G

Generally used with value of *g*o, but used in addition, in various languages, with value of *g*eneral, plea*s*ure, *y*et, si*ng*.

German—normally = *g*o, regardless of following vowel (*g*ehen); final, especially after *e*, *i*, = *h*uge or ki*ck* (salzi*g*); = plea*s*ure in recent French loan words; to represent sound of *g*eneral in loan-words, often uses *dsch* (Man*dsch*u).

French—before *a*, *o*, *u*, consonant = *g*o (*g*arçon); before *e*, *i* = plea*s*ure (*g*énéral).

Spanish—before *a*, *o*, *u*, consonant = *g*o (*g*abán); but between vowels, sound is fricative rather than plosive (force breath through small opening between back of tongue and back of palate; la*g*o); before *e*, *i* = strongly aspirated *h* (*g*eneral); strength of aspiration varies according to area.

Portuguese—before *a*, *o*, *u*, consonant = *g*o (*g*rande, *g*ula); before *e*, *i* = plea*s*ure (*g*eral).

Italian—before a, o, u, consonant = *g*o (la*g*o); before *e*, *i* = *g*eneral (*g*enerale); likewise in Rumanian.

Swedish—initially or after consonant, and before *ä*, *e*, *i*, *ö*, *y*, = *y*et; final is often silent (-li*g*, da*g*) or = ki*ck* (ty*g*); elsewhere = *g*o.

Norwegian—before *i*, *y* = *y*et; final = ki*ck* or fricative *gh*; elsewhere = *g*o.

Danish—final or between vowels generally silent; otherwise = go.

Icelandic—initial and followed by *e, i* = hoa*g*y (*g*efa); after vowel and followed by *i, j* = yet (kra*g*i); elsewhere = *g*o.

Dutch—strongly rasped voiced *h* (*g*ekken); in *ng* combination = si*ng;* in recent French loan words before *e, i* = plea*s*ure.

Japanese transliteration—regularly = *g*o, but between vowels and even initially is often pronounced as in si*ng* (ariga*t*ō).

Catalan—before *e, i* = mea*s*ure; final, after *i, oi, ui,* = *ch*urch or *sh*ort; final after other vowels = ki*ck;* elsewhere = *g*o.

Finnish—used only in foreign words and names.

Invariably = *g*o in Latin, Polish, Czech, Croatian, Lithuanian, Lettish, Irish, Welsh, Breton, Albanian, Hungarian, Turkish, Malay-Indonesian, Esperanto, transliterations of Sanskrit, Hindi, Arabic (save in Syrian and other dialects, where = *g*eneral), Hebrew.

With Diacritic Signs

ĝ—Esperanto: = *g*eneral.

ǧ—occasionally used in phonetic transcriptions to indicate sound of *g*eneral.

ğ—Turkish: = *g*o with fricative sound (force breath through small opening between back of tongue and back of palate).

g̗—Lettish: = sol*di*er or di*d* you.

In Combination

gg—Latin, Hungarian, Finnish, transliterations of Sanskrit, Hindi, Arabic, Hebrew, Japanese: prolong period before release of *g*o-sound (Lat. a*gg*er); Italian: prolong period before release of *g*o or *g*eneral, according to following sound (*g*o for *a, o, u,* consonant, *g*eneral for *e, i;* tra*gg*o, fa*gg*i).

gh—Italian, Rumanian: = *g*o before *e, i* (It. la*gh*i); Irish: = lo*ch* voiced, but sometimes silent; Arabic transliteration: = lo*ch* voiced (accompanied by vibration of vocal cords).

gi—Italian: before *a, o, u* = *j*oke (*Gi*orgio, pronounced JOR-jo).

gj—Swedish, Norwegian: = yet (Swed. *gj*öra); Danish: before *e, oe, ö* = *g*o; Albanian: = sol*di*er or ho*g* yard.

gli—Italian: final or followed by vowel, usually = mi*lli*on (*gli,* a*gli*o); followed by consonant, usually = *gl*ee (gero*gli*fico).

gn—French, Italian: = ca*ny*on (Fr. a*gn*eau, It. a*gn*ello).

gu—French: before *e, i,* usually = *g*o (*gu*etter); occasionally = an*gu*ish aig*u*ille); Spanish, Portuguese: before *e, i* = g*o* (g*u*erra), before *a, o* = ang*u*ish (Sp. ag*u*a, Pt. ág*u*a); Italian: always = ang*u*ish (g*u*erra).

gü—Spanish: before *e, i* = ang*u*ish (vergüenza).

gy—Norwegian: = *y*et; Hungarian: sol*di*er or di*d y*ou.

H

Save in combination with a preceding consonant (*ch, gh, lh, nh,* etc.) is generally silent in most Romance languages, and, in certain positions, in various other languages; otherwise, generally sounded as in English, or slightly more strongly.

German—as in English (*h*aben, *H*err); often indicates length of preceding vowel and is silent (wä*h*len, ze*h*n, Heimwe*h*).

French—generally silent (*h*omme); occasionally sounded as in English, by a dwindling number of speakers, in words usually, but not invariably, of Germanic origin (*h*aut, *h*ache, *h*éros); even if this "h aspirate" is not pronounced, it prevents both elision of definite article and *liaison* or "linking" (*la haute maison,* not *l'haute maison*).

Spanish, Portuguese, Italian—silent (Sp., Pt. *h*ora, It. *h*anno). In Spanish, often used before *u* to indicate *w*-sound (*Hu*esca, *Hu*aco).

Latin—some doubt attaches to its pronunciation; it seems likely that it was sounded as in English at an early period, then gradually became silent (*h*omo).

Approximately as in English: in Swedish (but normally silent before *j*); Norwegian and Danish (but silent before *j, v*); Icelandic, Dutch, Polish, Czech, Croatian, Lithuanian, Lettish, Irish, Welsh, Albanian, Hungarian, Turkish, Malay-Indonesian, Esperanto, transliterations of Sanskrit, Hindi, Arabic, Hebrew, Japanese. Perceptibly stronger than in English in Rumanian, Finnish; but in Rumanian its occurrence is rare save in combination with *c* or *g* (*h*ora).

With Diacritic Signs

ĥ—Esperanto: = lo*ch* (but seldom used).

ḥ—Arabic transliteration: more strongly and emphatically sounded than English *h* (the English sound is transliterated by *h*).

In Combination

hj—in Swedish, Norwegian, the *h* is silent.

hv—in Norwegian, Danish, the *h* is silent.

I

Generally indicates a sound fluctuating between p*i*n and mach*i*ne.

German—if long, mach*i*ne (m*i*r; the long value is normally indicated by a following *h* or *e* (*i*hnen, T*i*er); if short, = p*i*n (b*i*n; the sound is a little closer and longer than in American English).
French— = mach*i*ne (f*i*ls).
Spanish— = mach*i*ne (h*i*jo).
Portuguese— = mach*i*ne (f*i*lho).
Italian— = mach*i*ne (f*i*glio).

The German distinction holds approximately for Swedish, Norwegian, Danish, Dutch (which also prefers an *ie* spelling to indicate the sound of mach*i*ne), Latin (v*ī*num vs. f*ī*des).

Little or no distinction of length, save for factors of stress, appears in Rumanian, Polish, Croatian, Lithuanian, Welsh, Albanian, Turkish, Malay-Indonesian, Esperanto, where *i* generally = mach*i*ne. The *i* without a diacritic regularly indicates a short sound in Icelandic, Czech, Lettish, Irish, Finnish, Hungarian, and transliterations of Sanskrit, Hindi, Arabic, Hebrew, which use diacritics to indicate long value.

With Diacritic Signs

í—Spanish, Portuguese: indicates place of stress (maraved*í*, Marroqu*í*); Icelandic, Czech, Irish, Hungarian: indicates length (= mach*i*ne prolonged).

ì—Italian: indicates stress on final vowel (luned*ì*).

î—French: indicates occasional greater measure of length, more often a contraction (f*î*mes); Rumanian: = rhythm.

ī—Latin, Lettish, transliterations of Sanskrit, Hindi, Arabic, Hebrew: indicates length.

ı—(*i* without a dot over it)—Turkish: = rhythm.

į—Lithuanian: = mach*i*ne (former nasalization now lost).

i̯—occasionally used in historical linguistics to indicate a semivowel or glide value for *i;* = yet, boy.

In Combination

ie—German, Dutch: = mach*i*ne (v*ie*l, z*ie*k); Polish: = y*e*s, but the *i* is often inaudible, and serves only to palatalize the preceding consonant; Spanish, Portuguese, Italian: in combinations of *i* with a following *a, e, o, u,* the *i* normally functions as a glide, and the sound is *ya, ye,* *yo, yu* (famil*i*a, fam*í*l*i*a, famigl*i*a); but occasionally the *i* is stressed and then has the full value of mach*i*ne followed by *a, e, o, u* (Sp. v*í*a, Pt. fat*i*a, Bah*i*a, It. v*i*a, v*i*e); contrast Spanish Dios, where the *i* is unstressed and the pronunciation is a monosyllabic DYOS, with Italian DI-o, where the *i* is stressed and two syllables result; or Spanish farmacia, where the *i* is unstressed and the pronunciation is far-MA-sya, with Italian farmacia, where *i* is stressed and the pronunciation is far-ma-CHEE-a.

ieuw—Dutch: = *lee*way.

ig—Catalan: in final position, = b*i*t*ch* or f*ish*.

ih—German: = mach*i*ne (*ih*nen).

ii—Finnish, transliteration of Japanese: = mach*i*ne prolonged (but Japanese also uses *ī* in transliteration).

ij—Dutch: = v*ei*n.

ill—French: usually = fr*ee* year (f*ille*); occasionally = fr*ee* *l*ance (v*ill*e).

im—French: followed by consonant, = m*a*n with nasal passage closed (*im*possible); Portuguese: followed by consonant or final, = mach*i*ne with nasal passage closed (*im*poss*í*vel; s*im*).

in—French: followed by consonant or final, = m*a*n with nasal passage closed (*in*vers, v*in*).

io—Irish: = t*i*n or b*u*t.

ío—Irish: = s*ee*.

J

In a majority of the languages using this letter, it fulfills the function of an on-glide or off-glide (*y*et, bo*y*), being used regularly in combination with a vowel. This is true of German, Swedish (but in final position it is often silent in Swedish), Norwegian, Danish, Icelandic, Dutch, Polish, Czech, Croatian, Lithuanian, Lettish, Albanian, Finnish, Hungarian, Esperanto. The *j* used in modern Latin textbooks (also to be pronounced as *y*) did not exist in Classical times, the Romans making no distinction between the vowel and the semivowel value of their letter *i* in writing. Irish, Welsh, and present-day Italian do not use the letter *j*. The English value of *j*et prevails in Malay-Indonesian and in transliterations of Sanskrit, Hindi, Syrian and other dialects of Arabic, and Japanese (in Japanese, the value usually = sol*di*er or d*i*d *y*ou).

German— = *y*et (*j*a, *J*ahr).

French— = plea*s*ure (*j*eune); also Portuguese (*j*anela), Rumanian, Catalan, Turkish.

Spanish— = from strongly aspirated *h* to lo*ch,* depending on area.

Italian—used only in older writings to indicate contraction of two *i*'s in endings (avvolto*j*), where modern orthography would use *avvoltoi* as the plural of *avvoltoio.*

With Diacritic Signs

ĵ—Esperanto: = plea*s*ure.

In Combination

jh—Sanskrit, Hindi: = bri*dge h*ouse.

K

In the languages in which it is used, generally = *k*ing.

German— = *k*ing (*K*önig); likewise in Norwegian, Danish, Icelandic, Dutch, Polish, Czech, Croatian, Lithuanian, Lettish, Albanian, Finnish, Hungarian, Esperanto, transliterations of Sanskrit, Hindi, Arabic, Hebrew, Japanese.

French, Spanish, Portuguese, Italian—not used save in foreign words and names, where = *k*ing (Fr. *k*épi, Sp., Pt. *k*ilociclo, It. *k*aki). Likewise in Latin (save for archaic survivals like *Kalendae*), Rumanian, Irish, Welsh.

Swedish—before *e, i, y, ä, ö* = bu*t h*uge or *ch*ild; before *a, o, u,* consonant = *k*ing.

Turkish—followed by vowel bearing circumflex accent = qui*ck* yacht; otherwise = *k*ing.

Malay-Indonesian—in final position, becomes a mere glottal stop (similar to a catch in the breath); elsewhere = *k*ing.

With Diacritic Signs

ķ—Lettish: = for*t*une.

In Combination

kh—in transliteration of Arabic, Hebrew: = lo*ch;* of Sanskrit, Hindi: = blo*ckh*ouse.

kj—Swedish, Norwegian: = bu*t h*uge or *ch*ild; Danish: = *k*ing.

kk—Finnish, Hungarian, transliteration of Sanskrit, Hindi, Arabic, Hebrew, Japanese: prolong period before release of *k* (Jap. Ho*kk*aido).

kn—the *k* is sounded in all Germanic languages except English (Ger. *Kn*ie, *Kn*echt).

kw—occasional in Dutch: = *kv*.

L

Generally as in English, but the point of articulation shifts, as it does in English, from the front to the back of the mouth, depending on the nature of the following sound (compare English *l*eeway, *l*ot, Water*l*oo, mi*l*k). General equivalence with English appears in Swedish, Norwegian, Danish, Icelandic, Lithuanian, Lettish, Finnish, Turkish, Malay-Indonesian, Esperanto, transliterations of Sanskrit, Hindi, Arabic, Hebrew. The sound of *l* does not appear in Japanese.

German—more to the front of the mouth than in English, particularly before consonants, with slight mi*lli*on effect (Mi*l*ch, U*l*m).

French—slightly more frontal than in English, particularly before *e, i* (*l*iaison).

Spanish—as in French, above (*l*igero).

Portuguese—as in French, above; but before consonants and in final position, more to the back of the mouth than in English mi*l*k, to the point of reaching the sound of lo*w* (Brasi*l*); this effect is particularly noticeable in the Brazilian pronunciation of the Rio de Janeiro area.

Italian—slightly more frontal than in English (*l*eggero). This is also true of Dutch, Czech, Croatian, Albanian, Hungarian, and, presumably, Latin, to judge from its immediate descendants.

Polish— = mi*lli*on.

Irish—before *e, i* = mi*lli*on; elsewhere = *l*ove.

In Czech, Sanskrit, Hindi, *l* is sometimes used with the value of a vowel, and may bear the stress (Czech V*l*tava, p*l*n).

With Diacritic Signs

ł—Polish: = mi*l*k or *w*ar, depending on area.

ļ—Lettish: = mi*lli*on.

ḷ—Sanskrit transliteration, indicates use as a vowel.

In Combination

ld—Norwegian, Danish: in final position, *d* is usually silent.

lh—Portuguese: = mi*lli*on (fi*lh*o); likewise in Old Provençal.

lj—Swedish: = *y*es; Croatian: = mi*lli*on.

ll—Spanish: = mi*lli*on or *y*es, depending on area; likewise Catalan; Welsh: = *l* without vibration of vocal cords; sounds somewhat like *khl* or *tl;* Italian, Finnish, Hungarian, transliterations of Sanskrit, Hindi, Arabic, Hebrew: prolong sound of *l* (It. a*ll*a vs. a*l*a).

l.l—Catalan: prolong sound of *l*.

ly—Hungarian: sometimes = mi*lli*on; more often = *y*es.

M

Generally as in English, but see under vowels *a, e, i, o, u* for nasalizing effect on preceding vowel, especially in French and Portuguese.

Latin—in final position, probably became silent by the end of the Classical period (about 400 A.D.).

With Diacritic Signs

ṃ—in Sanskrit transliteration, indicates incomplete nasalization of preceding vowel.

In Combination

mh—Irish: = *v*at or *w*ish.

mm—Latin, Italian, Finnish, Hungarian, transliterations of Sanskrit, Hindi, Arabic, Hebrew, Japanese: prolong sound of *m* (Lat. fla*mm*a, It. fia*mm*a).

N

Generally as in English, but more dental and less alveolar (tip of tongue against back of upper teeth rather than against ridges of upper gums) in most languages outside the Germanic group.

German— = *n*ot (*N*ot); likewise in Dutch, Swedish, Norwegian, Danish, Icelandic; in Dutch a final -*n* is often silent (gekke*n*).

French—more dental than in English (*n*iais); see under vowels *a, e, i, o, u* for nasalizing effect on preceding vowel; when nasalization takes place, the *n*-sound itself disappears (bo*n*, pronounced BÕ).

Spanish—more dental than in English (*n*o).

Portuguese—more dental than in English (*n*ão); see under vowels *a, e, i, o, u* for nasalizing effect on preceding vowels; the *n* or *m* that causes nasalization tends to disappear (e*n*tender, home*m*).

Italian—more dental than in English (*no*). Likewise in Rumanian, Polish, Czech, Croatian, Lithuanian, Lettish, Welsh, Albanian, Finnish, Hungarian, Turkish, and, presumably, to judge from its descendants, Latin. Irish—when both preceded and followed by front vowels (*e, i*) = o*ni*on; otherwise = *no*.

With Diacritic Signs

ń—Polish: = o*ni*on.

ň—Czech: = o*ni*on.

ñ—transliteration of Sanskrit, Hindi: = si*ng*.

n̦—Lettish: = o*ni*on.

ñ—Spanish: = o*ni*on.

ṇ—Lithuanian: = o*ni*on; Sanskrit, Hindi transliteration: = English alveolar *n* (*no*).

In Combination

nd—Norwegian, Danish: *d* is usually silent.

ng—German: regularly = si*ng*er, not fi*ng*er (Fi*ng*er); final, in the speech of some, = thi*nk* (Gesa*ng*). Swedish, Norwegian, Danish, Icelandic, Dutch, Welsh, Malay-Indonesian, transcription of Japanese: = si*ng*er, not fi*ng*er.

ngg—Malay-Indonesian: = fi*ng*er.

nh—Portuguese: = o*ni*on (ni*nh*o); likewise in Old Provençal.

nj—Croatian, Albanian: = o*ni*on.

nn—Latin, Italian, Finnish, Hungarian, transliteration of Sanskrit, Hindi, Arabic, Hebrew, Japanese: prolong sound of *n* (Lat. a*nn*us, It. a*nn*o).

ny—Catalan, Hungarian: = o*ni*on.

O

Generally ranges between the open sound of *o*ven, or British n*o*t, and the sound of b*o*re, or g*o* without the final glide. Some languages make a phonemic distinction between the two sounds (a distinction of meaning between two words otherwise sounding alike; Italian *ho,* for example, with silent *h* and open *o,* means "I have"; *o,* with closed *o,* means "or"), while others do not; some make a distinction of length, others do not.

German—if long, = b*o*re or g*o* without final glide (l*o*ben); if short, = *o*ven or British n*o*t (v*o*ll); indication as to both length and openness is often given by what follows (*h* or a single consonant usually indicate long and close; double consonant, short and open). Similarly in Dutch, Norwegian, Danish. In Swedish, generally = p*oo*l.

French— = b*o*re (n*o*s), or *o*ven (m*o*de).

Spanish— = b*o*re (*o*jo).

Portuguese— = b*o*re (n*o*vo), or *o*ven (n*o*va); final = l*oo*k (amig*o*).

Italian— = b*o*re (m*o*nd*o*), or *o*ven (f*o*rte); generally only the closed value appears in unstressed syllables.

Catalan—unstressed, generally = l*oo*k.

Latin—long, = b*o*re (dōnō); short, = *o*ven (fŏlia); originally there seems to have been only a distinction of length; the distinction of openness and closeness arose probably during the Classical period and was well established by 400 A.D. Indication of length is given in modern textbooks (dōnō), but not in original Latin writings.

Japanese has a distinction of length, with long value generally indicated in transliteration by ō, but little distinction of open or closed quality (Tōkyō).

The sound of a single *o* unaccompanied by diacritics fluctuates between b*o*re and *o*ven in Rumanian, Polish, Croatian, Lithuanian, Lettish, Albanian, Irish, Welsh, Finnish, Hungarian, Turkish, Malay-Indonesian, Esperanto, transliterations of Sanskrit, Hindi, Arabic, Hebrew.

With Diacritic Signs

ó—Spanish, Portuguese: indicates place of stress (murió, cómico); Polish: = m*oo*n; Icelandic, Czech, Irish, Hungarian: indicates length (*aw*ful); Lithuanian: indicates length with rising tone, but seldom used in writing.

ò—Italian: indicates final stress, usually open quality, = *o*ven (andò); occasionally used in Lithuanian to indicate short vowel.

ô—French: = b*o*re, sometimes prolonged (nôtre); Portuguese: = b*o*re and indicates place of stress (alô).

ō—Lettish: indicates length; likewise in modern textbook Latin (dō), as in transliterations of Sanskrit, Hindi, Arabic, Hebrew, Japanese.

ŏ—occasionally used in modern textbook Latin to indicate short value (fŏrtis).

ö—German: = th*e*re with rounded lips, which may be long (Höhle) or short (öffnen); likewise in Swedish. In Finnish, Hungarian, Turkish indicates approximately the same sound, but with short quantity.

ő—in most languages that use ö, may be used interchangeably with it; in Hungarian, it indicates long quantity for the sound, while ö indicates short.

ø—Norwegian, Danish: = th*e*re with rounded lips; occasionally replaced by *ö* in older writings.

õ—Portuguese: = b*o*re with nasal passage closed (bot*õ*es); Lithuanian: indicates long value with falling tone, but not always used in writing.

ǫ—occasionally used in historical linguistics to indicate open quality for *o* (f*ǫ*rtem).

ọ—occasionally used in historical linguistics to indicate closed quality for *o* (p*ọ*ns).

In Combination

oa—Rumanian: n*o*t + f*a*ther, with stress on latter (f*oa*rte).

oe (or œ)—Dutch: + b*oo*k; also Malay (but Indonesian prefers *u*: cf. S*oe*rabaja, S*u*rabaya); Latin = b*oy* (p*oe*na).

õe—Portuguese: = l*oi*n, with nasal passage closed (leç*õe*s).

oei—French: = th*e*re with rounded lips + *yes* (*oei*l); Dutch: = L*oui*s, or ph*ooie*.

oeu—French: = th*e*re with rounded lips (*oeu*vre); more closed and shorter, usually, in final position (v*oeu*).

og—Norwegian, Danish: = b*oy*.

oi—French: = w*a*sp (m*oi*); Portuguese: = b*oy* (c*oi*sa).

oig—Catalan: in final position, = *i*tch or f*i*sh.

oin—French: final, or before consonant, = w*e*nt with nasal passage closed (m*oi*ns, C*oi*ntreau).

om—French: followed by consonant, = *o*bey with nasal passage closed (*om*bre); Portuguese: final, or followed by consonant, = *o*bey with nasal passage closed (b*om*).

on—French: final, or followed by consonant, = *o*bey with nasal passage closed (m*on*, *on*dine).

oo—Dutch, Finnish: = b*o*re, prolonged (D*oo*rn).

öö—Finnish: = th*e*re with rounded lips, prolonged.

ooi—Dutch: = *oi*l or b*uoy* (m*ooi*).

ouw—Dutch: = *ou*t (vr*ouw*).

P

Generally as in English. Initially, less explosive in the Romance languages. Not used in Arabic.

In Combination

pf—German: occurs frequently, in all positions (*P*f*e*ffer, O*pf*er, Kam*pf*); both *p* and *f* distinctly pronounced.

ph— = *f*irst in words of Greek origin in German (*Ph*iloso*ph*ie), Latin (*ph*iloso*ph*ia), French (*ph*iloso*ph*ie), Welsh, and occasionally other languages. The spelling *f* is regularly used instead in Dutch, Swedish, Norwegian, Danish (though *ph* may appear in some words in older writings), Icelandic, Spanish, Portuguese, Italian (Sp. *f*iloso*f*ía, Pt., It. *f*iloso*f*ia), Rumanian, Polish, Czech, Croatian, Lithuanian, Lettish, Irish, Albanian, Finnish, Hungarian, Turkish. In transliterations of Sanskrit, Hindi, *ph* = u*ph*ill.

pn—in words of Greek origin, both letters are fully sounded in German (*pn*eumatisch), French (*pn*eu), Portuguese (*pn*eumático), Italian (*pn*eumatico), and most other languages; but the *p* is silent, as in English, in Spanish, which drops it even in spelling (*n*eumático).

pp—prolong holding period before release in Latin (A*pp*ia), Italian (se*pp*e), Finnish, Hungarian, transliteration of Sanskrit, Hindi, Hebrew, Japanese (Sa*pp*oro).

ps—in words of Greek origin, both letters are fully sounded in German (*Ps*ychologie), French (*ps*ychologie), Portuguese and Italian (*ps*icologia), and in most other languages; but the *p* is silent, though it appears in writing, in Spanish (*ps*icología, pronounced *s*icología).

pt—in words of Greek origin, both letters are fully sounded in German, French, Portuguese, Italian (prefix *pt*ero-) and most other languages; but the *p* is silent, though written, in Spanish (*pt*ero-, pronounced *t*ero-).

Q

Not used save with a following *u*, except in Albanian (= sto*ck*yard or for*t*une; Sh*q*ipëtar), and transliteration of Arabic (= *c*ool, far back in mouth: Ira*q*); the same value appears in traditional Hebrew, but modern spoken Hebrew tends to equate it with *k*. Occasionally appears in French in final position (=*k*, co*q*).

Not used save in foreign words and names in Swedish, Norwegian, Danish, Icelandic (all four languages prefer the spelling *kv*); Rumanian, Polish, Czech, Croatian, Lithuanian, Lettish, Irish, Welsh, Finnish, Hungarian, Turkish, Malay-Indonesian, Esperanto, transliterations of Sanskrit, Hindi, Japanese (but appears in words of Persian or Arabic origin in the Urdu variant of Hindi).

In Combination

qu—German: = *kv* (*Qu*elle); likewise in Dutch. In French, the *u* is regularly silent (*qu*art); in Spanish, *qu* appears only before *e*, *i*; the *u* is silent and the *q* = *k*ick (*qu*into); in Portuguese, = *qu*art before *a, o* (*qu*adro), *k*ick before *e, i* (*qu*erela); likewise in Catalan; in Latin and Italian, both *q* and *u* are pronounced before any vowel (Latin *qu*ando, *qu*is; It. *qu*ando, *qu*esto).

qü—Portuguese: used optionally before *e, i* to indicate that the *u* is sounded (tran*qü*ilo or tran*qu*ilo); for the same purpose, Spanish uses *cu* (*cu*idado, *cu*esta).

qv—Norwegian, Danish: occasional in older writings, where the modern orthography uses *kv*.

R

Generally trilled or rolled, as in British ve*r*y, rather than pronounced as a lateral with cupped tongue, as in American English. This is generally true of Swedish, Norwegian, Danish, Icelandic, Rumanian, Polish, Czech, Croatian, Lithuanian, Lettish, Irish, Welsh, Albanian, Finnish, Hungarian, Turkish, Malay-Indonesian, Esperanto, transliterations of Sanskrit, Hindi, Arabic, Hebrew, Japanese (but in Japanese the trill is very light, amounting to a mere tap). In final position, it is seldom silent, as it is in British English and some American varieties (fathe*r*).

German—uvular (see French, below), or trilled (especially in stage pronunciation: *R*ose). Likewise in Dutch.

French—uvular roll, with uvula vibrating lightly, like a gentle clearing of the back of the throat (*r*are).

Spanish—trilled, = British ve*r*y (pe*r*o); initial and after consonant, trill is stronger and more prolonged (*r*osa, Hen*r*ique).

Portuguese—trilled, = British ve*r*y; in some areas, notably the Rio de Janeiro region of Brazil, uvular as in French (*r*aro).

Italian—trilled, = British ve*r*y (*r*a*r*o).

Catalan—final is often silent. In Czech, Croatian, is often used with vowel value, and may bear the stress (Czech B*r*no, Croatian T*r*st).

With Diacritic Signs

ř—Czech: trilled *r* combined with measure (Dvořák).

ŗ—Lettish: trilled *r* + yes.

ṛ—transliteration of Sanskrit, Hindi: = trilled *r* with vowel value, and may bear stress (v*ṛ*ka, m*ṛ*tiyu); but Hindi often prefers to insert a short *i* (m*r*ityu).

In Combination

rh—Welsh: aspirated trilled *r,* = *h* + *r.*

rr—Spanish, Portuguese, Italian, Catalan, Irish, Finnish, Hungarian, transliterations of Sanskrit, Hindi, Arabic, Hebrew: more strongly trilled and
prolonged, as in Irish bego*rr*a or Scottish mo*rr*nin' for morning (Sp.,
Pt., It. ca*rr*o, as opposed to ca*r*o). Likewise, probably, Latin (ca*rr*us, as
opposed to ca*r*us).

rz—Polish: = mea*s*ure.

S

Generally used with sound of *s*o or ro*s*e; but may be predominantly
dental (tip of tongue against back of upper teeth, as in most Romance
languages); alveolar (tip of tongue against ridge of upper gums, as in
English); or apical (tip of tongue against hard palate, back of ridge of
upper gums).

German—initial before a vowel, or between vowels, usually = ro*s*e (*s*o,
Ro*s*e); initial before *p, t* = *sh*ore (*s*prechen, *s*tehen); elsewhere = bu*s*
(wa*s*, be*s*te).

French—between vowels, even in two separate but closely linked words,
= ro*s*e (ro*s*e, le*s* avions); final, usually silent (le*s* mur*s*); elsewhere as
in English, but more dental (*s*oeur, Mi*s*tinguette).

Spanish—always = *s*o, never = ro*s*e, save by chance assimilation to following voiced consonant (de*s*mayarse, de*s*de); more hissed (apical) in
northern Spain; often turned into a light *h*-sound in southern Spain and
Spanish America (lo*s* cubano*s*, which may be heard as lo*h* cubano*h*, or
even lo cubano).

Portuguese—between vowels, even in two separate but closely linked
words, = ro*s*e (pre*s*ente, a*s* amigas); final and before unvoiced consonants = *s*ure (amigo*s*, e*s*cudo*s*); before voiced consonants, fluctuates
between ro*s*e and mea*s*ure (me*s*mo); elsewhere, as in English *s*o, but
more dental (*s*emana, acordar*s*e).

Italian—between vowels = ro*s*e generally in northern Italy, *s*o in southern Italy (ro*s*a); initial before *b, d, g, l, m, n, v* = *z*ero (*s*baglio,
*s*draiarsi, *s*magliante, *s*nidare, *s*vanire); elsewhere as in English but
more dental (*s*ilenzio, *s*tella, lapi*s*).

Latin—probably = *s*o universally in earlier period, changing after 400 A.D.
in the directions indicated by the modern descendants, according to
area.

Catalan—between vowels = ro*s*e; elsewhere = *s*o.

Normally = *s*o in Swedish, Norwegian, Danish, Icelandic, Dutch (more alveolar, as in English, in the Germanic languages); in Dutch, an *s* that gets to be between vowels regularly is changed in spelling to *z* (hui*s*, hui*z*en); = *s*o, but more dental, in Rumanian, Polish, Czech, Croatian, Lithuanian, Lettish, Welsh, Breton, Albanian, Malay-Indonesian, Esperanto, transliterations of Sanskrit, Hindi, Arabic, Hebrew, Japanese.

Hungarian— = *s*ure (*s*ajnálom).

Irish— = *s*o before a, o, u, consonant; = *s*ure before *e*, *i* (*S*ean, pron. *S*han).

With Diacritic Signs

ś—Polish: = *s*hin, lightly uttered.

ŝ—Esperanto: = *s*ure.

š—Czech, Croatian, Lithuanian, Lettish, transliterations of Arabic, Hebrew (but the last two may also use *s*h) : = *s*ure.

ş—Rumanian, Turkish: = *s*ure.

ṣ—Arabic: = emphatically uttered *s*, with blade of tongue pressed against roof of mouth; Sanskrit, Hindi transliterations: = apical *s*, while *s* indicates dental pronunciation.

In Combination

sc—Italian: = *sk*ull before *a, o, u*, consonant (*sc*oglio); = *sh*ell before *e, i* (*sc*elto, *sc*immia); a following *i* is normally absorbed before another vowel (*sc*ialare, pron. sha-LA-re).

śc—Polish: = A*shch*urch.

sch—German: = *sh*ore (*Sch*iff); likewise Swedish, but seldom used; Dutch: = *s* + lo*ch* (*sch*on, *Sch*eveningen); this written combination is borrowed by American English with the sound *sk* (*Sch*uyler, *Sch*ermerhorn); final = le*ss* (vle*sch*); Italian: = *sk*ill before *e, i* (*sch*eletro, *sch*izzo).

sh—Albanian: = *sh*ore (*Sh*qipëtar).

si—Polish: followed by vowel = sound intermediate between *sh*in and *Si*ena (*si*ę).

sj—Dutch, Swedish, Norwegian, Danish, Malay-Indonesian: = *sh*ore.

sk—Swedish, Norwegian: before *e, i, y, ä, ö, ø* = *sh*ore; Danish: = *sk*ull.

skj—Swedish, Norwegian: = *sh*ore; Danish: = *sk*it.

ss—Portuguese: between vowels = *s*o (po*ss*ível); Latin, Italian, Finnish, Hungarian, transliterations of Sanskrit, Hindi, Arabic, Hebrew, Japanese: prolong sound of *s* (Lat. amavi*ss*em, It. ama*ss*i).

stj—Swedish, Norwegian, Danish: = *sh*oe.

sz—Polish: = a*sh,* with tip of tongue curled upward; Hungarian: = *s*o.

szcz—Polish: = A*shch*urch, with tip of tongue curled upward.

T

Save in the Germanic languages, is generally more dental and less alveolar than in English (tip of tongue against back of upper teeth, not against ridges of upper gums).

German— = *t*op, ba*t* (*T*or, un*t*er, mi*t*).

French—more dental than in English (*t*erre); final, usually silent (fini*t*).

Spanish—more dental than in English (*t*engo, mache*t*e).

Portuguese—more dental than in English (*t*enho, presen*t*e); in the Rio de Janeiro area of Brazil, final -*te, -ti* usually = *chi*cken.

Italian—more dental than in English (*t*orre, ama*t*o).

Sanskrit, Hindi—distinguish between dental *t* (transliterated *t*) and alveolar *t* (transliterated *ţ*); Arabic—distinguish between normal *t* and emphatic *t* (transliterated *ţ*).

With Diacritic Signs

ťt̆—Czech: = hi*t* you.

ţ—Rumanian: = i*ts*.

t—Sanskrit, Hindi: = English alveolar *t*all; Arabic: strongly uttered, with blade of tongue pressed against palate.

þ —Icelandic: = *th*in; Anglo-Saxon: = *th*in or *th*is.

In Combination

tg—Catalan: = *j*oke.

th—appears in German, Dutch, Danish (occasionally), Latin, French, usually in words of Greek origin (Ger. *Th*eater, Lat. *th*eatrum, Fr. *th*éâtre), regularly with the value of *t* in the language that uses it. The combination is replaced in writing by *t,* even in words of Greek origin, in Swedish, Norwegian, Icelandic (but Icelandic uses þ and ð in native words for the sounds of *th*ing, *th*is); Spanish, Portuguese, Italian (*t*eatro), Polish, Czech, Croatian, Lithuanian, Lettish, Albanian, Finnish, Hungarian, Turkish, Esperanto, transliteration of Japanese; in the rare cases where *t* and *h* come together in compound words in these languages, they are given their separate values, as in Sanskrit and Hindi (below); Irish = *h*ill; Sanskrit, Hindi transliterations = ou*th*ouse (with dental value for *t*); Arabic, Hebrew transliterations: indicates a softly pronounced dental *t*, which in Hebrew often turns into *s* (matzo*th*), particularly in America, but in Israel remains a dental *t*, and is often transcribed that way.

ṭh—Sanskrit, Hindi transliterations: = ou*th*ouse, with English alveolar *t*.

ti—German: before vowel = i*t's* you (Na*ti*on); French: before vowel = ki*ss* you (na*ti*on).

tj—Dutch: = *ch*urch or hi*t* *y*ou; Swedish: = *ch*urch or *h*uge; Catalan: = joke; Malay-Indonesian: = *ch*urch.

ts—Hebrew, Japanese transliterations where it often appears in initial position, = i*ts* (*ts*ade, *ts*unami).

tsch—German: = *ch*urch (deu*tsch*).

tt—prolong holding period before release of *t*-sound in Latin, Italian, Finnish, Hungarian, transliterations of Sanskrit, Hindi, Arabic, Hebrew, Japanese (Lat. ba*tt*uo, It. ba*tt*o).

tth—Sanskrit, Hindi transliterations: prolong period before release of ou*th*ouse with dental *t*.

ṭṭh—Sanskrit, Hindi transliterations: prolong period before release of ou*th*ouse with alveolar *t*.

tx—Catalan, Basque: = *ch*urch.

ty—Hungarian: = hi*t* *y*ou.

tz—German: = i*ts* (je*tz*t).

U

Generally fluctuates between r*u*le and p*u*t. Distinctions of length appear in some languages, not in others.

German—if long, = r*u*le (g*u*t); if short, = p*u*t (M*u*tter). Likewise in Latin (senat*ŭs*, senat*ūs*), Norwegian, Danish, Lithuanian.

French—purse lips in position for f*oo*d, then pronounce m*ee*t (l*u*ne).

Spanish, Portuguese, Italian— = r*u*le (Sp., It. l*u*na, Pt. l*u*a). Likewise Rumanian, Polish, Croatian, Albanian, Turkish, Malay-Indonesian, Esperanto.

Czech, Lettish, Irish, Finnish, Hungarian, transliterations of Sanskrit, Hindi, Arabic, Hebrew, Japanese— = p*u*t (in Japanese is often silent, especially in final position in verb-forms; s*u*kiyaki, arimas*u*).

Swedish— = m*ee*t with rounded lips, or p*u*t, or th*e* man; Icelandic— = th*e*re with rounded lips; Dutch— = r*u*le, with or without rounding, or b*u*ck; Catalan— between vowels = *w*ill; Welsh— = b*u*sy, m*e*, or m*ee*t with rounded lips.

With Diacritic Signs

ú—Icelandic, Czech, Irish, Hungarian: = m*oo*n.

ù—Italian: indicates stress on final vowel (virt*ù*).

û—French: purse lips for f*oo*d, then pronounce m*ee*t; sometimes prolonged (s*û*r).

ū—Latin: in modern textbooks, = m*oo*n (l*ū*na); likewise Lettish, transliterations of Sanskrit, Hindi, Arabic, Hebrew, Japanese.

ŭ—Rumanian: in older documents, = very short, almost inaudible p*u*t; in modern textbook Latin = p*u*t (l*ŭ*p*ŭ*s).

ü—German: lips in position for f*oo*d, pronounce m*ee*t; may be long (H*ü*te) or short (H*ü*tte); Hungarian: same sound, short; Icelandic, Turkish: same sound, medium length.

ű—may generally be used alternatively with *ü;* but in Hungarian, denotes long value.

ų—Lithuanian: = m*oo*n, with original nasalization now lost.

ů—Czech: = m*oo*n.

ṷ—occasionally used in historical linguistics to indicate semivowel or glide value (*w*as, lo*w*).

In Combination

ui—French: = French sound of *u* (m*ee*t with pursed lips) quickly followed by m*ee*t (h*ui*t); Dutch: = *i*ce with rounded lips; Norwegian, Danish: = mach*i*ne; Irish: = b*i*t or w*i*t.

úi—Irish: = L*oui*s.

uig—Catalan: = *itch* or f*i*sh.

um—French: before consonant = b*u*t with nasal passage closed (h*um*ble); Portuguese: = r*u*le with nasal passage closed (*um*).

un—French: final or before consonant = b*u*t with nasal passage closed (l*un*di, chac*un*).

uu—Dutch: = m*oo*n with rounded lips; Finnish: = m*oo*n, prolonged.

V

Generally as in English, dentolabial voiced fricative (lower lip in contact with upper teeth, with breath escaping gradually, and vibration of vocal cords). This value holds for French, Portuguese, Italian, Rumanian, Swedish, Norwegian, Danish, Icelandic, Czech, Croatian, Lithuanian, Lettish, Albanian, Finnish, Hungarian, Turkish, Esperanto, transliterations of Sanskrit, Hindi, Hebrew. The letter *v* does not appear, save in foreign words and names, in Polish, Irish, Welsh, Malay-Indonesian, transliterations of Arabic and Japanese.

German— = *f*ather (*V*ater).

French, Portuguese, Italian— = *v*at (Fr. *v*in, Pt. *v*inho, It. *v*ino).

Spanish—initially and after consonants = *b*at (*v*erano, en*v*iar); between vowels, even in different but closely linked words, is a bilabial (not a dentolabial) voiced fricative (lower and upper lip in loose contact as breath escapes, with vibration of vocal cords) (a*v*e, la *v*aca).

Latin—originally = *w*as (*v*as); sound shifted to *v*at by 400 A.D.

Dutch—sound starts as *f*ull, becomes voiced like *v*ase before it ends (*v*eld).

Norwegian—generally silent when final after *l, n*.

In Combination

vv—prolong sound of *v* in Italian (a*vv*enire), Finnish, Hungarian, transliterations of Sanskrit, Hindi, Hebrew.

W

This typically Germanic contribution to the Roman alphabet appears in native words in relatively few languages (English, German, Dutch, Polish, Welsh, transliterations of Hindi, Arabic, Japanese). It does not appear, save in foreign words and names, in Swedish, Norwegian, Danish, Icelandic, Latin, French, Spanish, Portuguese, Italian, Rumanian, Czech, Croatian, Lithuanian, Lettish, Irish, Albanian, Finnish, Hungarian, Turkish, Malay-Indonesian, transliterations of Sanskrit, Hebrew.

German— = *v*est (*W*asser).

French— = *v*est in borrowed words (*w*agon-lit) likewise in Swedish, Norwegian, Danish, Icelandic.

Spanish, Portuguese, Italian—normally replaced, even in writing, by *v* (in French, recent geographic names where English normally uses *w* appear with *ou;* in Spanish, Portuguese, Italian, with *u* (Eng. R*w*anda, Fr. Ro*u*anda, Sp., Pt., It. R*u*anda); where the English *w* is initial in such terms, Spanish normally uses *hu,* with silent *h* and *u* pronounced as *w* (Eng. *W*aco, Sp. *Hu*aco).

Polish— = *v*est; final = o*ff* (L*w*ów, Polish name of Lemberg, pron. L'VOOF).

Dutch—initial generally = *v*est; elsewhere = *w*ater.

Welsh—used as pure vowel = b*oo*n or g*oo*d; also used as semivowel, =

*w*ater (dy*w*ed*w*ch, Bryn Ma*w*r, where the Welsh pronunciation is MA-oor).

Breton— = *w*ater.

In Combination

wh—peculiar to English, which reverses the spoken sounds in writing (Anglo-Saxon used *hw*); note corresponding words in other Germanic languages: *w*here = Norwegian *h*vor; *w*hat = *h*va; Swedish, German, Dutch eliminate the *h* both in speech and writing (Swed. *v*ar, *v*ad; Ger. *w*o, *w*as; Dutch *w*aar, *w*at).

X

Where used, generally as in English, with double value (unvoiced: a*x*; voiced: e*x*ample). Does not appear, save in foreign words and names, in Dutch, Swedish, Norwegian, Danish, Icelandic, Italian, Rumanian, Polish, Czech, Croatian, Lithuanian, Lettish, Irish, Welsh, Finnish, Hungarian, Turkish, Malay-Indonesian, Esperanto, transliterations of Sanskrit, Hindi, Arabic, Hebrew, Japanese.

German— = si*x* (O*x*ygen).

French— = si*x* or e*x*ample (se*x*uel, e*x*emple); final, usually silent (voi*x*) or = mi*ss* (si*x*, di*x*).

Spanish— = si*x* (e*x*acto, e*x*primir).

Portuguese—between vowels, generally = ca*sh* (cai*x*a); between *e* and another vowel = ro*se* (e*x*ato); elsewhere = si*x* (e*x*posição).

Italian—used only in foreign words, = si*x* (*x*ilofono).

Latin—probably always = si*x* in earlier period (se*x*, e*x*emplum); may have shifted to e*x*ample between vowels in later period.

Albanian— = a*dz*e.

Catalan— = *sh*ore, especially initial or after *i;* in initial group ex- before a vowel = a*x* or e*x*ample.

In Combination

xh—Albanian: = *j*et (fild*xh*án).

Y

A latecomer to the Roman alphabet, introduced to represent the Greek letter upsilon after contacts between Greeks and Romans became cultural (in earlier Latin borrowings from Greek, upsilon is represented by *u*). Where used, it appears generally with a semivowel or glide value (yes, boy). In the few languages where it is given full vowel value, it is generally equated with *i* (or m*ee*t with rounded lips).

German—normally only in foreign words and names: = yes or p*i*n (Malaye, Oxygen); likewise in Dutch.

French—as above (oxygène); occasionally used in native and Breton words with full vowel value: = m*ee*t (y, *Y*f, *Y*vonne); regularly used with semivowel value: = yes (crayon).

Spanish—seldom used with vowel value (archaic y); regularly used with semivowel value: = yes, boy (yerba, hay); but Greek upsilon is normally transcribed by *i* (ox*í*geno).

Portuguese—used only in foreign words and names; upsilon normally transcribed by *i* (ox*í*geno). Likewise in Italian (oss*i*geno).

Latin—used as vowel in Greek loan-words: = p*i*n or mach*i*ne, according to length (pyxida).

Icelandic, Polish, Czech, Hungarian—used as vowel, = p*i*n.

Swedish, Norwegian, Danish, Albanian, Finnish—used as vowel: = m*ee*t with rounded lips.

Turkish, Malay-Indonesian, transliterations of Sanskrit, Hindi, Arabic, Hebrew, Japanese—used only with semivowel value: = yet or boy.

Not used save in foreign words and names in Rumanian, Croatian, Irish, Esperanto.

Lithuanian— = mach*i*ne.

Welsh—used with full vowel or semivowel value; as vowel = rhythm or m*ee*t with rounded lips.

With Diacritic Signs

ý—Icelandic, Hungarian: = mach*i*ne; Czech: = mach*i*ne prolonged.

In Combination

yy—Finnish: = m*ee*t with rounded lips, prolonged.

Z

Another latecomer from the Greek to the Roman alphabet; in view of the different values the letter zeta had in the various Greek dialects, there is some doubt as to how it was pronounced in Classical Latin, and this fluctuation is perhaps reflected in its present-day values.

German— = i*ts* (*z*u, Na*z*i).

French— = *z*ero (*z*éro); final, generally silent (ne*z*, parle*z*).

Spanish— = *th*ing in northern Spain; *s*o in southern Spain and Spanish America (*z*orro, vo*z*).

Portuguese— = *z*ero (a*z*ul); final, generally = mea*s*ure (pa*z*).

Italian— = i*ts* or a*dz*e (*z*ucchero, *z*ero).

Latin—only in Greek words (*z*ona); probably = *z*one.

Swedish, Norwegian, Danish, Icelandic— = *s*o (seldom used save in foreign words and names).

Dutch, Rumanian, Polish, Czech, Croatian, Lithuanian, Lettish, Albanian, Hungarian, Turkish, Esperanto, transcriptions of Hindi-Urdu, Arabic, Hebrew— = *z*ero.

Japanese— = *z*ero or a*dz*e (mi*z*u).

Not used save in foreign words and names in Irish, Welsh, Finnish, Malay-Indonesian.

With Diacritic Signs

ź—Polish: = mea*s*ure, softly pronounced.

ž—Czech: = mea*s*ure.

ż—Polish: = mea*s*ure, strongly pronounced.

ẓ—Arabic transliteration: = strongly uttered *z*ero, with blade of tongue pressed against palate.

In Combination

zi—Italian: followed by vowel in same syllable, = *tsy* (giusti*zi*a, a*zi*one); Polish: followed by vowel in same syllable, = mea*s*ure.

zs—Hungarian: = mea*s*ure (*Zs*a*zs*a).

zz—Italian: = i*ts* or a*dz*e (po*zz*o, ra*zz*o). This is the only consonant where Italian has no phonemic or phonetic difference between the single and the double; but the single is used initially and in the *zi* combination described above, the double between vowels.

THE GREEK ALPHABET

The Greek alphabet was the earliest Western descendant of the Semitic. The letters took various forms and different directions of writing at different periods and in the various ancient dialects, between 1500 and 500 B.C. The precise pronunciation and chronological change in value of some of them is still in doubt. The Classical version of the sound values represented by the letters given here is based on the Attic (Athenian) of the period between 500 and 400 B.C., as reconstructed by Erasmus and other Renaissance scholars. Major sound transformations occurred at later periods, but were largely ignored in spelling. Centuries before the end of the Byzantine period (ca. 1450 A.D.) the sounds were approximately what they are in modern Greek, as indicated by the values of letters transferred to the Cyrillic alphabet (ca. 900 A.D.).

NAME OF LETTER	FORM OF LETTER	CLASSICAL VALUE	MODERN VALUE
Alpha	A, α	if long, = father; if short, = papa	father
		In Combination	
	AI, αι	aisle	met
	AΥ, αυ	our	before vowels or voiced consonants = lava; before unvoiced consonants = father + fat
Beta	B, β	bed	vase
Gamma	Γ, γ	go	before ε, η, ι, υ, αι, ει, οι, υι = yes; elsewhere = huge with vibration of vocal cords
		In Combination	
	ΓΓ, γγ	longer	longer
	ΓΚ, γκ	anchor	anchor
	ΓΞ, γξ	anxiety, lynx	lynx, anxiety
	ΓΧ, γχ	an + blockhouse at first; later = ankh	ankh
Delta	Δ, δ	do	this
Epsilon	E, ε	met	met

NAME OF LETTER	FORM OF LETTER	CLASSICAL VALUE In Combination	MODERN VALUE
	EI, ει ΕΥ, ευ	*eight* *met* + *look*	machine before vowels or voiced consonants = *never*; before unvoiced consonants = *left*
Zeta	Z, ζ	*adze, zone, Mazda*	zone
Eta	H, η	*there*, prolonged	me
	ΗΥ, ηυ	In Combination *there* + *look*	before vowels or voiced consonants = *never*; before unvoiced consonants = *left*
Theta	Θ, θ	*outhouse*; later *thing*	*thing*
Iota	I, ι	if long, = *machine*; if short, = pin	me
Kappa	K, κ	*king to skull*	*king to skull*

Lambda	Λ, λ	land		before η, ι, υ, ει, οι, υι = mil*l*ion; elsewhere = *l*and
Mu	M, μ	men		men
	MΠ, μπ		In Combination	*b*end or em*b*er
Nu	N, ν	now		before η, ι, υ, ει, οι, υι = o*ni*on; elsewhere = *n*ow
	NT, ντ		In Combination	*d*o or un*d*o
Xi	Ξ, ξ	fix		fix
Omicron	O, o	obey or British not		obey or British not
	OI, οι OΥ, ου	boy so; later group	In Combination	me gr*ou*p
Pi	Π, π	pet		pet

NAME OF LETTER	FORM OF LETTER	CLASSICAL VALUE	MODERN VALUE
Rho	Ρ, ρ	British very	British very
Sigma	Σ, ς (s in final position)	sit	us, with tip of tongue touching palate back of upper gum ridge (apical)
Tau	Τ, τ	stall, more dental	stall, more dental
Upsilon	Υ, υ	if long, = moon; if short, = look; later = meet with rounded lips	me
		In Combination	
	ΥΙ, υι	quit	me
Phi	Φ, φ	uphill; later graphic	graphic
Chi	Χ, χ	Buckhill; later loch	before ε, η, ι, υ, αι, οι, υι = huge; elsewhere = loch
Psi	Ψ, ψ	upset	upset
Omega	Ω, ω	bore, prolonged	obey or British not

Extra Letters Appearing in Some Ancient Dialects

Digamma	F	F	*w*ar
Qoppa	Q	Q	*c*ool or *qu*ell
San or Sampi	⋺	⋺	song (precise value undetermined; used instead of sigma in some dialects)

Diacritic Signs

Smooth breathing	'	used before initial vowel; indicates lack of *h*-sound	still used in writing, but both now silent; generally omitted at all times before capital letters
Rough breathing	'	used before initial vowel or *rho;* indicates preceding *h*-sound	
Acute accent	´	indicates rising tone and place of stress	indicates place of stress
Grave accent	`	used only on vowel of final syllable; indicates falling tone and place of stress	indicates place of stress
Circumflex accent	^	used only over long vowels or second vowel of diphthong of final or penultimate syllable; indicates rising-falling tone and place of stress	indicates place of stress

Accent marks generally omitted over capitals at all periods. Still used in modern orthography, but with loss of distinctions of vowel-length and tone, they all indicate merely the place of stress.

Marks of punctuation, both ancient and modern, include the period (.), the comma (,), used as in Roman-alphabet languages; but what in the Roman system is a semicolon (;) is in the Greek system a question mark.

THE CYRILLIC ALPHABETS

The original Cyrillic alphabet, devised in the late ninth century by two Christian missionaries from Constantinople for the use of the Slavic tribes that had penetrated the Balkan region, was eventually adopted, with individual modifications, by those Slavic nations that had accepted the Eastern, or Greek, form of Christianity. Its inventors, Cyril and Methodius, variously described as native Byzantine Greeks or as Hellenized Slavs, based themselves upon the Greek alphabet as far as it would go in approximating Slavic sounds; for other Slavic sounds that had no counterpart in Greek they either modified Greek letters, borrowed from the Hebrew alphabet, or created their own symbols. The Cyrillic system appears today in Russian, Ukrainian, Byelorussian, Serbian, Bulgarian, and Macedonian variants, and is widely used by Soviet linguistic authorities in devising written forms for Soviet Union languages that were formerly unwritten or had unwieldy written forms. Early Rumanian documents were also written in a variety of Cyrillic, but this was given up in favor of the Roman alphabet used today in Rumania (though it has to some extent been brought back to life for the use of the Moldavian SSR). Russian Cyrillic underwent minor modifications in the early days of the Soviet Union, but the forms used under the czars are still encountered in older books and documents; these symbols are here labeled OR (Older Russian). Other abbreviations used are R (Russian); U (Ukrainian); S (Serbian); B (Bulgarian). For reasons of space, only these four are here described in full, with occasional references to Byelorussian.

LETTER	LANGUAGES USING	VALUE
А, а	RUSB	A—stressed, = *father*; unstressed, = *bacon* U— = *aisle*; no important difference of length or quality S— = *father*, long or short B— = *father*
Б, б	RUSB	generally = *but* A—in final position, = u*p* U—in final position, = *rub* S—in final position, fluctuates between so*b* and u*p* (Usku*b*) B—in final position, = u*p*
В, в	RUSB	generally = *voice* RB—final = ski*ff* U—final = *low* S—final, fluctuates between li*ve* and ski*ff*
Г, г	RUSB	generally = *good* (save in U) R— = *voice* in genitive adjective and pronoun endings -го, -ого, -его, and in сегодня (today); final = kic*k*. This letter is regularly used to transliterate *h* of English or German (гитлер, Hitler) U— = *hand* S—final, fluctuates between le*g* and kic*k* B—final = kic*k*

LETTER	LANGUAGES USING	VALUE
Г, г	U, Byelorussian	*gear* to *good* (appears mostly in foreign loan-words)
Д, д	RUSB	generally = *dear*, but more dental. R—final = *lit*; followed by palatal vowels (е, ё, и, ю, я, ь) = *did you* U—final = *lid*; followed by vowels ю, я, ь , occasionally i, = *did you* S—final, fluctuates between *did* and *it* B—final = *lit*
		In Combination
ДЖ, дж	U (may also appear exceptionally in R, B)	= *jam*
Дз, дз	U (may also appear exceptionally in R, B)	= *adze*
Ђ, ђ	S	= *did* you (represented in Croatian version of Serbo-Croatian by *dj*)
Е, е	RUSB	R—initial stressed, = *yes*; initial unstressed, = *yip*; elsewhere, stressed, = *met* (with palatalization of preceding consonant); unstressed, = *it* (with palatalization of preceding consonant)

U— = met (with no palatalization of preceding consonant)
SB— = met

Ё, ё	R, Byelorussian	= *yore*; not usually indicated in writing or printing, save as reading aid to children or foreign learners; palatalizes preceding consonant
Є, є	U	= *yes*, with palatalization of preceding consonant unless this is a labial (б , в , м , п , ф)
Ж, ж	RUSB	generally = *measure* R—with tip of tongue touching palate farther back than in English (retroflex); final = *ash* U—not retroflex; final = *measure* S—not retroflex; final fluctuates between *measure* and *ash* B—not retroflex; final = *ash*
З, з	RUSB	generally = *zeal* RB—final = *so* U— = *measure* when followed by е, ю, я , ь , occasionally i S—final, fluctuates between *less* and *says*
И, и	RUSB	R—stressed, = *year*; unstressed, = *yip* (with palatalization of preceding consonant) U—*sister* or *rhythm*; does not palatalize preceding consonant SB— = *machine*
І, і	OR, U	= *machine* OR—used under czars only before another vowel; now replaced by и

LETTER	LANGUAGES USING	VALUE
		U—palatalizes preceding dental, sibilant, or l, but not labial or palatal
Ï, ï	U	= yip; does not palatalize preceding consonant, and is often preceded by apostrophe in writing
Й̆, й̆	RUB	RB—never used initially; normally offglide, = boy / U—used initially, internally, finally; = yes, boy
Ј, ј	s	= yes, boy
К, к	RUSB	ranges from kill to skull, depending on following vowel
Л, л	RUSB	R—before back vowels, = look or milk; before front vowels (я, е,и, ё, ю, ь), = million / U—before є, ю, я, ь, sometimes i, = million; elsewhere = look / SB— = leave to love, depending on following vowel
Љ, Љ	s	= million; represented in Croatian version of Serbo-Croatian by lj
М, м	RUSB	from meet to moot, depending on following vowel
Н, н	RUSB	R—before front vowels (я, е, и, ё, ю, ь), = canyon; elsewhere = not

U—before ε, ю, я, ь, sometimes i, = ca*n*yon: elsewhere = *n*ot
SB— = *n*ot

Њ, њ	S	= ca*n*yon; represented in Croatian version of Serbo-Croatian by *nj*
О, о	RUSB	R—stressed, = *aw*ful, occasionally *war*; unstressed, in syllable immediately before or after stressed syllable, = American n*o*t; elsewhere = b*u*t U—stressed, = *o*bey to m*o*rning; unstressed, approaches l*oo*k SB— = *o*bey to m*o*rning
П, п	RUSB	ranges from *p*eel to *p*ool, depending on following vowel
Р, р	RUSB	trilled *r*, = British ve*r*y
С, с	RUSB	*s*eat to *s*oot, depending on following vowel U—before ε, ю, я, ь, sometimes i, = thi*s y*ear
Т, т	RUSB	R—before back vowels, = s*t*ool, but more dental; before front vowels я, е, и, ё, ю, ь), = hi*t y*ou U—before ε, ю, я, ь, sometimes i, = hi*t y*ou; elsewhere = s*t*ool, but more dental SB— = s*t*eal to s*t*ool, depending on following vowel, but more dental
Ћ, ћ	S	= hi*t y*ou or *ch*ick; represented in Croatian version of Serbo-Croatian by *ć*

LETTER	LANGUAGES USING	VALUE
У, у	RUSB	stressed, = tool; unstressed, = look
Ў, ў̃	Byelorussian only	= low
ф, ф	RUSB	= father
X, x	RUSB	generally = loch U—from loch to huge, depending on following vowel
Ц, ц	RUSB	from tsar to what's your, depending on following vowel
Ч, ч	RUSB	generally = church U—if doubled and followed by ю, я, = strongly uttered ch + you
Ҷ, ҷ	S	= jet; represented in Croatian version of Serbo-Croatian by dž
Ш, ш	RUSB	R— = shore, with tip of tongue touching palate farther back than in English (retroflex) U— = shore, not retroflex; doubled and followed by ю, я, = strongly uttered sh + you SB— = shore, not retroflex

Щ, щ	RUB	RU— = *Ash*ch*urch* В— = *Ash*ton
Ъ, ъ	RB	R—silent; used today only in the interior of words to indicate non-palatalization of consonants that would otherwise be palatalized by following front vowel (объявление), and may be replaced by apostrophe; used in OR also after final consonant to indicate non-palatalized value В— = *bu*t; silent in final position
Ы, ы	R	= rh*y*thm
Ь, ь	RU	silent, but palatalizes preceding consonant
Ѣ, ѣ	OR, B	OR— = *ye*s; replaced today by e В— = m*e*t or *ya*rd
Э, э	R	= m*e*t
Ю, ю	RUB	generally = f*ew* RB—palatalizes preceding consonant U—does not palatalize preceding labial consonants, and is often preceded in writing by apostrophe
Я, я	RUB	R—stressed, = *ya*rd; unstressed, = *yuh* going? U—does not palatalize preceding labial consonant, and is often preceded in writing by apostrophe; = *ya*rd В— = *ya*rd

LETTER	LANGUAGES USING	VALUE
Θ,θ	OR	= *f*ather; replaced today by φ
V, v	OR	= *m*achine; replaced today by *u*
ꙟ,ꙟ	B	= *b*ut
ꙟ,ꙟ	B	= *y*ummy

Appendix II. Some Recent Developments in Language-Learning Methodology

Since the first appearance of this book, in 1966, there has been one significant type of scientific experiment that has been carried out in the field of language-learning. Some of its aspects should hold interest for our readers.

The experiments in question, reduced to their simplest terms, consisted of taking two large groups of college beginners in a given language who had previously been judged to be approximately equal in IQ, language ability, and general preparation, and imparting instruction to them in their first year of the foreign language by two radically different methods: the old, traditional method of grammar, reading, translation, composition, which concentrates mainly on the written form of the language; and the new methodology that came into vogue during the Second World War, which centers about the spoken language and stresses the ability to speak and understand rather than the ability to read and write (in fact, the written form of the language is normally withheld from the students during the first six weeks of instruction).

The two groups were then tested at the end of the year to determine what significant differences might result between them in their ability to read, write, speak, and understand the language they had been taught. The progress of the two groups was then followed into their second year of the foreign language, though here the methods were generally blended.

The results were, by and large, what might have been expected. At the end of the first year, students trained by the traditional method surpassed their fellows in the ability to read and write, those trained by the spoken-language methodology were better in speaking and understanding. What had not been expected was that by the end of the second year the differences between the two groups had largely been ironed out.

Specific reports on two large-scale experiments of this type include one in Spanish, involving 169 beginning students, and conducted at Purdue University, which was discussed at length by the men who had directed it, Professors K. D. Chastain and F. J. Woerdehoff, in *Modern*

Language Journal for May 1968, and again by Professor Chastain in the April 1970 issue of the same journal; and an earlier one involving some 300 beginning students of German at the University of Colorado, fully described in the book *A Psycholinguistic Experiment in Foreign-Language Teaching,* by Professors G. A. C. Scherer and M. Wertheimer, published by McGraw-Hill in 1964.

The conclusions of the directors of the Purdue experiment favor what they call the "cognitive code-learning theory" (the traditional grammar-reading-translation-composition system): "The students in the cognitive classes were able to understand and speak Spanish as well as, if not better than, those who used the language laboratory and practised with pattern drills. Their scores in the written aspects of the language were better. . . . The implications were: 1) that deductive presentation of material was superior to inductive; 2) that analysis was superior to analogy; 3) that drills stressing understanding were superior to pattern practice; 4) that using all the senses in assimilating material being studied was superior to the 'natural' order of presentation."

In his later article, Professor Chastain reiterates these conclusions, but adds that "the large amounts of drill work in the audio-lingual method seemed to help students with low verbal ability in some language skills," the implication being that the best of both methods should be combined into a synthesis for all students, or that the student should be guided into the method that best suits his particular abilities.

The earlier and somewhat more comprehensive experiment at the University of Colorado reaches the following conclusions (Scherer and Wertheimer, *A Psycholinguistic Experiment,* pp. 243–4): ". . . there was no clear-cut evidence of a statistically significant superiority of the audio-lingual over the traditional group" but "the audio-lingual method yields more desirable attitudes in students than does the traditional method. . . ."

In listening, the audio-lingual students were far superior to the traditional students at the end of the first year, but this difference disappeared by the end of the second year. In speaking, the audio-lingual students were far superior at the end of the first year, and maintained this superiority throughout the second. In reading, the traditional students' ability exceeded that of the audio-lingual students at the end of the first year, but the difference disappeared during the second. In writing, the traditional students were better at the end of the first year, and maintained their superiority during the second. In English-to-German translation, the traditional students were much better at the end of the first year, but this difference disappeared by the end of the second. The audio-lingual group, while it did occasionally reach, never did surpass the traditional in reading, writing, and translation during the two years of the experiment. Lastly, "a combination score, weighting audio-lingual and non-audio-lingual skills equally, showed no significant difference at the end of any of the four semesters. . . . The two methods, while yielding occasionally strong and persisting differences in various aspects of proficiency in German, result in comparable over-all proficiency."

Here are some considerations offered on these experiments by two of the nation's foremost experts in the field of language-learning, Professor John B. Carroll of Harvard University and Dr. Theodore Huebener, for many years Director of Foreign Languages in the New York City Board of Education. The former, in the May 1965 issue of *Modern Language Journal,* states (p. 279): "The average differences between the groups were small enough to suggest that it does not make any material difference whether one uses the audio-lingual method as opposed to the traditional grammar-translation method. . . . The dramatic superiority that an ardent audio-lingual habit theorist might have predicted failed to appear." He goes on to claim (p. 280) that "The more meaningful the material to be learned, the greater is the facility in learning and retention. . . . The audio-lingual habit theory tends to play down meaningfulness in favor of producing automaticity . . . materials visually presented are more easily learned than comparable materials presented aurally . . . conscious attention to the critical features of the skill, and understanding of them, will facilitate learning. . . . The more kinds of association that are made to an item, the better is learning and retention." His final conclusion (p. 281) is: "The audio-lingual habit theory which is so prevalent in American foreign language teaching was perhaps, fifteen years ago, in step with the state of psychological thinking at that time, but it is no longer abreast of recent developments. It is ripe for major revision, particularly in the direction of joining it with some of the better elements of the cognitive code-learning theory."

Huebener's comment, offered in *German Quarterly,* May 1965 (p. 387) is: "In connection with the consideration of the language laboratory, the gains [for the audio-lingual method] are meagre. The superiority of the audio-lingual students in auditory comprehension and speaking certainly is nothing startling; it was to be expected. According to the principle of the specificity of learning, we learn what we practise. If the student speaks the foreign language every day, he learns how to speak it; if he practises reading, he learns how to read it."

For our readers, the basic significance of these experiments is that there is no universal, "royal road" method to learning a foreign language. There are different methods, each of which works out best in connection with the native equipment, inclinations, and needs of the individual.

If you are taking a regular course in a high school, college, university, or private language school, the methodology is laid out for you. Make sure, before you register for the course, that it is at least partly in accord with your own abilities, preferences, and desires.

If you are studying a language on your own, and are faced with a choice between studying from traditional grammars, readers, and exercise books, or from records or tapes, follow your own bent, remembering that the first will enhance your reading and writing abilities, at least at the outset, the second your speaking and understanding. But remember also that in the long run, if you persist in pursuing the language of your choice, you will probably have a chance to shift from one approach to the other, and that in the final analysis the results will not be so far apart as they may seem at first glance.

Consider, above all, your needs and purposes. For immediate use, do you want to acquire some facility in understanding the spoken tongue and in speaking a number of set phrases so that you will be understood? If so, the tapes and recordings will be of greater help. Do you want to be able to read the language, and perhaps express some of your thoughts in written form? Then the written, grammatical approach will be of greater immediate value.

There is no reason in the world why the two approaches should not be combined, as they are in our more progressive schools and colleges. If your ultimate goal is proficiency in all four skills, you will have to combine them. Let your own wants and inclinations be your guides.

Above all, do not fall for any propaganda that tells you: "There is only one way to learn foreign languages, and that is *my* way."

Appendix III. What to Do and What Not to Do in a Foreign Country

Prices, Tips, and Alms—The Words That Go with Each—Local Customs, Linguistic and Otherwise—The Traffic Signs—The Courtesy Code and its Language

FOREIGN travel is implied in at least 75 per cent of language learning, whether it materializes or not. Hence it may not be amiss to pass on a few hints connected with foreign travel in general, even if they are not strictly or primarily linguistic.

To dispose of the linguistic part first, the best advice that can be given you is to try to learn as much as possible of the languages of the countries you are planning to visit, using them on every possible occasion, even in the form of clichés, or in pidgin form, with verbs in the infinitive. This effort on your part will be generally appreciated. Only the French, British, and Americans, as a rule, think that everyone ought to know their languages, to the point of speaking them like natives.

If the language fails to work in spoken form, try it in written form, as did my Chinese friend from Chung King to a Cantonese waiter in a New York Chinese restaurant. Most people you are apt to encounter are literate in their own tongues.

If you have a phrase book, and are unable or unwilling to try the pronunciation indicated by the English transcription, it will not be amiss to point to the phrase in its own authentic spelling. This has been done, with some success, by a few users of my own phrase books. Also, do not forget to try your available substitute languages, including English.

For the rest, remember you are faced with fellow human beings, and try to act accordingly. Be careful about any services that may be offered you. Do not let yourself be swindled in any business transaction of the buy-and-sell variety; but don't try to beat down the other fellow on the assumption that if an object doesn't cost one quarter to one half what it would cost you in the States you are being robbed. Different countries have different price lists. Some of the prices hinge on the system of taxation. As a smoker, I found the price of cigarettes absurdly high in England, and much more reasonable in some countries, like Portugal.

Learn to take these things in your stride, and do not let them get under your skin. If you must have home conditions, then there is no place like home, and you should stay there.

In most foreign countries a percentage is added to your hotel or restaurant bill as a service charge. This is supposed to do away with the need of tipping, and many European travelers and tourists take it literally or leave only the loose change in addition. Most Americans abroad do not. Be generous, but don't overdo it, because it establishes precedents that will work out badly for subsequent American tourists. If you want to add 5 per cent to the amount you are already charged on your bill, it will be gratefully accepted, save in a few localities where more is expected of you, and in these cases they'll let you know about it. In many instances, your extra tip is appreciated not only for its monetary value but also because it is regarded as indicating satisfaction on your part with the way you have been served or treated, and constitutes an element of professional pride to the person serving you.

Responding to the pleas of beggars is your own responsibility, as in your home locality. It can be overdone, in some countries. It can also be underdone. If you choose not to, do so with courtesy, for beggars, too, can have their human dignity. In Spain there is a formula that has always intrigued me. It is *"Perdone, hermano"* ("Forgive me, brother").

Beware of the traffic rules and customs, particularly if you are a pedestrian. Some cities have excellent systems of traffic lights, similar to our own. Obey them. They are enforced even on pedestrians, though with courtesy (the policeman will take you by the arm and escort you back to the sidewalk you started from). Other cities have few or no traffic signals. In these cases, do not assume that the pedestrian always has the right of way, as in California. Many Europeans are the kindest and most considerate people in the world, save when they are behind a steering wheel. Then they turn into fiends, and seem to take grim pleasure in preventing you from crossing the street. You have no recourse but to wait, and wait, and wait.

Local customs are what they are. Study them, comply with them to the best of your ability, and try not to be or at least not to appear to be shocked by them. In many European countries you will encounter more ceremony and politeness but less informality than is customary in the United States. In many countries an inquiry for directions is not made abruptly, but is preceded by an exchange of "Good day!" Do not be surprised if the person you ask walks blocks out of his way to see that you get safely to your destination. Don't be surprised, either, if your European acquaintances invite you out to bars and restaurants, but not to their homes. Home dinner invitations are reserved for very intimate friends. It is no longer fashionable, in most parts of the United States, to be shocked at seeing whites and Negroes together in public places. In Europe it has never been fashionable. Negroes are treated exactly like everybody else, and you may see mixed groups anywhere, including the very best hotels and restaurants. Europeans have little patience with intolerance and boorishness, black or white.

Do not expect ingrained customs, particularly if based on religious beliefs, to be set aside for you. Do not demand alcohol in Arab coffeeshops, or meat and dairy products together in Israeli restaurants. Do not object to putting on a skullcap if you visit a Hebrew temple, or to removing your shoes before entering a Moslem mosque. Show the same respect for the institutions of the countries you visit that you would expect foreign visitors to display for yours. Rise for the national anthem, and remove your hat at the passage of the national flag.

Unless there are special reasons to the contrary, it is unwise to discuss religious beliefs, local, or even international politics with chance acquaintances. You may not even realize that you are giving deep offense. By all means talk about the weather, but do not criticize it, or the local climate; as with us, it's the only climate and weather they have. If it gets to be 110 degrees in the shade in Córdoba, stay in the shade. If you must be out in the sun, keep your head and the back of your neck covered. If they close down between twelve and three, there is likely to be a good reason for it. Do not make fun of the local currency; it means a great deal to the inhabitants, and they don't like to have it described as "unreal," even by implication.

There is little point to criticizing the local food, once you have ordered it. If you don't like it, pocket your loss and ask for something more to your taste. If you are suspicious of the local water, you'll find it more expeditious to order bottled water than to discuss it with the waiter; he drinks it, and it's safe for him, because his system is inured to the local germs. Remember that in spite of all our chlorination, Europeans coming to America occasionally come down with gastric complaints, which they, too, attribute to our water. Also, you may get the reply that a finicky lady of my acquaintance got in a German town when she inquired about the water: "I don't know, lady; I never drink water."

Even if you don't appreciate to the full some of the antiquities you are shown, don't be like the American soldier who inquired of his Roman guide: "Don't they ever throw anything away around here?" Visitors to the United States, missing some previously admired landmark that had come down to make room for a new forty-story office building, have been known to voice the query in reverse: "Don't they ever save anything in America?"

Courtesy is a currency that has universal validity. If your attitude is courteous, it will get across to the natives, even if you miss up on some of their customs and practices. There are very few countries where such expressions as "Good morning!", "Please," "Thank you!", "Don't mention it!", "Pardon me!" are not current. "How are you?", "Good-by," "Glad to meet you!" may be added for full measure. Extremely helpful also are "Come in!", "I should like" (much better than "I want," which sounds a little brutal to most foreign ears), "Please speak more slowly," "Please repeat." It is not too difficult to learn these dozen expressions in a number of languages—as many as are the countries you plan to visit. Any good phrase book will have them.

Do not try to be outlandish, merely because you happen to be abroad. The chances are you wouldn't walk down Fifth Avenue in short shorts. Why expose your pulchritude on Rome's Via Veneto, or Paris' Champs-Elysées? In fact, women are not allowed into some churches with their arms uncovered. There is a time and a place for everything.

On the other hand, don't think you have to go native in every land you visit, and slavishly follow everything the natives do. You have your own legitimate customs and your own human dignity. Girls need not submit to being pinched if they don't like it. The local police will generally protect you from unwanted attentions as much as, if not more than, your own American bluecoats; they have special instructions to that effect. Do, however, submit gracefully to the Spanish *piropo*, the flowery compliment which the Spaniard feels it his duty to offer to any good-looking woman, even if she is fully escorted. And do not object too strenuously to the cluck which is the Italian version of our wolf whistle. Human emotions have a way of being similar everywhere.

Appendix IV. A Few Useful Addresses

(Following are a few names and addresses of organizations that may be useful in your language-learning process. Non-inclusion in this list is in no sense to be interpreted as an unfavorable reflection. There are, in addition to the few mentioned here, many reputable private language schools, producers of language recordings, publishers of foreign-language grammars, dictionaries, and books of all kinds, booksellers that specialize in such works. The ones here mentioned simply happen to be those with whom I have had some measure of direct contact. Also, there are numerous publishers and producers of language books and recordings which are specifically aimed at classroom use rather than at the individual learner.)

FOR GENERAL INFORMATION ON ALL THINGS CONNECTED WITH
    LANGUAGES AND LANGUAGE-LEARNING:
Secretary, Modern Language Association of America, 62 Fifth Ave., New York 10011

FOR GRANTS AND THE POSSIBILITY OF STUDYING ABROAD:
U.S. Office of Education, 26 Federal Plaza, New York 10007

FOR LANGUAGE RECORDINGS FOR PRIVATE RATHER THAN CLASSROOM USE:
Cortina Academy of Languages, 136 West 52 St., New York 10019
Dover Publications, Inc., 180 Varick St., New York 10014
Folkways Records and Service Corp., 701 Seventh Ave., New York 10036
Funk & Wagnalls, Inc., 201 Park Ave. South, New York 10003
Holt, Rinehart & Winston, 383 Madison Ave., New York 10017
Linguaphone Institute, 207–209 Regent St., London W. 1R, 8 AV England
Living Language, Crown Publishers, 419 Park Ave. South, New York 10016
David McKay & Co., 750 Third Ave., New York 10017

PRIVATE LANGUAGE SCHOOLS:
Berlitz Schools, 40 West 51 St., New York 10020
Language Guild, 75 East 55 St., New York 10022

BOOKSELLERS AND IMPORTERS OF FOREIGN LANGUAGE BOOKS:
Adler's Foreign Books, 162 Fifth Ave., New York 10010
Baker & Taylor, Kirby Ave., Somerville, New Jersey 08876
Barnes & Noble, 105 Fifth Ave., New York 10003
Brentano, Inc., 586 Fifth Ave., New York 10019
McGraw-Hill Publishing Co., 1221 Avenue of the Americas, New York 10020
Stechert-Hafner, 31 East 10 St., New York 10003
S. F. Vanni, 30 West 12 St., New York 10011

FOR INFORMATION CONCERNING LANGUAGES FOR INTERNATIONAL USE:
International Language Review, P.O. Box 393, Denver, Colorado 80201
Esperanto Information Center, 156 Fifth Ave., New York 10010
Esperanto Information Center, 410 Darrell Road, Hillsborough, California 94010
(See also Mario Pei's *One Language for the World,* Bibb & Tannen, 63 Park Ave. South, New York 10003)

Index

ABBREVIATIONS